# The Complete Book of
# QUILTING

## *Gianna Valli Berti*

Sterling Publishing Co., Inc.
New York

We gratefully thank the quilters, collectors, and museums who, in their attempt to help spread this art, have so generously contributed their pieces to this book.

Title page: "Le oche giulive" ("The merry geese"), by G. Berti, based on an idea of Jocelyn Detournay's.
Photography: Alberto Bertoldi and Mario Matteucci.

**Library of Congress Cataloging-in-Publication Data**

Berti, Gianna Valli
    The complete book of quilting / Gianna Valli Berti.
        p. cm.
    ISBN 1-4027-0662-6
  1. Quilting--Patterns. 2. Patchwork--Patterns.
3. Appliqué--Patterns. I. Title.
TT835 .B35815 2003
746.46'041--dc22

                                        2003015718

10  9  8  7  6  5  4  3  2

Published by Sterling Publishing Co., Inc.
387 Park Avenue South, New York, NY 10016
Originally published and copyright ©1998 in Italy by RCS Libri S.p.A., Milan
under the title *Mille Idee Con Il Patchwork*. Translated into English by Deborah
Folaron and Cosimo Calabro
Translation ©2004 by Sterling Publishing Co., Inc.
Distributed in Canada by Sterling Publishing
℅ Canadian Manda Group, One Atlantic Avenue, Suite 105
Toronto, Ontario, Canada M6K 3E7
Distributed in Great Britain by Chrysalis Books Group PLC,
The Chrysalis Building, Bramley Road, London W10 6SP, England
Distributed in Australia by Capricorn Link (Australia) Pty. Ltd.
P.O. Box 704, Windsor, NSW 2756, Australia

Sterling ISBN 1-4027-0662-6

# CONTENTS

# A SHORT HISTORY OF QUILTING

# QUILTING THROUGH THE AGES

## SOME WORD STUDY

As we begin to explore the world of quilting, let's start with a look at the terminology itself. The word *quilt* derives from the Latin *culcita* (something that is stuffed, like a pillow, or stitched through, like a mattress), which we find again in the Spanish word *colcha* and in the Italian word *coltre*. In modern English the term *quilting* (from *to quilt:* to stuff or stitch) indicates a kind of creation in which three layers of material (quilt top, batting, and backing) are sewn together by stitching that goes through all three. A quilt, then, is a cover or blanket that is stuffed or batted and stitched together, but also any other kind of quilted work, no matter what its use.

As far as the term *patchwork* is concerned, it includes various types of work, but basically involves piecing, the joining of pieces of fabric together. Another basic type of quilting is appliqué, joining fabrics by sewing or applying small pieces of fabric on a background fabric, which then becomes the quilt's top layer. A third type of quilting is wholecloth quilting, in which the top surface is not cut or patched, but is decorated with quilting stitches overall. The word *quilting* also may refer to the decorative stitching that binds the three layers of a quilt together.

*Opposite: Square quilt with flower basket in broderie perse (Persian embroidery) has Ohio Star pattern and sawtooth and straight narrow quilted borders in several colors. M. Hood (US, 1850).*

## ORIGINS

Some historians maintain that Western civilization was born on the banks of the Nile; others, on the banks of the Ganges; and still others in the valley between the Tigris and Euphrates rivers. Whatever the case, in each of these areas proof has been found that local populations have been familiar with the technique of quilting for at least 5000 years. It was practiced in the Middle East and Persia as well as in Egypt, Greece, and ancient Rome.

At the Academy of Sciences in Leningrad there is a preserved sample of a quilted funeral carpet that was found in a tomb, dating between 100 B.C. and 200 A.D. The British Museum in London has an ivory statue from the second millennium B.C. that shows a Pharaoh wearing patchwork clothes. These examples confirm the idea that quilting has existed as long as fabric has existed—in fact, even before fabric, because pieces of hide were sewn together using the same system.

However, it was a long time before quilting, in its path from East to West, arrived in Europe. Quilted garments are known to have played an important role during the Crusades. Under their armor, the Crusaders who returned from the Middle East wore multilayered garments, which were sewn together to protect them from the harsh climate and the discomfort that resulted from wearing shirts of mail.

Returning Crusaders brought quilted garments back to Europe and the British Isles in the 11th and 12th centuries. The padded and stitched garments offered some protection against arrows, as well as adding comfort, for common soldiers, who couldn't afford armor.

On p. 10: Picture of Guidoriccio da Fogliano, victorious over the castles of Montemassi and Sanoforte of Maremma. By Simone Martini (1328).

It's likely that sewing women, first employed in big houses of hereditary estates, learned about quilting there and returned with the skills to incorporate them in their own work at home, spreading the knowledge of quilting. The quilting frame was invented and became a part of domestic equipment. Quilting skills were passed on from mother to daughter as they worked together in the evenings over the quilt frame. Thus European women came to know about the technique of quilting and made it their own.

The spread of quilting seems to have been favored later by a natural calamity: the big chill that invaded the continent for several winters during the 14th century. The cold was so frigid that it caused the Thames, Rhine, and Rhone rivers to freeze. During this period, women, who were necessarily restricted to their homes for long stretches of time, began to produce articles from pieces of fabric that were sewn together and then quilted. As time passed, the stitches became more regular and the pieces less random, and the finished prod-

ucts became beautiful rather than just warm. At this point we could say there already was true patchwork: first in England and later in America, to follow only these two main lines of quilting evolution (although quilting was done all over the world).

## QUILTING IN EUROPE

Over the centuries, every European country added its own contributions to the development of quilting, enriching it with many styles and techniques and creating well-crafted, artistic works out of basic, utilitarian objects.

The French contributed the custom of cutting figures from a piece of fabric and then superimposing them on a different base, a method known as appliqué. Later on, when the figures were cut from printed fabric (with designs of leaves, flowers, fruit, animals, people, etc.), this very refined method became known as *broderie perse* (Persian embroidery). Catholic Spain introduced techniques of quilting in the creation of sacred vestments and raised this work to a high level, even in women's clothing. Women who sewed in the northern countries specialized in the use of wool, motivated by the need to stay warm in the very frigid climate.

Italy embraced quilting as its own, even if it did not become as rich a national tradition as that of the other European countries. There is an example of very famous patchwork in the diamond costume of a harlequin and another in the painting by Simone Martini of Guidoriccio da Fogliano (facing page). The clothing of the cavalryman and the harness of the horse are luxurious examples of patchwork and testimony to an art that was already flourishing in the 14th century. In the 15th century, in several regions of Italy, people wore undergarments that were quilted. Quilted costumes, banners, and horse harnesses served to confer wealth and liveliness to the *Palio di Siena,* in which every quarter of the city competed with the others to have the richest displays.

Quilted works were also produced in Sicily. Their main virtues were not to add warmth, which was not needed in the climate of the island, but rather their artistic merits. The beauty of the design and the skillfulness of the execution of Sicilian work are shown in a blanket dating back to the 14th century representing the legend of Tristram and Isolde, which has figures of people, flowers, and animals worked in appliqué.

In Italy, a technique of Florentine quilting called *trapunto* was developed that was different from that of other regions. The quilter inserted extra batting between the lines of stitching from the back of the quilt, which created stuffed areas of relief and shadow.

## QUILTING IN ENGLAND

We now come to the country that reached the heights of quilting production, at least until others in the New World would challenge it: England.

European women were exposed to and adopted the technique of working various layers of stitched fabric—i.e., quilting—upon the return of their cavalrymen from the Crusades. It is easy to imagine how well appreciated the warmth-giving properties of these works were, not only by those who wore mail garments but also by the inhabitants of cold castles. Quilting, in fact, became widely used in what today we would call undergarments—underskirts, waistcoats, etc.

Quilted items were produced of fabrics that were refined and valuable, like silk, taffeta, and satin, because of the demands and economic status of royalty and the nobility, the only ones who initially had the privilege of wearing such fabrics.

As time passed, women from lower social classes, including countrywomen, learned the art of quilting and applied it to the creation of their own garments and bedcovers. Confronted with the difficulty of getting fabrics, they cleverly used scraps of fabric that had been discarded. Scraps or remnants from tailors were especially valuable, because they came from the luxurious clothes of the nobility.

We know that in the 16th century, quilting was already very widespread in England, but the first work we have dates back to 1708 and is testimony to the custom of using remnants of Indian chintz for appliqués. The importing of this fabric had been banned by Parliament in 1701, and this restriction caused even the smallest scraps of Indian fabric to become valuable. In the quilt illustrated below, the appliqués are sewn with tiny stitches (35 to the inch or 14 to the cm). The stitching is unusual—red rather than white thread is used. In England, quilting was widely accepted because of the harsh climate.

*Patchwork bedcover, worked with appliqué of Indian chintz. This is the oldest existing piece of patchwork produced in England (1708).*

The spread of quilting at first served to satisfy the basic needs of the family, but was then followed by the creation of products for exchange or sale. In this way, the quilted bedspreads moved out of the humble country milieu into the houses of aristocrats and castles. Wealthy women learned to appreciate these works, which in the meanwhile had become refined in their decoration and precise in their execution. Many women became deeply involved in their own personal creations.

Period paintings frequently show women intent on their work in their salons, where quilting became a constant and prestigious activity. Even Queen Elizabeth was won over, to the point of wearing clothes that were so heavy (due to the heavy, worked fabric and precious decoration) that they needed to be mounted on small wheels in order to allow her to move about more easily. During the Elizabethan period (1558 to 1603), characterized by a booming economy and significant cultural growth, quilting moved from being a simple craft to an authentic art form.

Mary Stuart, Queen of Scotland, devoted herself to quilting while being held prisoner in the Tower of London, in order to withstand twenty years of seclusion. We can still see some of the items made by her, preserved in her chambers.

# THE GOLDEN AGE OF QUILTING

Quilting traveled a long road in its evolution in England and underwent many changes during its development, enriched by contributions from other countries.

Quilt production of the general English populace during the early period was characterized by poverty, lack of technical experience, and scarcity of material. In the beginning, sewing was done at home. The growing national economy allowed needlewomen to get more remnants and discarded fabric directly from top textile factories. The advent of the sewing machine (1779) and the power loom for weaving (1785) enormously increased the production of wool, cotton, and silk fabrics, both solid-colored and printed. This stimulated quilters to express themselves with new enthusiasm. In 1856, the Singer sewing machine came out on the market, which gave new impetus to quilting. In this way, machine stitching existed alongside hand stitching; the latter is still typical of the English method today. The rich and very refined works created during the reign of Queen Victoria (1837 to 1901) caused that era to be called the Golden Age of Quilting. During this period, more than any other time in England, quilting was done by people at all levels of English society, from the least well-off to the wealthiest, but it was the refined production that developed the most. The most valuable creations even appeared in wills, as they were highly sought after furnishings passed on from one generation to another.

At times very rich women who had fallen into tight economic times did quilting in order to turn a profit, and in so doing contributed to the creation of an increasingly refined esthetic in this art form.

Quilting was also taught at school, and the items produced were often given as charity donations or as gifts to people of special merit. It was not unusual for quilting to become a family activity in which everyone was involved. Children did the simplest tasks, like threading needles. Men prepared the frames; cut the templates from metal, wood, or cardboard; or marked out the preparatory designs. On specific occasions, such as an upcoming marriage, family members and friends were invited over to collaborate in the making of a quilt and at the same time to enjoy the pleasure of each other's company. These meetings were called quilting parties; we have several records of them in the paintings of the period.

It was also not unusual to find itinerant quiltmakers, who stopped over to live and work in homes in any given place until the work was complete and paid for (on the basis of the amount of thread used). Then they would move on elsewhere, taking their own frames and experience with them.

Even men sometimes dedicated themselves to quilting, beyond their role in family collaboration in the activity. Soldiers and sailors, for example, devoted free time to this activity, which furnished them with extra sums of money. Mostly, it was wounded or convalescing men who created quilts, which were somewhat austere, as they used remnants of old uniforms.

From the 18th century onward, the activity of the quilt marker or stamper developed alongside the activity of the quilters. When the design of the stitching was particularly important or difficult, there was a need for specialized skills. The value that these stampers brought to quiltmaking was so highly appreciated that it became the custom to leave on the fabric a trace of the pencil markings used during the preparation phase. We know that the most appreciated marker of the 1700s was a Joe Hedley, who came to his profession after working as a tailor, as was often the case. At some point English patchwork began to lose its creative liveliness, although it did not die out. In fact, it found new inspiration in the colonies in America, where it was introduced during the 1600s by European immigrants, and from there it rebounded in England more vigorously and richer than ever, continuing to live on, through high and low times, up to our own day.

# QUILTING IN AMERICA

European immigration to America, especially of English, French, and Dutch people, created a new socioeconomic reality from the 17th century onward. The early colonizers settled initially on the Atlantic coast and encountered every kind of difficulty there. They managed to attain a certain degree of organization only in the early 1700s, after acquiring the means to take advantage of the area's natural riches in a systematic way and after carrying out profitable commercial exchanges. In early colonial times, poverty constrained women to produce only blankets and articles of clothing. Patchwork, already practiced in Europe, became a widespread activity. Transplanted to a world far away from the mother country and deprived of fundamental resources, pioneer women created works that were quite different from those of their European counterparts. They needed to work creatively with the very limited materials they had at their disposal, recycling what remained of old blankets brought over from Europe and garments stretched to the maximum, and even using sacks from flour, seed, or feed.

Material for stuffing quilts was hard to come by and rudimentary, and included dried leaves, husks from Indian corn, and pieces of paper. Even fragments of letters mailed from Europe have been found in some quilts. It was not possible to think of stitching through blankets of this kind, since the crudeness of the stuffing didn't allow for it. The goal instead was to hold everything together with tied knots of every type.

Only later, when the top (the upper part of the quilt), the backing, and especially the batting, became less coarse was it possible to join the three layers of the quilt with regular quilting stitches and to begin to make true and proper quilts. A long time passed, however, before the pioneers attained this result. The European mother country did not encourage autonomous development in the colonies, but rather held them in a state of subservience. Only much later could the colonies cultivate cotton or raise sheep, and thus carry out activities advantageous for creating quilts. Before gaining these rights, transgressors of the laws were punished severely.

Raising sheep did not immediately guarantee that American quilts would have batting that was comfortable like those that grace and warm our beds today. Early American wool had the characteristic smell of sheep when it was moistened or overheated. Likewise, the early batting made of cotton certainly wasn't uniform like today's, since the cotton used still was full of seeds, as there was a lack of machinery to remove them.

*Tablecloth with squares dyed in delicate color combinations.*

For a long time, housewives dyed the fibers (in addition to making thread and weaving the cloth) with whatever they could get from the surrounding natural environment. Generally yellow was obtain from lilies, orange from marigolds, red from madder, blue from delphiniums, green from mistletoe, and brown from walnuts. Often they made quilts that were quite a bit larger than those necessary for a normal bed, since they had to cover all the members of the family, who normally slept together in the single room of a modest house: parents and little children in the bed above, and the others in makeshift beds underneath.

As new dyes were invented, people incorporated them into their designs, which let them increase their color "vocabulary."

# THE QUILTING BEE

Patchwork took on a particularly high social value at the time of quilting bees, which were already present in the English tradition but which became more prominent in the American colonies. For a pioneer family, the quilting bee was a particularly important and pleasurable event. Everyday life was too rough to allow for time simply to enjoy the company of friends and family. Home and chores were set aside only to attend church, to give assistance to other families (to construct or repair houses or farm buildings, often devastated by fire), or at times when circumstances were dire. The quilting bee, then, was a splendid opportunity to enjoy a little relaxation.

For these outings, the women wore their best clothes and went with their whole families to visit friends or relatives, who more often than not lived far away, since settlements were scarce in this very vast land. They came to spend the day doing needlecrafts to create something for a special event, such as an upcoming wedding.

It was an occasion for socializing, conversation, and catching up on news that the newspapers certainly wouldn't be reporting, while everybody worked around the same quilting frame. In the evening, men and women dined together, sang and danced, and new loves were

*Quilting bee in Kansas, 1890. We see women carrying out their work individually or collectively around the same quilting frame, and men also are present.*

sparked. Quilting bees were an authentic moment of solidarity for a people whose survival depended on collective action.

From this early period of American quilting we have very little in the way of patchwork examples, since poverty constrained families to recycle the materials into utility quilts, unless new scraps were available. Scraps of the old quilts were used for new quilts. We find one literary description of quilting from the time of the famous Harriet Beecher Stowe novel, *Uncle Tom's Cabin:* "Young and old set about to working with brisk fingers while conversation proceeded endlessly ... and the day was spent in happily chattering away while the women composed the remnants," clearly a reference to patchwork.

Undoubtedly the quilts produced in the colonies of the New World were very different from those done in England. The American ones, in fact, were inferior from the technical point of view and production, but were more highly esteemed for their compositional strength, especially when compared to those of the refined English ladies who by now had become less creative and whose work suffered from excessive use of embroidery and other kinds of decoration.

Frequently the first design used by early American quilters was Crazy Quilting, which allowed the crafter to use fabrics that were completely different from each other. Crazy Quilting let the sewer cut pieces of any shape and apply them to a base layer of fabric, with very pleasing results. The base fabric, no matter how ugly or worn out, did not interfere with the aesthetics of the product, because it was completely covered up; its function was to support the work.

*Crazy Quilt bedcover in a photograph dated 1900 (US).*

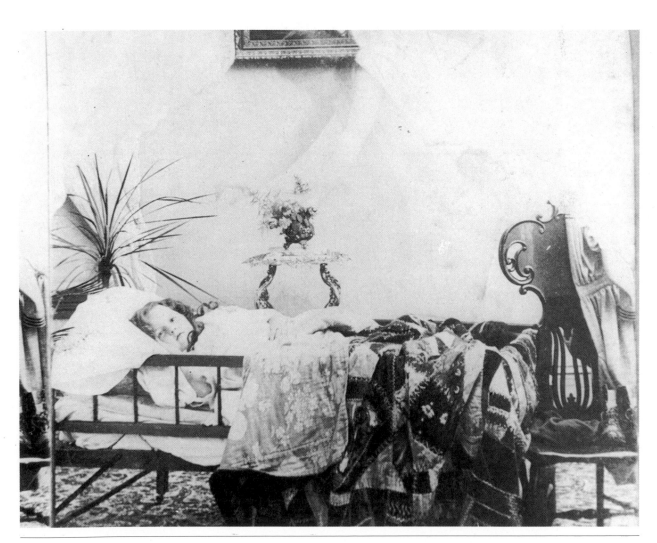

# COMPARING AMERICAN AND ENGLISH QUILTING

Living conditions in the colonies produced fundamental differences, even in the method of quilt assembly commonly used. In Europe it was customary to make a quilt with a central design or medallion, working out from the center and adding pieces all around until the desired dimensions were reached, but in America people adopted a system of making separate squares and then joining them to form the top of the quilt. Although it also existed in Europe, this method of production was very widespread throughout the colonies because of the need to create in the tiny dimensions of the dwelling places of the time, where it certainly was not as easy to manage a large work as it would have been in a comfortable-sized English parlor. We must recall that often in pioneer life, patchwork was done on long trips by wagon train or during a break in fieldwork, so the small dimensions of the quilt components were decidedly more practical. Many patchwork designs therefore arose, and innumerable ideas were sparked as to the layout and combinations of quilts. It is difficult to pinpoint any unique moments in the development of American patchwork, since the production features of any quilting group were added onto those of others.

*Quilt with Honey Bee squares and lattice strips in printed multicolored fabric (US, about 1840).*

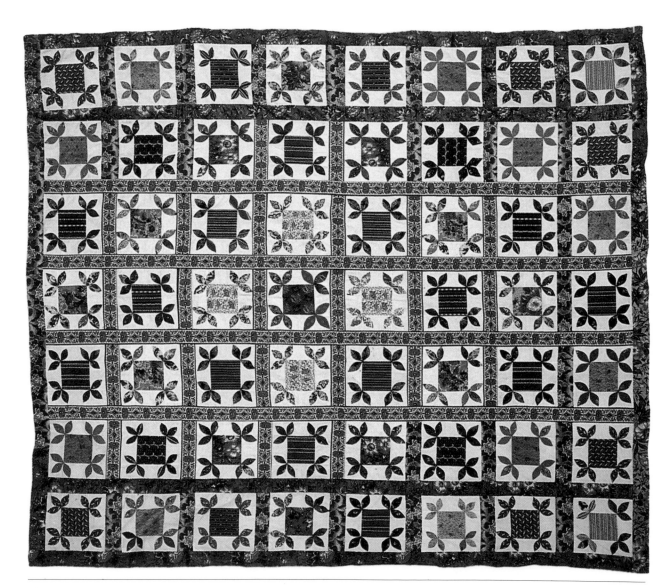

*Medallion tablecloth in the English style, done in chintz in a pleasing assortment of colors.*

This occurred either through the voluntary exchange of techniques, designs, and materials or because of the frequent uprooting of families and small communities which, after initially settling on the Atlantic coast, moved ever westward in order to improve their own living conditions or follow their dreams.

Even the names given to some of the designs can be difficult to ascertain, since the same design might have a different name in different localities.

With time, the beauty and richness of American quilting won over even traditional England, and so the best patchwork from the colonies eventually made a return trip across the ocean, and the skill came full circle.

There then began a period of intense and varied exchange: England sent over highly valued fabrics, while the New World continued to revitalize English quilting, sending back new creations, rich in imagination and full of novelty.

Thus, the country that had been the cradle of quilting witnessed a renaissance in its own production, thanks to those who had moved far away.

The greatest era in American quilts was the early 1800s, when quilters were able to count on a wide range of fabrics that could replace the English ones. Quilting had its own space in the family life of every person, since everyone participated from a very young age on in some way or another. This was especially important for girls of marriageable age, who were creating their hope chests. In these cases, the quilts were not finished completely. Instead, the quilt tops were pieced in preparation for batting, backing, and stitching. Only when the young girl became engaged was the work completed. To do so ahead of time, in fact, was thought to bring on misfortune.

If enthusiasm for filling the hope chest could at times get the better of tradition, observation of the rules was strict in the case of the final quilt, the Bride's Quilt, which was finished off shortly before the wedding, generally during a quilting bee.

We shouldn't be surprised at the large number of quilts that made up the hope chest (around 12), since they were in fact necessary in order to survive the rigors of the climate, which required the use of several layers of bedcovers. There were other reasons for needing many quilts. For example, if a person needed to prepare an additional bed, an improvised

*Quilt made by Albert Small (Illinois, 1945-1950) which holds the world prize for the number of its pieces: 123,000 hexagons forming stars and other multicolored shapes.*

guest room was set up by placing a pile of quilts on the floor to serve as a mattress and others on top for covers. For these reasons, the stock of quilts had to be abundant. In a novel of the period, we read of a woman teacher who, on a very cold night, slept with twenty quilts, none of which seemed superfluous to her. This might remind us of the tale of the Princess and the Pea, in which the princess seems to have used many quilts, judging from the traditional drawings showing her on top of a mountain of quilts, which she found indispensable for lessening the harsh discomfort of one tremendous pea.

## THE RENAISSANCE OF QUILTING

*Indian quilt from the late 1800s, done in fanciful designs and warm earth tone colors.*

Although the development of quilting in the United States unfolded over several centuries, accompanying the historical events of the country itself, the period of the pioneers is surely the most striking.

In the early 1900s, many women worked outside of the home and the huge output of industrial textiles on the market caused a temporary decline in artistic quilt production.

Factory-made blankets became a substitute for quilts, but the quilting tradition did not become extinct.

Quilting, especially the production of quilts, was revived along with the desire to connect up with one's own roots by practicing traditional crafts. During the 1920s and 1930s, the Great Depression struck the United States on the heels of the famous Wall Street crash. Because of the difficult nature of these times, American women made a virtue of necessity. With the experience they had already acquired, women created well-made patchwork, in which tradition appears to have been renewed with new interpretations.

What followed was an authentic attack of quilting fever. The daily newspapers systematically published patchwork patterns in order to satisfy the insistent demands of their readers. Designs or patchwork kits (containing all the materials necessary for any given patchwork project, precut and ready to sew) could be mail-ordered from women who were particularly entrepreneurial and expert at quilting. Manufacturers of fodder and animal feed supported these needs and introduced the custom of printing feed sacks with designs; the sacks became very popular with quilters.

Outside of the United States, quilting was done in very unique ways in countries on every continent: in Japan, where the quilting stitch is called sashiko (literally "tiny stylets"), and in India and Africa. We should not forget that this tradition was never interrupted. Quilting is still being enthusiastically done today. In London as well as Paris or New York, it is currently the trend to have at least one quilted work at home or to wear an article personalized in this style. Architects are increasingly introducing patchwork elements in their planned rooms, and antique dealers compete for fine examples of quilting.

Furthermore, quilting continues to be increasingly linked to other forms of visual art and is popularized in specialized publications, fairs, and local or traveling exhibitions.

In closing this section on the historical development of quilting, we must note that although contributions to this activity have been predominantly made by women, there were also contributions by men. By way of example, we recall the story of George W. Yarroll, an engraver from Kentucky. This artisan, convinced that patchwork would help keep his precious hands agile, devoted himself to quilting with so much zeal that he produced *Spectrum,* the quilt which held the world's record for its number of pieces (more than 66,000) until it was toppled in the mid-1900s by Albert Small of Illinois, who created a quilt out of 123,000 tiny little hexagons. Beginners should not be deterred by these numbers. Great satisfaction can come from patchwork that is much less ambitious!

# SUPERSTITIONS

One unusual aspect of the world of quilting is the superstition linked to quilting. For example, it was thought that God might be offended by the beauty that some quilts attained, as if their creators had wished to compete with God for perfection. This reverential fear caused women making the quilts to voluntarily insert an error in their work. Another superstition is linked to the binding that often appeared on the borders: it never could be broken, even in the corners, because this was thought to cause a premature interruption in the life of whoever used the quilt. Nor, in the many designs on wedding quilts, was there to be any lack of hearts. At least one was required to be appliquéd or embroidered somewhere, since the absence of a heart would make it impossible to look forward to a happy union.

*Delightful Album Quilt in delicate tones, made up of 25 patchwork squares with patterns that include some classical ones: Basket, Bear's Paw, Double T, Spools, Palms, Tree of Life, and 9-Patch.*

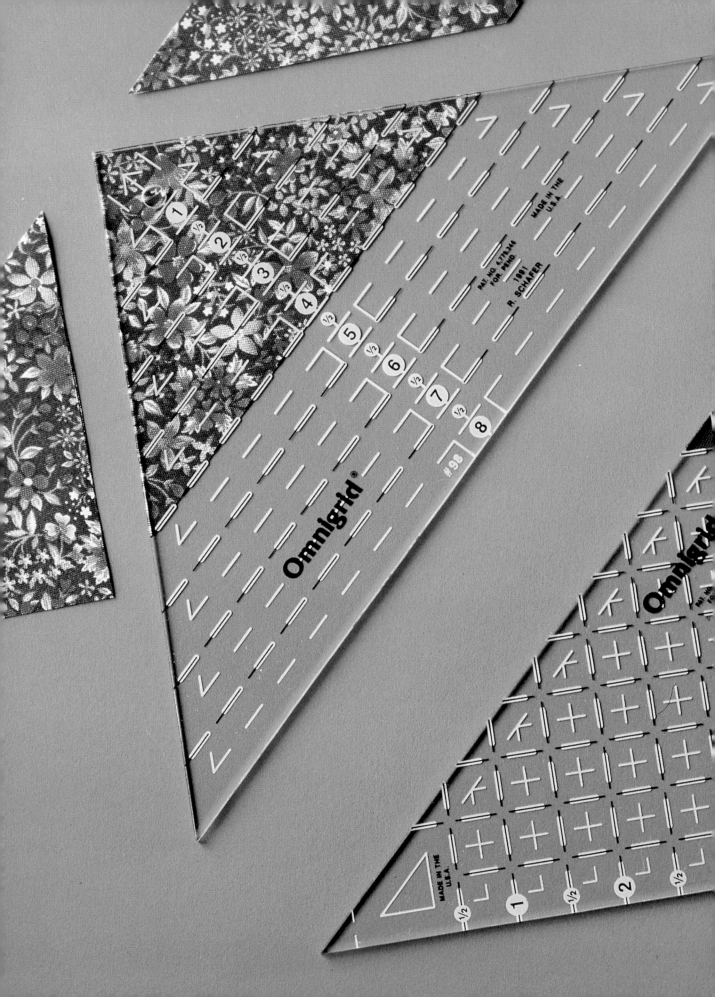

# TOOLS AND FABRICS

# EQUIPMENT

Quilting does not require a particularly complex set of tools. Most likely everything that is needed is already available in your home, if you sew.

As you become more involved in quilting, you may want to add other tools. The aim of this book is to be a primer of quilting basics. Once you have learned them, it is up to you to choose more complicated projects and techniques, as you desire.

The basic tools and supplies that you should have at your disposal, besides a sewing machine and an iron, are:

◆ Thread: Strong 100% cotton thread is what is most commonly used. You will need silk thread for silk fabrics. Synthetic thread should be avoided as much as possible, because it tends to cut the fabric with time and is hard to work with. Special quilter's thread also is available for hand quilting.

◆ Needles: You will need needles of varying sizes, according to the type of fabric being used and the phase of work. Experience will be the best guide to your choice; fine needles usually are good to use.

◆ Pins: Pins should be sharp and fine, otherwise they may leave marks on the fabric. For the same reason, don't leave them pinned in the fabric for longer than necessary.

◆ Safety pins: These are curved and are specially designed for working on patchwork during the quilting phase.

◆ Scissors: You'll need a pair for paper and cardboard, a sharp pair of dressmaker's scissors, and a small pair of embroidery scissors.

◆ Pencils: Use graphite pencils for tracing the patchwork patterns and marking paper templates and fabric patches, colored pencils for the preparatory drawings, and special quilter's pencils to trace quilting designs on the fabric.

1

◆ Ruler and set square.

◆ Compass and protractor: A compass for marking circles and a protractor for measuring angles.

◆ Tracing paper and graph paper.

◆ Quilter's hoop.

For faster procedures and for large projects, where the pieces to be cut are very numerous, it is useful to have the most up-to-date equipment, namely:

◆ Rotary cutter: A cutter with a circular blade; it can cut several layers of fabric at the same time.

◆ Synthetic cutting mat with ruled grid: For use with the rotary cutter. A mat with different colors on its opposite sides is recommended, since this lets you choose the side with greatest contrast to the color of the fabric to be cut. Available in many sizes, from very small to very large.

◆ Rulers, triangles, and squares specifically for quilting: These have a wide range of uses and are extremely helpful for novices and experts alike. They are transparent, designed to facilitate precise cutting of pieces with different angles and sizes, and are also very useful for calculating seam allowances. Available for left-handed people as well.

3

1. *You probably already have the basic equipment for quilting at home, including a compass and protractor.*

2. *Specific tools for patchwork: see-through quilter's rulers, also available for left-handed people.*

3. *A rotary cutter is very useful for large projects because it cuts several layers of fabric at once.*

4. *Using a rotary cutter and a quilter's ruler, marked for cutting pieces with straight, acute, or obtuse angles, on a cutting mat.*

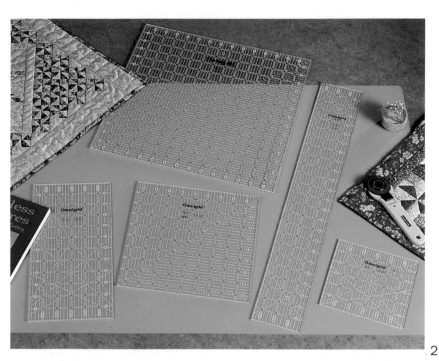

2

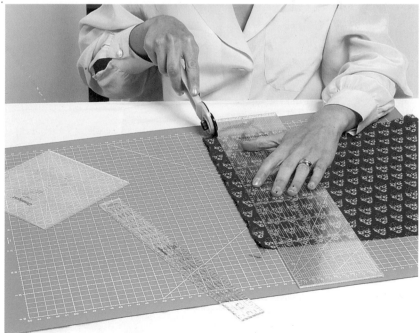

4

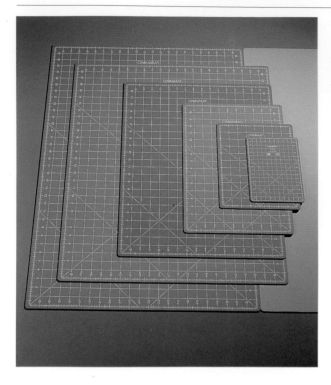

# QUILTING HOOPS AND FRAMES

The choice of hoop or frame for quilting depends on the size of the work as well as on your preference. However, it is recommended that you use a hoop or frame, because it is only by working on taut fabric that you can end up with uniform, smooth quilting stitches. There are various types of hoops and frames on the market, and with a little bit of creativity, they can also be made at home.

◆ Homemade frame: A frame made of four pieces of wood, fitted or nailed together in the desired size, enables you fasten the quilt to be quilted onto it with large whipstitches. The homemade frame has the advantage of being easily put away; it can be propped up against a wall. A large frame, positioned on two sawhorses, serves wonderfully for a quilting bee, as many people can work around it at the same time.

◆ Round hoop: Used most commonly for embroidery, it is also helpful for small quilting projects. The outer ring should be adjustable to adapt to the thickness of the batting.

◆ Frame on pedestal: This is very comfortable, because it leaves the hands free to carry out the quilting.

◆ Square frame made of plastic: Truly practical as it can be taken apart and reassembled. However, it can only be used for projects requiring batting of medium thickness. Usually, extra segments may be added to increase its size.

◆ Table frames are ideal for stitching very large pieces. They are set up on two to four legs; manufactured by specialized factories.

In the past, in the small homes of American pioneers, large square quilt frames were often raised with pulleys until they touched the roof when not in use, freeing up space. However, I would not recommend this system for our needs. I don't think we could get family approval for this one!

*Above left: Synthetic cutting mats of several sizes with two different colors on the opposite sides, offering the possibility of choosing the greatest contrast with the color of the fabric to be cut. Above right: Rulers and drawing compass for patchwork (courtesy of Omnigrid USA).*

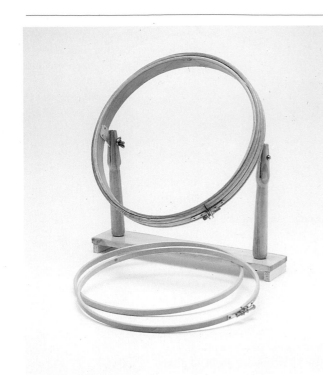

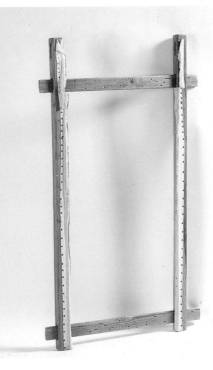

*Above left: Round hoop, equipped with adjustable outer ring. Above right: Old homemade quilting frame.*

*Square frame in plastic can be taken apart and reassembled. Has extra segments that let you increase its size.*

*Table frame, especially useful for quilting large projects.*

# TEMPLATES

*Facing page, top: Pairs of solid templates of semi-rigid materials: use A for the cutting lines and B for the sewing lines.*

In order to create certain quilting designs, templates are needed. Let's see now what they consist of. Templates serve as the basis for patchwork carried out in the English method, but they are also useful in other ways. Various types exist, but they basically are of two kinds: solid (whole) and window.

*Facing page, middle: Templates for the Ohio Star and Baby Blocks (Cube) designs.*

◆ Solid templates may be of semi-rigid material (cardboard or plastic of the weight of X-ray film) or rigid material (heavy cardboard, plastic, wood, or metal). We will call them the base templates, since they are the basis for producing paper ones. Solid templates are particularly useful if you have a pair. The larger one (A, p. 31) can be used to cut the fabric. A includes the seam allowances. The smaller template (B) can be used to draw the paper template that is indispensable for the English method. B is the size of the final patch when sewn in place.
◆ Window templates are made of semi-rigid or rigid material. They serve to mark the patches on a particular part of patterned fabric, generally corresponding to a particular design. Window templates show the stitching lines and the cutting lines at the same time. Both types of template can be acquired at specialized shops, but you also can make them at home. Templates made of rigid material are particularly useful for working on large-sized projects, where a form is repeated very often. If we recall how certain quilts are composed of several thousand patches, we can understand the wear that a template can undergo.

*Facing page, third: Window templates of the hexagon and shell, to trace cutting lines and sewing lines and to trace the pieces at the desired points on the fabric.*

In the diagrams below, intended to serve as a guide for preparing templates, the most commonly used geometric shapes are reproduced. The long straight arrows indicate the straight grain of the fabric. The little arrows show the degrees of an angle.

To construct a 6-pointed star, for example, use a diamond with 60- and 120-degree angles (360/6 = 60). The central angle is 60 degrees in the 6-pointed star. To make an 8-pointed star, use a diamond with 45- and 135-degree angles (360/8 = 45). The central angle is 45 degrees in the 8-pointed star.

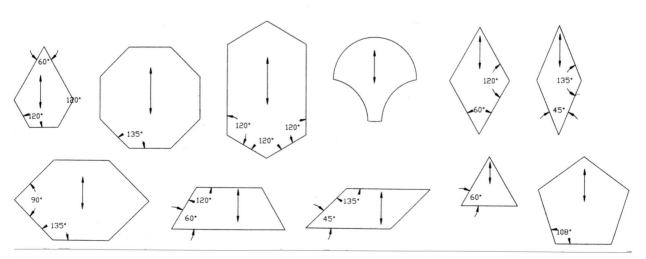

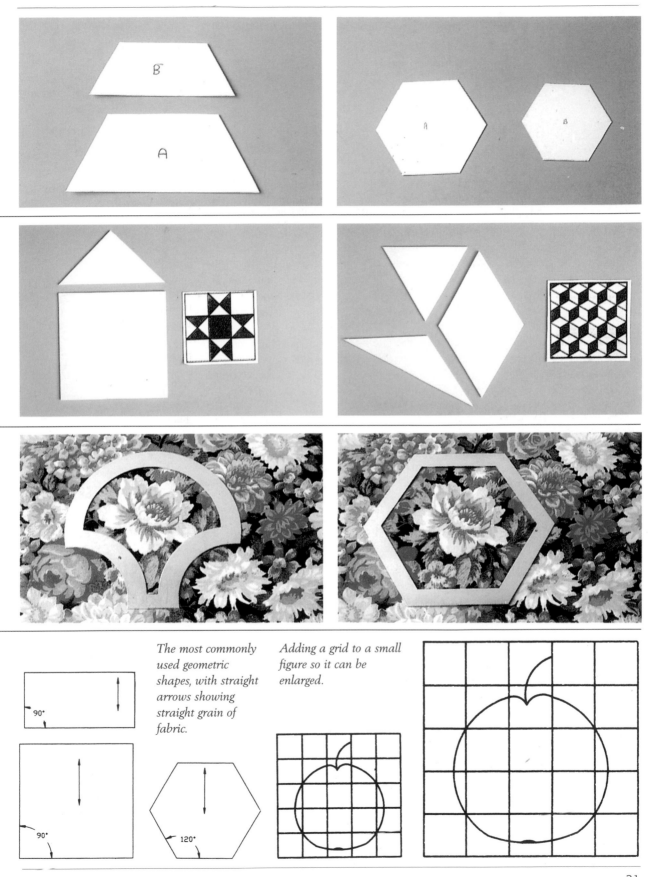

The most commonly used geometric shapes, with straight arrows showing straight grain of fabric.

Adding a grid to a small figure so it can be enlarged.

# FABRICS

The ideal quilting fabric is not too tightly or too loosely woven. If too loose, it frays, and if too tightly woven, it is hard to quilt through it. Pure cotton fabric is ideal but wool, silk, or fabric blends will also yield good results. It depends on the use and kind of quilting you plan to do.

Silk and velvet are somewhat difficult to work with. Silk tends to slip easily and retains the marks from pins, needles, and basting. Velvet has a nap and requires that the pieces always be joined with the nap going in the same direction. Although the special qualities of such "rich" fabrics are fascinating and showcase the talents of those who use them, they aren't the wisest choices for beginners. For your first projects, it's best, without a doubt, to use 100% cotton fabric.

In general, it is best to use fabrics that have the same weight and consistency throughout a project, in order to have overall unity to your work. In some types of work, however, this precaution is not necessary. For example, the Log Cabin design is worked on a base fabric, so differences between the pieces are not too important because of the mitigating effect of the underlying fabric layer. In Crazy Quilting, the variety of fabrics is an important decorative element. It, too, has an underlying fabric layer.

In the past, worn-out pieces of fabric were infinitely recycled. Even today it is alright to cut pieces from used fabric, but take care when joining them to new fabric, because they wear out earlier.

Before choosing fabric, consider what the specific use of the quilted item will be. If the quilt is to be used exclusively or mainly as a decorative piece, fabrics with a strong visual effect should be chosen. Silk, synthetics, velvet, brocade, satin, or taffeta can be used along with any other fabrics that could enrich the quilt's aesthetic quality. Of course, such a work would not be washable, and would have to be dry-cleaned. If the item mainly will be used for practical purposes and will be subject to frequent laundering (for example, a baby blanket), choosing fabric that can hold up to this treatment should be your main consideration. Good sense and workmanship should guide your choices.

## HOW TO PREPARE FABRICS

In order to prepare the fabric for quilting, first prewash it in hot water. Wash each color of fabric separately. This will allow you to find out how stable the dye is. Fabrics that need dry cleaning, such as wool and silk, should not be prewashed. After this trial run, be sure to eliminate any fabrics that lose their color (bleed), otherwise they could cause irreparable problems in the finished quilt. It's crucial to prewash fabrics anyway, as many shrink a bit. We suggest you prewash as soon as the fabric is bought, in order to avoid mixing fabric that is already prewashed with fabric that is not, which could cause problems.

After your fabric is washed, press it so there are no wrinkles in it, if possible while it is still a little damp. If you have space, try to arrange your fabrics by color so when you are planning a pattern you will have your materials ready and in order.

*Opposite: Cotton quilt with vivid colors. Pinwheel design (US).*

# HOW TO ANTIQUE FABRICS

The fact that many of today's fabrics are colorfast is of course positive. However, it is a disadvantage if you want to achieve that used look typical of antique items. To achieve this effect, try repeatedly washing the fabric in hot water and using a light bleach.

Another way to give a more early American look to fabrics is to rinse them in tea, which dims the brightness of the white and brings the various dyes into less intense shades of color. Try this on little swatches first before moving on to a whole piece of fabric.

By studying Early American quilts, you can get an idea of the color harmonies and patterns that were used in that era.

Fabric should be pressed carefully before being cut because the initial wrinkles will not go away in later phases of the work and will affect the accuracy of cutting.

*Coverlet with hexagons in heavy cotton fabric (D. E. Sassi).*

34

# BEFORE CUTTING

When preparing fabric for cutting, it is important to remember that:
◆ At least one side of each piece should be on the straight grain (except for Crazy Quilting, where all the pieces are irregular);
◆ Velvet has a nap and printed fabrics should not be used with their wrong side up;
◆ You should cut off the selvages of the fabric, because they usually have a different texture from the main fabric, look different, and can cause wrinkles;
◆ **IMPORTANT: Remember to add seam allowances to the piece sizes given in this book. This also is true for strip widths and appliqués.**

   You have many choices of fabric and design, but the cutting and sewing of pieces must be done with precision.

*Log Cabin quilt in satin-finish fabric has lively colors (R. D. Sassi).*

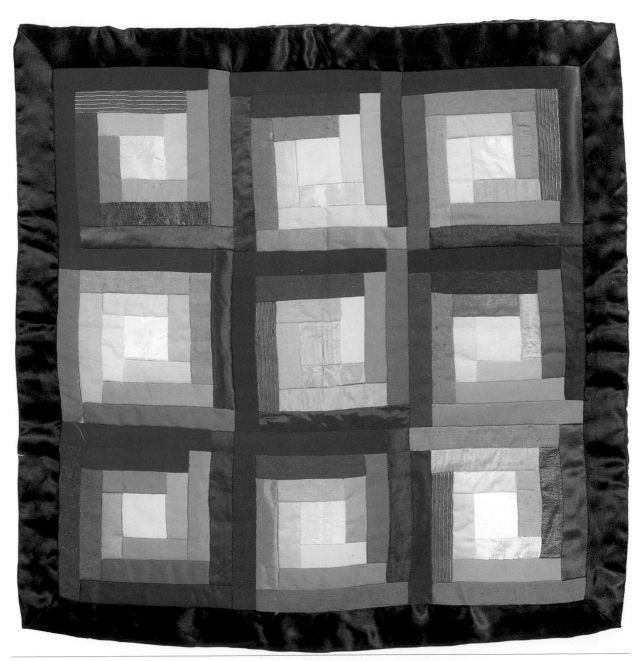

# MAKING A QUILT

# PLANNING A QUILT FOR A ROOM

The basic steps in making a quilt are:
- ◆ Getting an idea
- ◆ Planning colors and choosing fabrics
- ◆ Making templates and cutting the pieces
- ◆ Making the quilt top
- ◆ Preparing the quilt layers for quilting
- ◆ Doing the quilting stitches
- ◆ Finishing the quilt.

 Considerations that contribute to the planning of a quilt are its use, the environment, and person who will use the quilt. All of these will influence the choice of fabrics and colors.

*Delicate tones, good for mini-quilts and wall hangings for children's rooms, result when you use harmonious pastel colors such as light blue, pink, yellow, and lavender. It is a good idea to add a touch of bright color to keep from flattening the composition too much.*

Log Cabin baby blanket uses printed fabrics with designs that appeal to children (N. Betral).

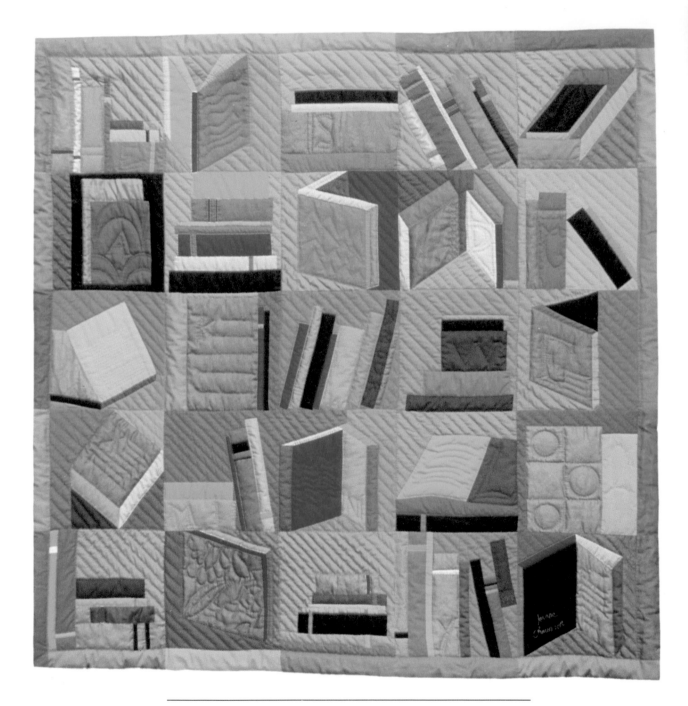

*Quilts with lively designs and vivid colors are ideal for children's rooms. This square panel has a complete library done in patchwork in an ingenious composition with lively colors, accented by quilting stitches (J. Chausson).*

*In order to liven up a dull room, you can create contrast with a wall hanging that emanates brightness. The quilt below has its blocks designed to create a pleasing contrast between the vivacious colors of the Bow Tie pattern and the lighter background fabric (R. Ferré).*

Abstract, geometric, or figurative compositions, especially ones with an interplay between line and color, are particularly welcome in a modern environment. The quilt below, which is restrained-looking because of its limited color range, suggests a labyrinth (A. Woringer).

*If you want to create a quilt with elegant and refined tones, like those typical of the English in the 18th century, select costly fabrics such as velvet, silk or brocade and complex designs with an especially prominent quilting stitch. The medallion quilt below, typically English, is noteworthy for its design, color harmony, and fine stitching (Jinny Beyer).*

# COLOR STUDY

Although it is not necessary to follow fixed rules in the selection of colors for planning a quilt, it is useful to understand color characteristics and basic color theory.

## THE COLOR WHEEL

Beyond the meanings attributed to colors by various civilizations at different moments in time, color itself possesses a language all its own. It is important to understand the messages—even the unconscious ones—that we receive through a quilted composition. The choice of colors and their combinations are very important to the success of the work. Keeping in mind every person's tendency to "feel" colors, it is good to be familiar with colors and to know their main characteristics. Since the colors in a patchwork composition are not read separately, because they interact with each other, it is important to know the characteristics of color combinations in addition to those of individual colors. The color wheel helps us to understand the relations between various colors and allows us to predict the final effect of a patchwork composition that results from its color harmonies.

## PRIMARY AND SECONDARY COLORS

The primary colors (also known as pure colors, because they can't be obtained by mixing other colors) are: red, yellow, and blue. They are found at the vertexes of an equilateral triangle inscribed within the color wheel. If the primary colors are put next to each other, they give off vibrations. The secondary colors, which are obtained by mixing the primary colors, are: orange (red + yellow), green (yellow + blue), and violet (blue + red). The secondary colors are found at the vertexes of an equilateral triangle that is upside down compared to the primary color triangle.

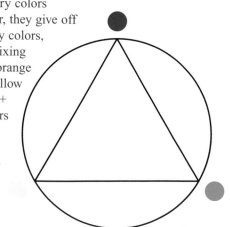

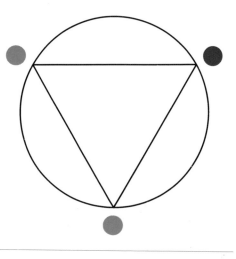

# COMPLEMENTARY AND ADJACENT COLORS

Complementary colors, meaning those directly across from each other on the color wheel (for example: yellow and violet, red and green, blue and orange), "ignite" each other when placed side by side. Adjacent or nearby colors on the color wheel (for example yellow and orange, blue and violet) create a harmonious effect.

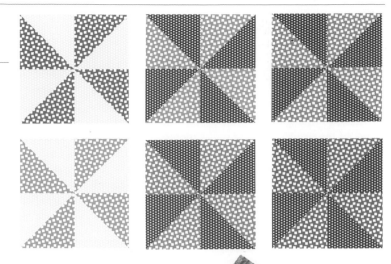

# WARM AND COOL COLORS

The visual stimuli provoked by colors sometimes are associated with warmth and coolness. For this reason, red, orange, and yellow, colors visibly linked to the sun and to fire, are called the warm colors, while blue and violet, associated with ice, snow, and water, are called cool colors, as is green. When warm and cool colors are put side by side, the warm colors advance, in other words they give the impression of moving to the foreground, while cool colors retreat, giving the impression of receding into the background. These properties should be kept in mind if you want to achieve a three-dimensional effect. Adding white or black to a color gives you a lighter or darker color. When placed side by side, the light colors advance and dark ones retreat. Comparing two figures of equal sizes, the lightest one seems to be the largest. It is good to keep these concepts in mind if you want to give the effect of symmetry or balance.

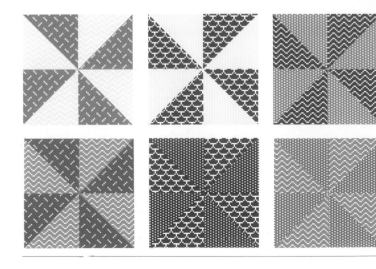

*Above: Detail of a quilt by R. Peel.*

# COORDINATING COLORS

A work based only on solid-colored fabrics can give results that are rigid or excessively dramatic. In order to soften this effect, we suggest using one or more fabrics that are multicolored (e.g., prints). Multicolored fabrics are useful for emphasizing the design and the chromatic value of the whole. In using multicolored fabrics, it is good to keep in mind the visual properties that they will have in a composition. For example:

◆ Fabrics with tiny designs are a pleasing complement to solid-colored fabrics and don't distract the eye from the overall design, so they don't visually confuse the

design. Small overall patterns are a good alternative to solid colors and combine well with colorful fabrics printed in larger designs.

◆ Large colorful prints can be distracting if put side by side with other large colorful prints, because the two designs tend to compete, thus taking away from the overall quilt design.

◆ Stripes, checks, and plaids can give movement to the composition but they can also be a problem if the perpendicularity of their design is cut into geometric pieces done in an imprecise way.

*Grids using the Pineapple pattern, in various color combinations.*

Combining and positioning colors in patchwork is a little bit like cooking; you need to "taste" and adjust when necessary. It is good to experiment with the colors, doing color pencil sketches in different color combinations on a grid of your chosen design. A patchwork piece needs to be pleasurable to the eye, whether viewed from close up or from afar. While experimenting with colors, it is useful step back from time to time in order to observe the results at various distances and angles. By knowing the properties of colors, you can plan a better composition, whether it is achromatic, monochromatic, or polychromatic.

◆ Achromatic compositions—ones done in neutral colors such as white, gray, and black—require a certain skill so that they do not end up monotonous or dismal. It is always advisable to use a touch of bright color to add a more pleasurable appearance to the whole.

◆ Monochromatic compositions, carried out with colored fabrics based on a single hue (e.g., light blue, dark blue, and sky blue), do not present any particular difficulty. It is helpful to use fabrics with different levels of color intensity and brightness.

◆ Polychromatic (many-colored) compositions are the most common ones. Along with the design itself, the colors used give the quilt its character.

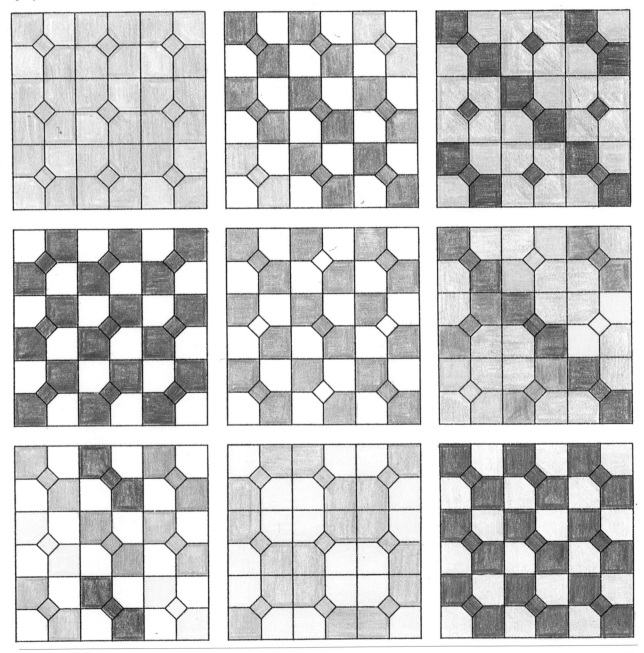

*Grids using the Bow Tie pattern.*

# PLANNING THE DESIGN

After deciding upon the tones (light and dark) and colors of your fabrics, it is useful to draw a diagram of the quilt top. It might have:

◆ A central composition (in other words, an English style one); one with squares (American style); one with strips; or a mixture;

◆ Blocks laid out horizontally or diagonally;

◆ Lattice strips or no lattice strips between blocks;

◆ Borders or no borders;

◆ Whole-cloth or patchwork borders.

*Quilt with geometric composition can be put together by laying out squares horizontally or diagonally (V. Martin).*

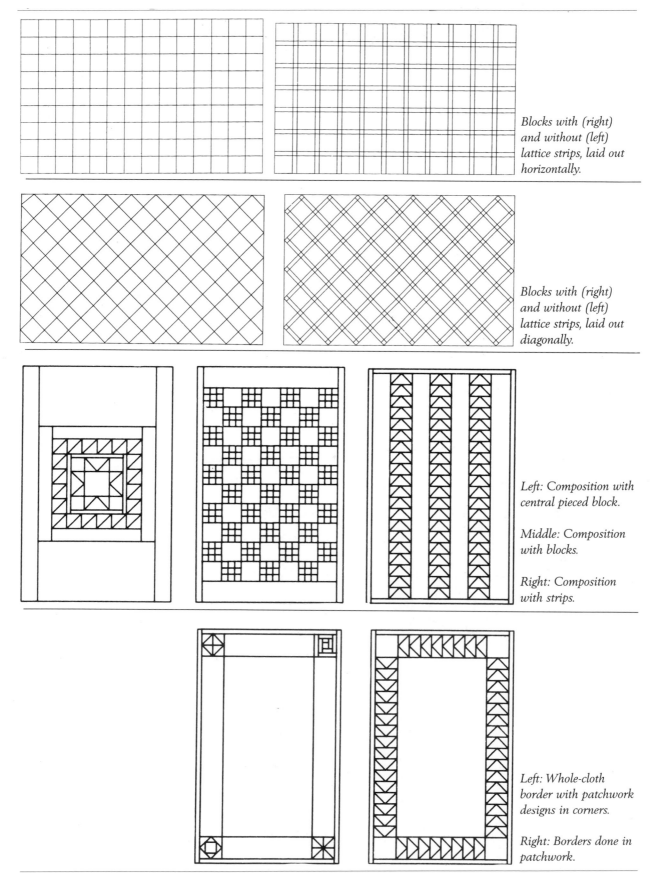

*Blocks with (right) and without (left) lattice strips, laid out horizontally.*

*Blocks with (right) and without (left) lattice strips, laid out diagonally.*

*Left: Composition with central pieced block.*

*Middle: Composition with blocks.*

*Right: Composition with strips.*

*Left: Whole-cloth border with patchwork designs in corners.*

*Right: Borders done in patchwork.*

# ASSEMBLING THE QUILT TOP

To make the top, cut and piece various parts that compose it:

◆ For compositions based on a central design (English style), piece the center, join the side pieces to the central one, and continue to work from the center outward.

◆ For compositions with quilt blocks (American style), piece the blocks and then add the lattice strips so you first make horizontal pieced rows and then join the rows vertically.

◆ For compositions with strips, piece the various vertical strips and stitch them together, working horizontally.

◆ Add the inner border (if any), first sewing on the top and bottom border pieces and then the side ones; add the other borders using the same system.

◆ Carefully press the quilt top with an iron.

*Composition with central pieced block (J. de Bailliencourt). Diagrams show order of piecing.*

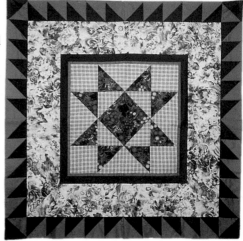

  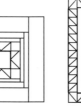

*Composition with quilt blocks (C. Flocard). Diagrams show assembly of blocks and lattice strips to make the center of the quilt top.*

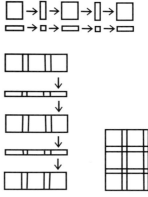

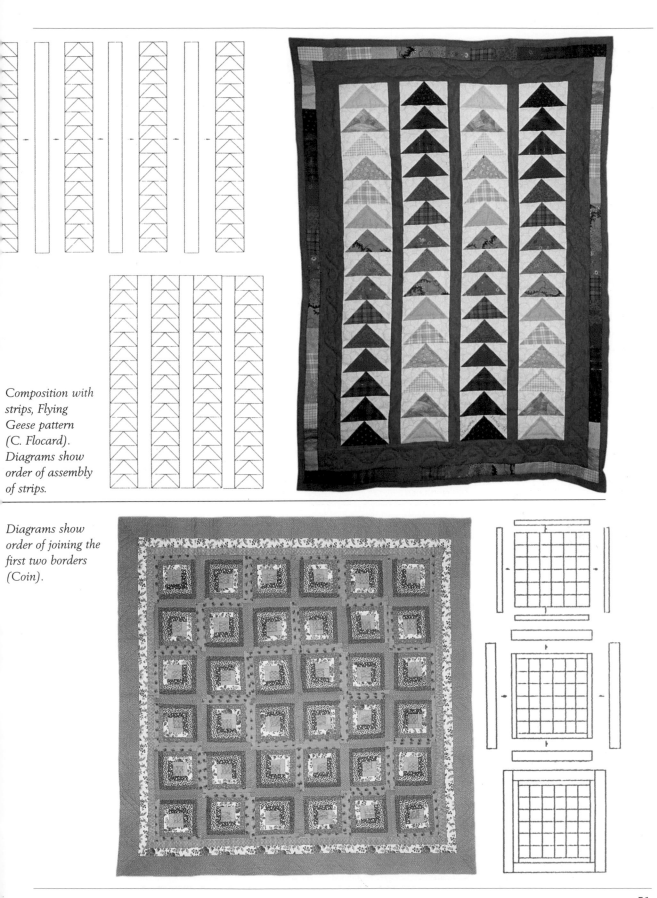

*Composition with strips, Flying Geese pattern (C. Flocard). Diagrams show order of assembly of strips.*

*Diagrams show order of joining the first two borders (Coin).*

# QUILTING STITCH DESIGNS

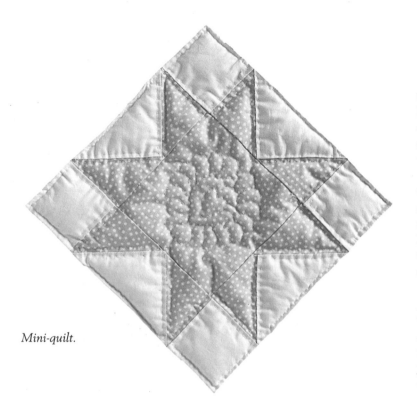

*Mini-quilt.*

Quilting stitch designs are practically limitless and depend on the tastes and design abilities of the quilter, as well as on your work style and the reason for which the quilt is being made, etc.

The quilt stitches can be worked over the piecing lines or next to them. The stitching may be geometric or decorative, may extend over the entire quilt, may be limited to specific areas, may highlight the shapes of the pieces, and may give the quilt nuances, contrast, etc.

Whatever the design, if the choice is guided by good taste, quilting stitches will be a much-appreciated final touch, in addition to their primary function—serving to keep the three layers of the quilt joined together. They are the icing on the cake.

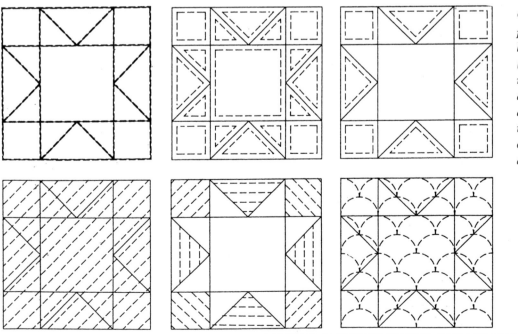

*Quilting along piecing lines (top left), parallel to them (top row, center and right), at a particular angle (bottom left and center), or totally independent of the patchwork design (bottom right).*

*Above: Classic designs for quilting stitches.*

*Below and to the right: Quilting stitches in the Shell design.*

# ASSEMBLING LAYERS AND BASTING

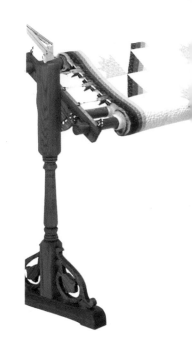

In order to join the three layers that make up a quilt:

◆ Place the quilt backing on the work table (or on the floor if it's too big to fit on the table) with the right side facing downwards.

◆ Tape the quilt backing in place around the sides with pieces of adhesive tape if necessary.

◆ Put the batting layer over the quilt backing and put the top, with its right side up, over the batting.

◆ Pin together the three layers and hand-baste (in grid style or in rays), moving out from the center in alternating directions on the grid to avoid having the three layers slip out of place. For quicker work, the basting can be replaced by curved safety pins designed specifically for quilting.

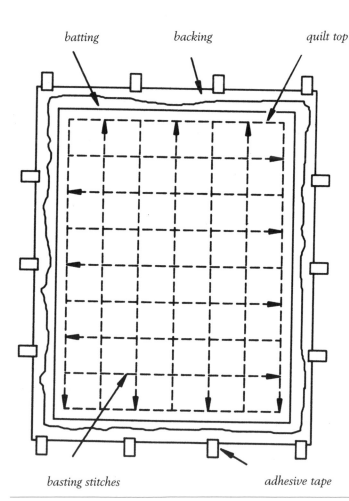

*batting*    *backing*    *quilt top*

*basting stitches*    *adhesive tape*

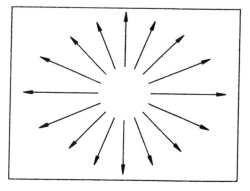

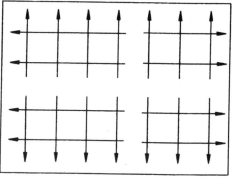

*Above: Basting in rays. Below: Basting in a grid.*

# QUILTING STITCHES

Quilts can be pieced by hand or by machine. In addition, the quilting stitches that join the layers can be sewn by hand or by machine, as long as your machine can accommodate the quilt.

In hand quilting, a few running stitches at a time can be taken, provided that the batting is not too thick. If the batting is thick, the hand-quilting stitch needs to be done in two steps: First push the needle straight downwards and pull it through all the layers of the piece from underneath. Second, push the needle up through all the layers and pull it out on top (see diagram). For best quilting results, use fine, short needles (betweens) and a thimble. If you do not have thread specifically designed for quilting (quilting thread is very smooth and strong), regular sewing thread (preferably 100% cotton) can be used. If the thread tends to knot up, rubbing it with a piece of beeswax will help. For smaller works it is not essential to use a hoop or frame, although it's helpful, but it is essential for larger pieces or for those with thick batting. To start using a thread, tie a knot in one end, insert the needle from the back of the piece, and pull the thread upwards until the knot passes through the backing and gets caught in the batting. To end off your thread, make a knot in the thread on the front of the piece and then push the needle down through all layers until the knot passes through the fabric and gets embedded in the batting. Trim off excess thread. A backstitch at the beginning and at the end of the stitching will strengthen your work greatly. Very thick quilts may need to have individual stitches sewn through them and tied at intervals of a few inches (or a few cm), instead of using running stitches.

*Table frame, especially useful for quilting large pieces.*

*Right: Cross-section of quilting stitches through the 3 layers.*

*Round hoop, with adjustable outer ring.*

*Tubular square plastic frame.*

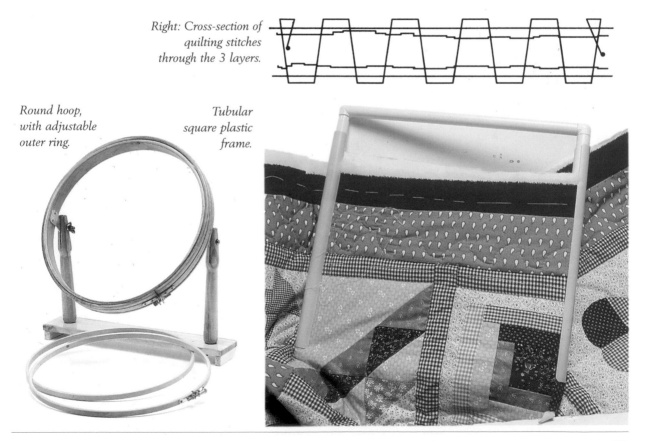

# FINISHING THE EDGES

To finish the edges of the quilt, you can proceed in one of several ways, for example:

◆ Trim off any excess batting that extends beyond the quilt edge. Then fold the excess fabric on the sides of the quilt top to the back of quilted piece, turn the raw edges of the outer fabric (e.g., the border) under, and secure them to the backing with hemstitching;

◆ Fold the excess fabric at the edges of the backing to the front side of the piece to form a border; pin and hand- or machine-stitch in place.

◆ Bind the edges with strips of fabric.

If the work will be hung as a wall hanging, it is good to stitch an extra sleeve of fabric to the back of the quilt, a few inches (5 or 7 cm) down from the top, in order to keep the work from losing its shape. A rod can be run though the sleeve to hang the quilt.

*Quilt with sawtooth border (Coin)*

# PARTS OF A QUILT TOP

pieced border of fabric strips    quilt block    lattice (joining strip)    whole-cloth border    patchwork design    pieced square

# QUILTING METHODS

In this section, I have decided to present the most basic, most commonly used methods: the English method, the French method (appliqué), the American method, and the speed-quilting method.

The most well-known and most unique patterns found in traditional patchwork, the Log Cabin and Crazy Quilting, as well as versatile strip piecing, are explained separately. We also cover the paper-piecing method, which uses translucent paper as a base, a method that, compared to the traditional ones, is surprisingly easy, fast, and precise. The paper-piecing method may be new, even to those who have done quilting for a long time; we think knowledge of it will become invaluable for every quilter.

# ENGLISH METHOD

*In the Mini-Quilt with Hexagons (p. 61), the central part is worked according to the English method, while the borders are stitched in the American method (G. Berti).*

The English method is the preferred one for patterns with straight sides and small dimensions. You need to:

◆ Draw on the cardboard and cut the basic templates, A and B (one with and one without seam allowance; see pp. 30 and 31).

◆ Cut the fabric pieces with the bigger template (A), which includes the seam allowances. Cut paper templates with the smaller cardboard template (B) to the size of the finished piece. Make one paper template for each fabric piece.

◆ Pin a paper template to the center of every fabric piece (on the wrong side), fold the seam allowances over, baste them in place, and press.

◆ Place one prepared fabric piece over the other, right sides together, and sew them together on one side from corner to corner with a small, regular whipstitch, without catching the paper. To start and end the stitches, overstitch two stitches to secure the thread.

◆ Keep sewing on the other pieces in the same way; then press the whole thing. Take out the basting stitches and papers at the end of the process.

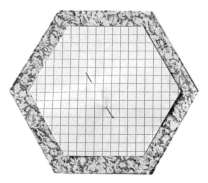

*Template pinned to wrong side of the piece.*

*Piece with seam allowances folded over and basted.*

*Pieces joined with whipstitching.*

# FRENCH METHOD (APPLIQUÉ)

*Paper template in place on wrong side of fabric piece.*

The French method, or appliqué, is very useful for works with curved designs on a background fabric. For hand appliqué:

◆ Draw templates on cardboard and cut out the basic templates (A and B; see pages 30 and 31).

◆ Cut the fabric pieces with the bigger template (A), including the seam allowances, and cut the paper templates with the smaller template (B). B should have the measurements of the finished piece, without seam allowances.

◆ Pin the paper template to the center of the fabric piece on the wrong side, turn over the seam allowances, baste seam allowances in place, and press.

◆ At the points where the form has a very concave curve, make a couple of snips in the seam allowances in order to fold them over more easily. At the point where the curve is convex, it is good to first make a running stitch; pulling the thread creates a gather that makes the seam allowances fall into place perfectly.

*Seam allowances folded, clipped, and basted.*

◆ Press the prepared appliqué, take out the basting stitches and the paper, and place it on the background fabric. Baste the piece down and attach it with hidden, regular hemstitching. Then remove basting.

◆ When an appliqué is made up of overlapping parts, these parts should be superimposed and stitched and then sewn to the background fabric in a logical order.

For machine appliqué with zigzag or couching stitch, prepare only a small cardboard template (B) the size of the finished piece. Using this, cut the fabric pieces without seam allowances.

Depending on the appliqué and the background fabric (which can be the usual cotton fabric, terrycloth, felt, or a knit), it is sometimes useful to put a thin piece of stabilizer under the background fabric before stitching. After the sewing is done, the excess stabilizer may be trimmed off. The stabilizer will strengthen the work considerably, both at the time of sewing and later during washing and pressing.

A very helpful method for hand or machine appliqué uses fusible webbing or stabilizer, a very thin layer of synthetic material, protected on the front and back by paper that can be drawn on and removed when the stabilizer is used. It doesn't cause any problems during washing or ironing of the piece, and it has many advantages:

◆ It eliminates the need to baste.

◆ It gives greater substance to the work, without adding stabilizer below the background fabric.

The instructions on how to use fusible stabilizer are given with the product itself.

*Appliqué stitched on by hidden hemstitching to the base fabric.*

*Baby's book, in soft padded fabric, is decorated with figures and letters that were hand-appliquéd (G. Berti).*

# AMERICAN METHOD

*Opposite: This strictly geometric composition excels in the play of its nuanced colors. Note 3 plaid borders and plaid lattice strips (Coin).*

Quilting with the American method, in which the pieces are placed next to each other and joined with right sides of fabric facing, can be done by hand or by machine. The American method is preferred for straight-sided pieces and can be done in one of several ways:

◆ The traditional method, using paper templates and markings on the fabric.
◆ The speed-quilting way, using a rotary cutter.
◆ The paper-piecing method on a translucent paper base (we will have a section devoted to this method).

## TRADITIONAL METHOD

◆ Trace and cut out basic templates A and B from cardboard (see pp. 30 to 31).
◆ Cut out the fabric pieces using the bigger template (A), which includes the seam allowances.
◆ Cut out paper templates using the smaller basic template (B), which has the dimensions of the finished piece.
◆ Pin each paper template to the wrong side of its corresponding fabric piece and mark the seam allowances with a pencil on the wrong side of the fabric. Remove the paper.
◆ Pin two pieces together (with right sides together) and sew one side, following the marked seamlines; press the seam allowances open.
◆ Continue to stitch together pieces in the same way.

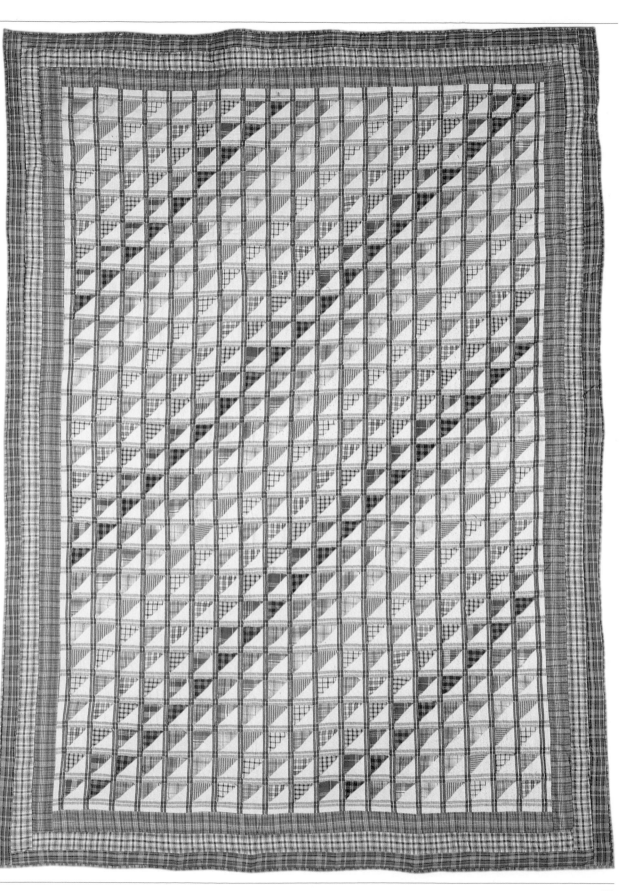

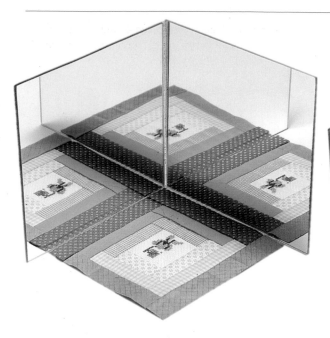

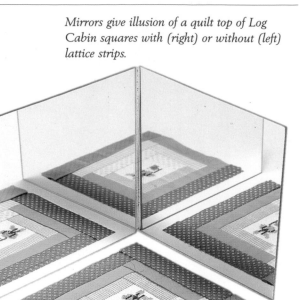

# THE LOG CABIN BLOCK

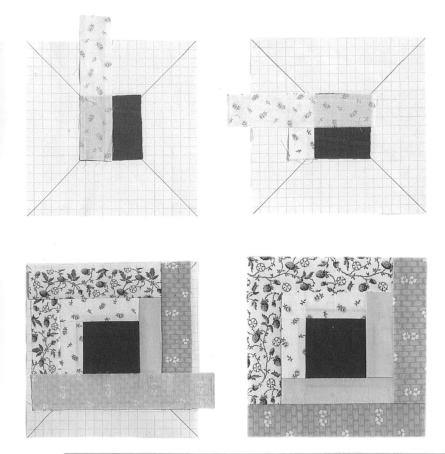

The Log Cabin block can be created in several ways:

◆ On a base of graph paper, which is torn off at the end of the piecing;

◆ On a fabric base to give greater substance to the work (checked fabric is ideal as it serves as a guide for aligning block pieces so they are perfectly parallel and perpendicular);

◆ With no base layer at all.

DIRECTIONS FOR 1st METHOD
(also useful for the other two):

◆ Cut out the base square from graph paper and mark diagonals with a pencil or an iron.

◆ Cut the fabric pieces. (Note: Photos show untrimmed length of pieces 2, 3, and 9).

◆ Pin piece 1 (right-side up) in the center of the paper square, and pin piece 2 (right-side down) on it.

◆ Sew together on one side, trim excess fabric, and fold back piece 2; press or flatten with your fingernail.

◆ On the adjacent sides of pieces 1 and 2, pin, stitch, trim, unfold, and press piece 3.

◆ On the adjacent sides of pieces 1 and 3,

pin, stitch, unfold, and press piece 4, and so on for all the other pieces, moving in a clockwise direction until the base square is covered.

◆ For pieces 2 to 9, instead of cutting each piece to the desired length before stitching, it is faster to cut long strips of the various colors and trim them one by one after sewing, as is shown in the photos.

*Little apron with Log Cabin design (G. Berti).*

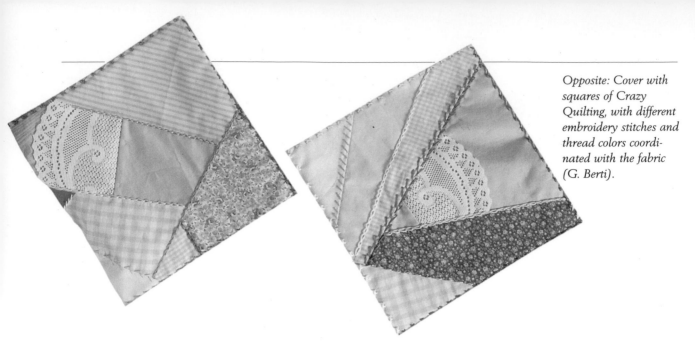

# CRAZY QUILTING

Crazy Quilting is assembled on a layer of base fabric, which neutralizes the problems that using fabrics of many different weights and fibers might cause. The quilt can be livened up with embroidery and appliqués of lace, ribbon, or fabric printed with lively patterns.

Crazy Quilting can be done in various ways; for example:

◆ Appliqué all the pieces onto a single piece of fabric that is as big as the whole quilt top, starting in a corner.

◆ Appliqué the pieces onto many base fabric squares, which later on will be joined to make up the quilt top.

We will present the latter method, which can also serve as a guide for the others.

◆ Cut the base fabric squares.

◆ Pin the first patch (right-side up) in a corner of a base square and put the second one on it (right-side down); stitch them together on one side, fold open the second piece, and flatten the stitching with an iron or with the pressure of your fingernail; trim if necessary.

◆ On one of the sides of the first two joined pieces, pin a third piece, stitch it on, press it, and trim it.

◆ Add other pieces, proceeding in the same way until you have covered the base square completely.

◆ Press the completed square and trim the sides.

◆ Make the other squares the same way, and join them together to form the quilt top; press and trim.

Creating a composition is easier this way, and the square method eliminates having to add pieces that are too long as you proceed, as well as other problems. To avoid inserting pieces that are very long, you can prepare fabric made up of more than one section, thus in effect creating squares of pieced strips.

If you don't manage to get a straight line with two adjacent pieces, fold the protruding piece back under and stitch it on the right side. The decorative embroidery will cover this different stitching.

# STRIP PIECING

Strip piecing (also called string piecing) is very easy and versatile, yielding interesting results, especially as a design element in other creations. You can use this technique with strips of many kinds:

◆ Parallel or diverging, of equal or unequal thickness, laid out horizontally or at an angle.

◆ With strips composed of various pieces.

◆ In coordinated colors or contrasting ones, in tones or shades of the same color, etc.

To conserve fabric, cut strips of about the same length that are not too short.

From the strip fabric, you can cut designs (flowers, fruit, animals, geometric shapes, and so on) for hand or machine appliqué.

One single design can be done using its positive or negative (see p. 71), which doubles the range of options possible.

Strip fabric, because of its versatility, is particularly valuable for borders because it quickly gives a very pleasing effect.

*Pieced placemat with border of strip fabric and hexagon design.*

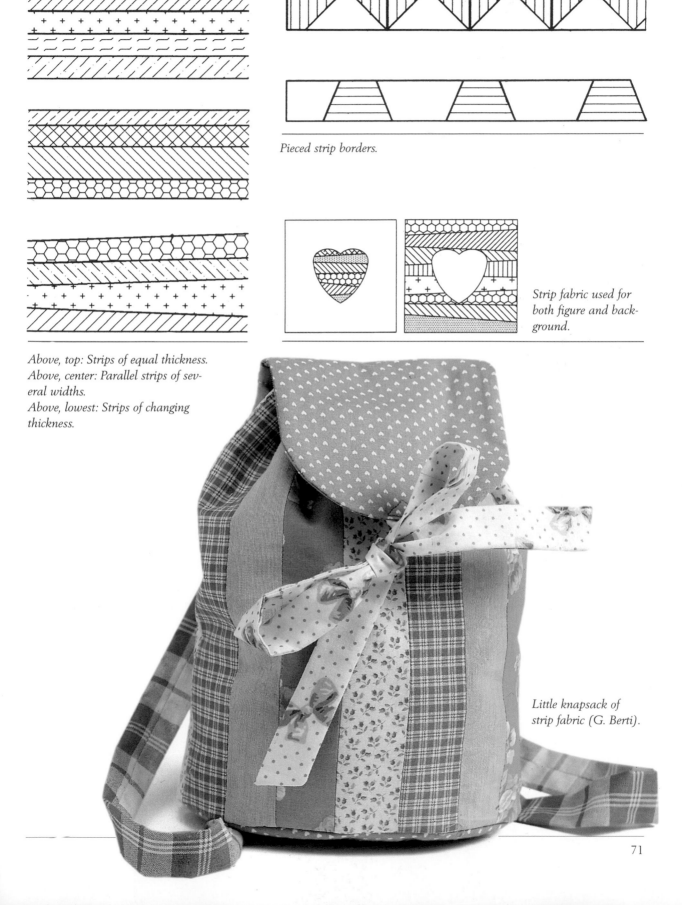

Pieced strip borders.

Strip fabric used for both figure and background.

Above, top: Strips of equal thickness.
Above, center: Parallel strips of several widths.
Above, lowest: Strips of changing thickness.

Little knapsack of strip fabric (G. Berti).

# SOME MORE ABOUT FABRIC

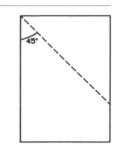

## CHOOSING FABRIC

In order to best use fabric for quilting, it is good to be familiar with its characteristics. Here are some additional facts:

◆ A good weight of cotton is like shirting material. Pure cotton is the most highly recommended fabric for quilting, although other fabrics such as wool, silk, and other natural and synthetic fibers can be used.

◆ Many people avoid cotton-polyester blends or pure polyester, because polyester holds stains and is difficult to sew. However, people over the years have made do with the fabrics at hand, frequently using remnants from clothing for quilting.

◆ Be sure to prewash all fabrics before starting to cut pieces, if the quilt will be washed.

◆ If you have a fabric you love that is not colorfast, try boiling it in a solution of white vinegar (1 cup to a gallon of water) to see if this sets the dye. Otherwise discard it.

◆ Pressing should be done on moist fabric, because otherwise the remaining creases or ripples can cause problems and they will not be able to be eliminated after the quilt has been batted and backed. Don't move the iron back and forth, but press up and down.

It's important to understand the straight grain and bias of woven fabrics, in order to cut pieces correctly.

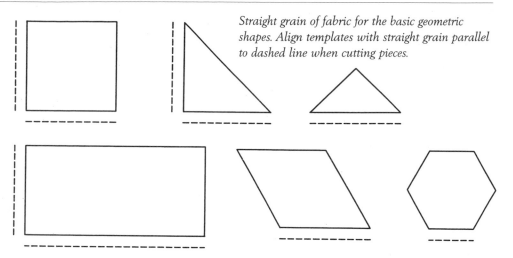

*Straight grain of fabric for the basic geometric shapes. Align templates with straight grain parallel to dashed line when cutting pieces.*

The straight grain is the line that is parallel either to the warp (corresponding to the width of the fabric) or the woof (corresponding to the length). Any other line is either the true bias or another bias.

## THE BIAS

The true bias (usually just called "the bias") is a line that forms a 45-degree angle with the straight grain of the fabric (see diagram, p. 72).

The fabric, when pulled straight up and down on its width, doesn't stretch much and its length is only slightly stretchy. The true bias, however, is the angle at which the fabric stretches the most.

It is important to know about this characteristic because in putting together a piece, especially one of large size or one intended to be hung (such as a wall hanging), it is good to avoid placing the bias lines on the sides of a square or on the sides of the whole piece: it could lose its shape and become distorted with use.

Strips, squares, and rectangles should be cut on the straight grain of fabric. Other shapes, like the triangle, hexagon, or diamond (rhombus) cannot have all their sides on the straight grain, but one or more sides can be.

When deciding which sides to cut on the bias, think of the position that the pieces will have in the quilt and try to avoid stitching bias edge against bias edge.

Above are diagrams that give the best location for the straight grain on the geometric pieces used in the projects made in this book. Keep this in mind when you go to cut your pieces. Be sure your fabric is in square, and not twisted before you cut anything, also.

Refer to the diagram that shows the alignment of the straight grain of fabric for cutting the geometric pieces used in this book.

# SPEED CUTTING AND PIECING

## EQUIPMENT

This method is based on using a rotary cutter and a sewing machine.

The essential equipment for cutting with a rotary cutter is:

◆ The rotary cutter;
◆ See-through rulers and squares;
◆ Gridded, self-healing cutting mat.

Each of these pieces of equipment is available for either right- or left-handed people.

## ROTARY CUTTER

The rotary cutter is produced in several sizes: large, medium, and small.

◆ The large one is best for large works since the blade stays sharp longer.
◆ The medium is good for general use, very manageable, and easy to hold right against the ruler while cutting.
◆ The small rotary cutter is particularly useful for cutting curved pieces or small ones.
◆ There are refill cutting wheels for all types of cutter. Because the blades are very sharp, be very careful when using and storing rotary cutters.

You should:

◆ Protect the blade, clicking the safety device every time you finish a cut.
◆ Store the cutter in a safe place (such as an eyeglass case), out of the reach of children.

There are various ways to handle and use the cutter. I think it is best is to:

◆ Stand up when cutting;
◆ Press the index finger on the concave curve of the handle, where the area is purposely notched to help grip it and to keep it from slipping loose;
◆ Grip the handle end in the palm of your hand;
◆ Push with the thumb on one side and with the middle, ring, and little fingers on the other, and tighten them while wrapping your grip; your hand needs to be in control of the tool as if it were a part of you;
◆ Cut by holding the cutter so it is touching the margins of the ruler;
◆ Press the cutter downwards as hard as needed for the type of fabric and number of layers to be cut; practice will be your best guide;
◆ Make sure that the cut obtained is absolutely clean, and that no threads are uncut; uncut threads mean that you need to replace the blade;
◆ Be sure the cutter blade edge is always perfectly smooth and make sure it is clean, especially the central part where it turns on the pin; use a drop of lubricating oil when necessary.

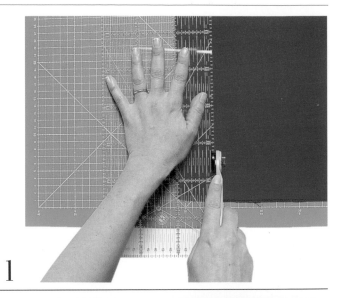

◆ To cut, press on the ruler with the whole left hand or with the fingertips; with the right hand, run the cutter from the bottom upwards, moving away from your body.

1

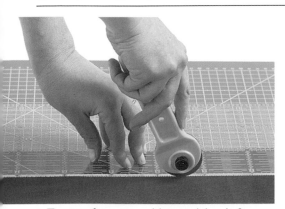

◆ To stop the cutter without raising it from the fabric when you have reached the level of your left-hand fingertips, move the left hand upwards, contracting and spreading your fingers cautiously.

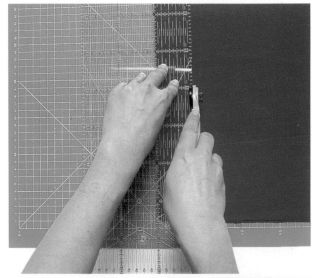

2

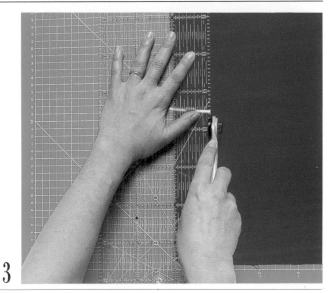

◆ Cut only up to the level of your fingertips and then move the left hand upwards;
◆ Keep cutting and moving your left hand up until the cut is complete.

3

# SEE-THROUGH RULERS AND SQUARES

There are many kinds of gridded quilting rulers and squares, available with different shapes, measurements, and markings. It is a good idea to choose tools manufactured by the same company as the gridded cutting mat. Otherwise, make sure that the markings on the ruler and grid coincide perfectly.

For the basic set, you should have at your disposal:

◆ A long ruler, e.g., 23½ × 6" (60 × 15 cm), with angle markings of 30, 45, and 60 degrees;
◆ A short ruler, e.g., 12 × 1¼" (30 × 3 cm);
◆ A quilter's square showing the bias angle (45-degree line), about 6 × 6" (15 × 15 cm).

Rulers and squares should be cleaned of stains or lint from time to time by wiping them gently with a little cloth soaked in alcohol. Acetone should be avoided.

*Ruling compass (at left) and see-through squares and rulers.*

# CUTTING MAT WITH GRID

To cut with the rotary cutter, you need to use a synthetic cutting mat. Cutting on another surface (such as wood, glass, linoleum, etc.) will cause irreparable harm for it damages the cutter and the surface on which you work and results in imperfect cuts as well.

Cutting mats are self-healing and are made in various sizes. Generally it is preferable to work with a large mat, as large your work space permits. There is also a huge size, 94½ × 47¼" (240 × 120 cm), which is designed for working on very large pieces. With a 23½ × 18" (60 × 46 cm) mat, you can adequately measure and cut almost everything you will need.

Among the different types of mat, one of the most useful is the one that displays two different colors on the opposite sides. It offers the possibility of working on the side that provides the greatest contrast with the color of the fabric to be cut. A mat can also be cleaned without dimming the markings by wiping it gently with a little cloth soaked in dishwashing detergent and rinsing it with cold water. It is good to keep the mat far away from sources of heat, such as an iron. Store it flat in a place that is neither too hot nor too cold.

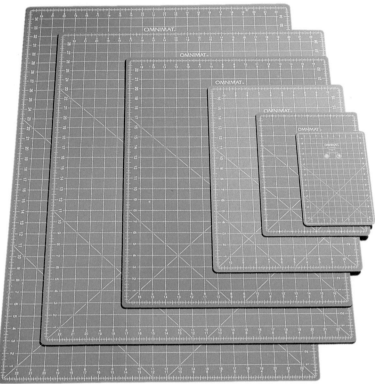

*Above: Synthetic cutting mats with printed grids in various sizes, green on one side and gray on the other, which offers you the possibility of using the side that contrasts best with the fabric to be cut.*

# CUTTING THE PIECES

If you only need a few equal-sized pieces for a project, it is easy to cut them individually from a whole piece of fabric. When, on the other hand, many equal-sized pieces are needed, the best way to proceed has three basic phases:

◆ Squaring up of the fabric
◆ Cutting fabric strips
◆ Cutting the strips into the smaller geometric shapes needed (patches or pieces).

## SQUARING UP THE FABRIC

It is always necessary to square up the fabric. Even when it has been torn on the straight grain rather than cut, fabric never has its width and length lines perfectly perpendicular to each other, because of fabric type, yardage, ironing, etc.

Let's imagine that we have some fabric that measures 43¼" (110 cm) in width from selvage to selvage, as is often the case with cotton fabrics used to do quilting. Because the width of the fabric is the dimension that has least stretch, the fabric strips should be cut in that direction:

◆ Fold the fabric along its length, matching the two selvage edges;
◆ Lay out the gridded mat vertically on the work surface, and on top of it put the fabric with the edges to be squared up on the right (edges without selvages);
◆ Position the ruler with a short side lying on the fold of the fabric;
◆ One final tip is to put a gridded square between the ruler and the lower edge of the fabric, since this helps to determine the best alignment of the ruler;
◆ Press down on the ruler with the left hand and cut with the right. If the fabric to be squared up is very wide, you will need to fold it twice; you will then have 4 layers to cut through at the same time, which should present no particular difficulty.

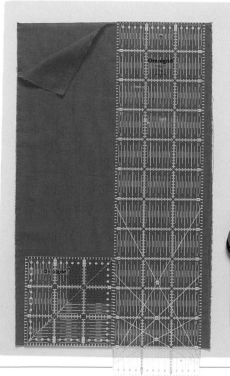

*Squaring up the edge of two layers of fabric.*

# CUTTING STRIPS ON THE STRAIGHT GRAIN

To cut strips on the straight grain:

◆ Place the squared-up fabric on the cutting mat with the side to be cut on the left. Then position the ruler, decide on the width of the strip, press down on the ruler with the left hand, and cut with the right.

◆ Position the ruler to cut the next strip.

◆ To calculate the width of the strip to cut, add seam allowances of ⅝" (1.5 cm) to the width of the finished patch or piece. This is the seam allowance of ⁵⁄₁₆" (.75 cm) multiplied by 2, because it's added to both sides of the strip. **Important: in this book, strip widths are given WITHOUT SEAM ALLOWANCES. You must add them before you cut.**

If you intend to cut many strips, it is good to check the squareness of the fabric edge from time to time. What might happen is that a strip seems to resemble a "V", which means that perfect squaring has been lost. You then need to square up the fabric again as you did when you first began.

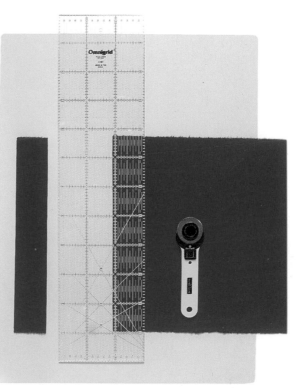

# CUTTING STRIPS ON THE BIAS

To cut strips on the bias:
◆ Square up the fabric;
◆ Rotate it 180 degrees;
◆ Position the bias square ruler with its diagonal line on the left vertical side of the fabric;

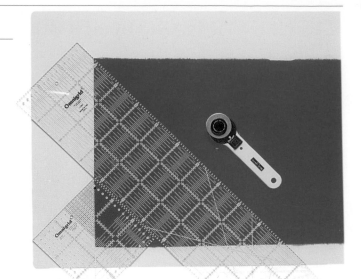

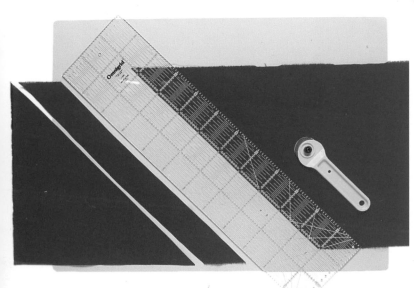

◆ Position a long ruler along the side of the square ruler (see above) and cut the first edge of the strip;
◆ Move the square away, position the ruler at the width desired for the strip, and cut the second edge.

A simpler system for cutting strips on the bias consists of positioning the ruler so that the lower edge of the fabric aligns with the 45-degree angle line marked on the ruler (you don't need to use the square).

If you have little fabric at your disposal, instead of cutting a true bias, you can cut an imperfect bias, using as a reference point the 60-degree angle line on the ruler.

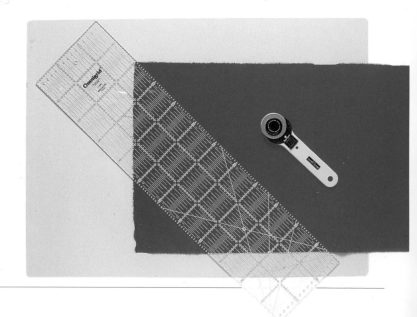

# CUTTING A STRIP INTO PIECES

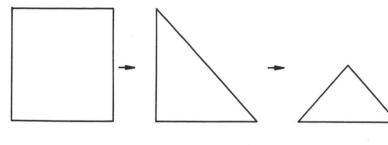

If you want to cut many small pieces from a strip, it is good to work on several layers of strips. If you work on 2 or 4 layers of strips, you will be cutting 2 or 4 pieces at the same time.

Before giving specific directions for cutting the necessary pieces for the projects given in this book, we will assume that we are starting with the basic geometric shapes of the square, rectangle, or diamond (rhombus).

From these forms we can cut other forms: triangles and rectangles from squares and hexagons from diamonds with two 60-degree angles.

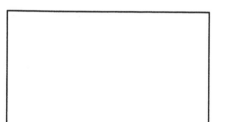

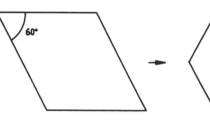

# CUTTING SQUARES

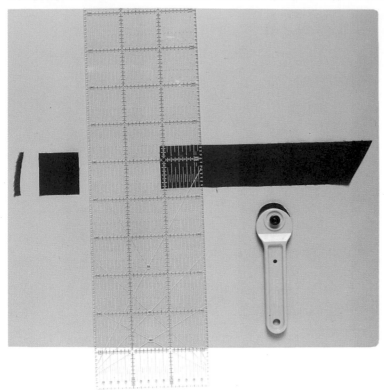

To cut squares from strips:

◆ Place the mat horizontally and put the strip (always horizontal) with the selvage on the right on top of the mat;

◆ Square up strip, cutting off selvages;

◆ Rotate the mat 180 degrees;

◆ Position the ruler at the width necessary for the side of the square piece (including seam allowances) and cut;

◆ Square up the strip as necessary.

◆ To add seam allowances, add ⅝" (1.5 cm) to the height and width of a finished square. This is two times the seam allowance of 5⁄16" (.75 cm). If the side of the finished square is 1½" (4 cm), the side of the square to cut is 2⅛" or 5.5 cm (1½" + ⅝" or 4 cm + 1.5 cm).

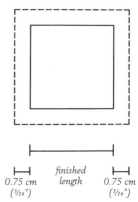

|  | finished length |  |
|---|---|---|
| 0.75 cm (5⁄16") | | 0.75 cm (5⁄16") |

# CUTTING HALF-SQUARE TRIANGLES

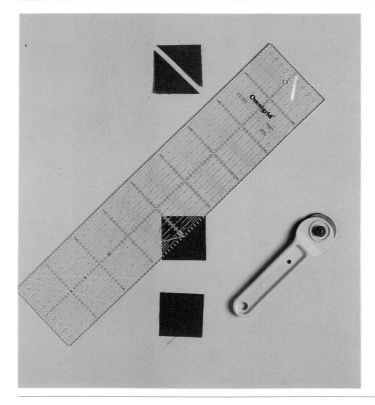

To cut right triangles that are the size of half a square, all you need to do is cut a square along its diagonal. The triangles that are formed have two short sides on the straight grain and a long side on the bias. To calculate the seam allowances (and thus the size of the initial square), you should add 1" (2.5 cm) to the length of one short side of the finished triangle.

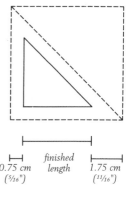

If the short side of the finished piece is 1½" (4 cm), the short sides of the piece you cut should be 2½" (1½" + 1") or 6.5 cm (4 cm + 2.5 cm).

|  | finished length |  |
|---|---|---|
| 0.75 cm (5⁄16") | | 1.75 cm (11⁄16") |

**Important: Seam allowances must be added to all triangle, rectangle, and square measurements given in this book before cutting.**

# CUTTING QUARTER-SQUARE TRIANGLES

To cut quarter-square right triangles, cut a square along both of its diagonals. The triangles cut have two short sides on the bias and one long side on the straight grain of fabric.

To calculate the seam allowances (and thus the length of the sides of the square to cut), add 1⅜" (3.5 cm) to the length of the long side of the finished triangle. If the long side of the finished triangle is 2" (5 cm), then the long side of the triangle to be cut (and thus the side of the square it comes from) is 3⅜" (2" + 1⅜") or 8.5 cm (5 cm + 3.5 cm). See diagram below.

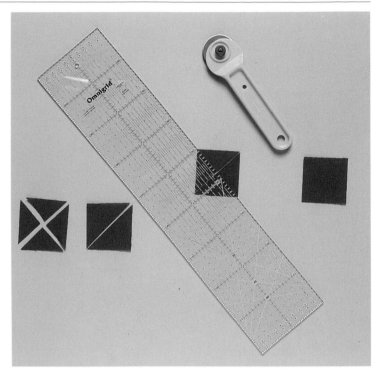

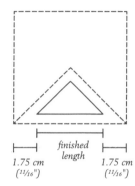

finished length

1.75 cm
(¹¹/₁₆")

1.75 cm
(¹¹/₁₆")

# CUTTING RECTANGLES

The rectangle is cut from the strip by the same method used for cutting squares, but you should position the ruler's edge at the measurement needed to get the width of the base of the rectangle.

To calculate seam allowances, add ⅝" (1.5 cm) to the height and to the base of the finished rectangle. If the finished rectangle is 1½" × 3⅛" (4 cm × 8 cm), the rectangle to cut is 2⅛" × 3¾" (5.5 cm × 9.5 cm).

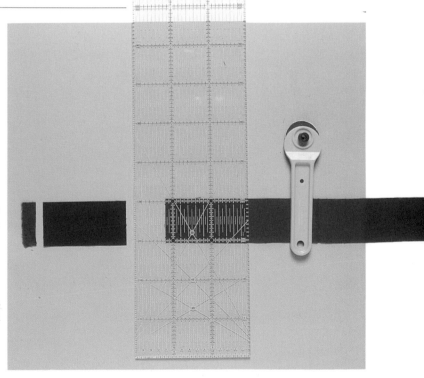

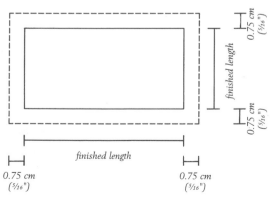

0.75 cm
(⁵/₁₆")

finished length

0.75 cm
(⁵/₁₆")

finished length

0.75 cm
(⁵/₁₆")

0.75 cm
(⁵/₁₆")

## CUTTING DIAMONDS

◆ To create diamonds from a strip of fabric, use a ruler that shows 30- and 45-degree angles. Place the strip on the mat;

◆ Position the ruler at the desired angle with the fabric strip, make the first cut;

◆ Reposition the ruler with its side at the height of the diamond and parallel to the first cut, and make the second cut.

◆ To calculate seam allowances, add ⅝" (1.5 cm) to height (h) of finished diamond. For example, if the height of the finished diamond is 2" (5 cm), then the height of the diamond to cut is 2⅝" (2 + ⅝") or 6.5 cm (5 + 1.5 cm).

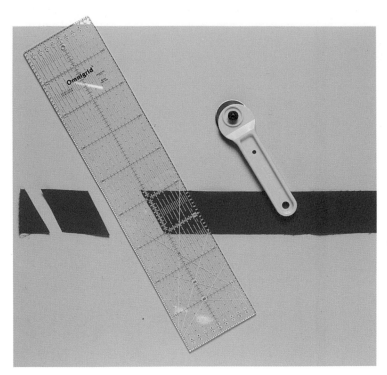

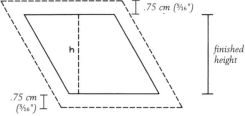

## CUTTING HEXAGONS

◆ To cut hexagons, cut two diamonds with acute angles of 60 degrees.

◆ Place the diamond vertically on the mat;

◆ Halve the height (e.g., 4/2 = 2), and position the ruler with the 2" (5 cm) line on the vertical line between the closer points;

◆ Cut off the triangle section that extends on the right (see photo);

◆ Rotate the mat 180 degrees, reposition ruler, cut off the second triangle section.

◆ For seam allowances, add ⅝" (1.5 cm) to the height (h) of the finished hexagon.

**Important: Add seam allowances to hexagon measurements given in this book before cutting.**

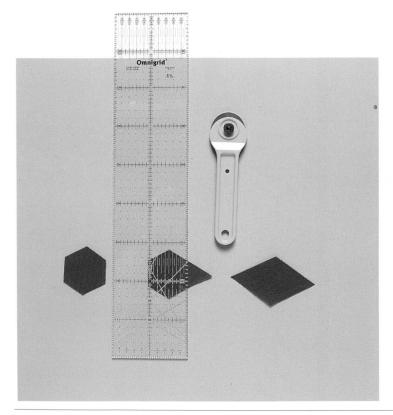

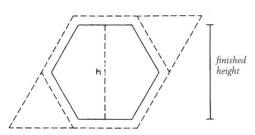

# ALTERNATE CUTTING METHOD

To avoid all of the mathematical calculations necessary for cutting every piece, rather than using the markings on the ruler we can use the paper template method, in which a template is attached underneath the ruler. The system is very helpful for cutting multisided pieces like hexagons and octagons. You should:

◆ Prepare the paper template of the shape and size desired (adding seam allowances);

◆ Attach the template underneath ruler with clear tape;

◆ Position ruler on fabric and cut one side;

◆ Rotate ruler and position it so that another side of the shape coincides with the edge of the fabric; cut the next side;

◆ Keep rotating the ruler and cutting the other sides.

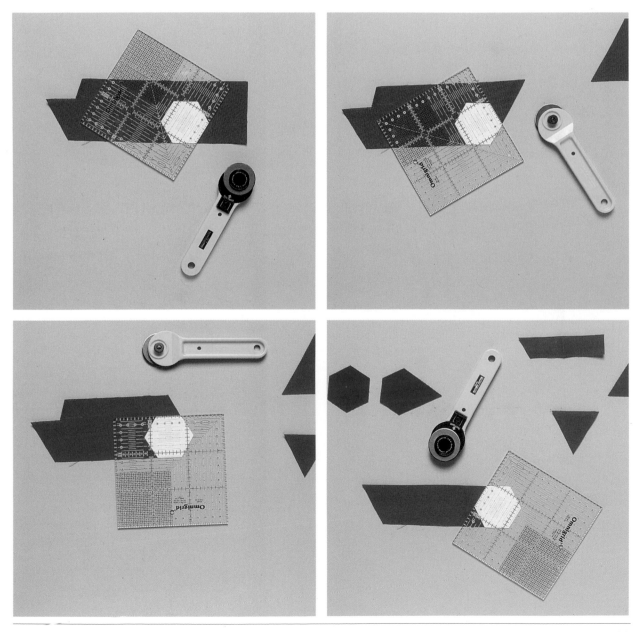

# SEWING

*Simple Easter eggs worked with English/American style patchwork (M. P. Vettori).*

In speed quilting, the second great asset, along with the rotary cutter, is the sewing machine. Sewing by machine is undoubtedly a significant step forward compared to endless hand sewing; sewing without first having to mark seam allowances on every piece is even better.

For people used to marking stitching lines, it may seem impossible to work without them, but if you have good control of the machine, the task is easy to do as long as the pieces are cut precisely.

*Adhesive tape is useful for indicating seam allowances.*

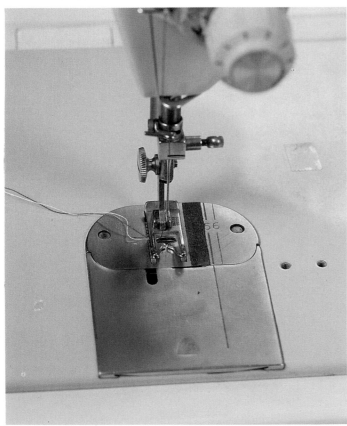

## THE SEWING MACHINE

Some modern sewing machines are specially adapted for patchwork (some can even do machine quilting), but if you wish to use the machine you already have, there is no problem. A few small tricks adapt any machine to machine piecing. For optimal use of the machine:

◆ Adjust the thread tension to the fabric;

◆ Adjust the stitch length, which for normal fabrics such as cotton is about 10 or 12 to the inch (4 or 5 stitches per cm);

◆ Use a fine, perfectly sharp needle.

◆ There are several ways to measure the seam allowances you need, using the settings and layout of the machine. Some have marks on the throat plate to the right of the needle. Check to see if there is a line measuring ⁵⁄₁₆" (.75 cm), a line that indicates its distance from the contact of the needle with the fabric. To check this distance, put a piece of graph paper or a ruler underneath the needle, just touching it, and see if there is a mark on the metal plate that corresponds to ⁵⁄₁₆" (.75 cm).

If this mark does not exist, you can:
◆ Replace the current throat plate with one that has the markings;
◆ Get a presser foot that is wide enough to serve as a seam allowance guide at ⁵⁄₁₆" (.75 cm);
◆ Move the needle from the central position and see if you can get a distance of ⁵⁄₁₆" (.75 cm)—this is certainly possible in machines set up for zigzag stitching;
◆ Stick a piece of adhesive tape on the throat plate at a distance of ⁵⁄₁₆" (.75 cm) to serve as a guide.

Once the machine is set up for the kind of sewing you want to do, you can proceed to do patchwork, as you would with any other kind of sewing.

# CHAIN PIECING

If you need to join many equal-sized squares, it is good to prepare them and sew them in a series, in other words in a chain, following a system that avoids wasting time or thread.
◆ At the beginning of the chain, we suggest that you to sew a piece of scrap fabric folded in 2 or 4 layers, in order to avoid having the machine do any irregular stitches in your work.
◆ Then, without cutting the thread, put two pinned-together pieces under your needle, right sides together, and sew them together on one side. Experts manage to avoid raising the presser foot between sewing pairs of pieces, which helps to save time and thread. By not cutting the thread after sewing every pair of pieces, you will avoid having your work space covered with little pieces of thread, which inevitably end up in another part of the house, where they aren't welcome!
◆ At the end of the chain of pieces, insert another piece of folded scrap fabric; sew it and cut the thread before the folded fabric, so that the fabric stays on the machine for the next chain.
◆ To save time, press open the seam allowances of the chained pieces before cutting off the extra lengths of thread that join the chained pieces together.
◆ To create a whole quilt of squares, we suggest you cut and sew the first squares, which will serve as a pattern, and then cut in a group and chain-stitch all the other pieces.

# PRESSING

Keep in mind the following:
◆ It is good to press each line of stitching first, before it is crossed by later stitching. You can flatten seam allowances by pressing with your fingernail, without using an iron;
◆ Turn seam allowances toward the darkest fabric; in the case of light-colored pieces, let the seam allowances show through;
◆ Turning the seam allowances away from the same section will make the work stronger;
◆ Pressing seam allowances open will make the stitched work smoother and better-looking but, especially when the quilting stitches run parallel to the sewing stitches, the batting might escape through the spaces;

◆ Pressing seam allowances open decreases the strength of the piece, especially a large one;
◆ Turning seam allowances toward the fabric of the lightest weight (if you have fabrics of different weights) makes the work smoother and more uniform;
◆ It is very important to press all of the seam allowances in the same direction if the design is a radial one; for example, the Lemon Star;
◆ Press all the seam allowances of one strip of pieced fabric towards the right and then the seam allowances on the next strip towards the left, so you will not need to sew through four layers when you join the strips.

These suggestions might seem to contradict each other at times, but with experience you'll know which method to use for pressing.

# MORE USES OF THE ROTARY CUTTER

Up to this point we have presented a system for rotary-cutting simple geometric shapes; the shapes then are assembled, sewn, and pressed in a way that is close to the traditional method. There is an innovative work method in which the steps of cutting, sewing, and pressing follow a different order. Working with fabric in bias strips, this method lets you create many patchwork designs very quickly and easily. Many traditional designs, such as the Basket or the California Star, contain squares formed out of two triangles (2-triangle squares) whose short sides are on the straight grain of fabric and whose long sides are on the bias.

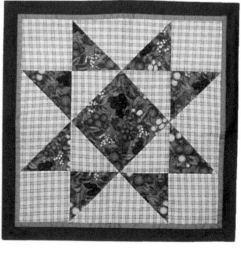

A 2-triangle square, when cut along the other diagonal, generates two pieced triangles made of quarter squares. The quarter-square triangle is the basis of many classic patterns, such as the Ohio Star and Card Game. Using the bias strip cutting method, you can prepare half-square and quarter-square triangles surprisingly quickly and easily. You can even contemplate creating fantastic king-size quilts which, if you worked in the traditional method, would seem impossible to do.

To make half-square and quarter-square triangles, you need to:

- ◆ Create fabric in strips;
- ◆ Create 2-triangle squares from the strips;
- ◆ Create quarter-square triangles from the 2-triangle squares.

*California Star pattern (Le Rouvray).*

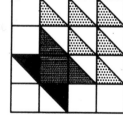

Basket

California Star

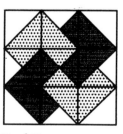

Ohio Star

Card Game

# FABRIC FROM BIAS STRIPS

To create bias strip fabric, instead of first cutting the strips of a single color and then those of another, and then proceeding to join, sew, and press them, it is faster and easier to cut them all at the same time from two pieces of fabric, one on top of the other:

◆ Align two pieces (and colors) of fabric, right sides together, and place them on the mat horizontally;

◆ Cut the strips on the bias;

◆ Stitch together pairs of bias strips on one long side, with a seam allowance of 5⁄16" (.75 cm);

◆ Press the strips open.

*Strip-pieced tablecloth.*

# CUTTING 2-TRIANGLE SQUARES

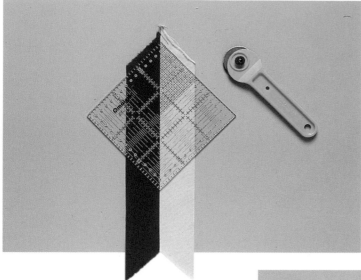

Once the strip fabric is prepared:
- Lay out the sewn and pressed fabric on the mat, right-side up;
- Square up the fabric, i.e., position bias square on the upper part of the strip (with the diagonal line of the square on the stitching) and cut the first two sides of the pieced square (see photo left).

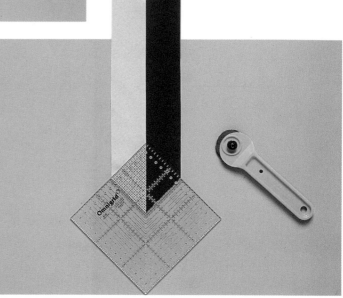

- Rotate the mat 180 degrees, position the square on the lower part of strip (having the diagonal coincide with the stitching), and cut the other two sides of the pieced square;
- To cut more squares, rotate the mat 180 degrees again, and cut the first two sides above at the top, then rotate the mat and cut the other two below;
- Continue in the same way to make all the squares.

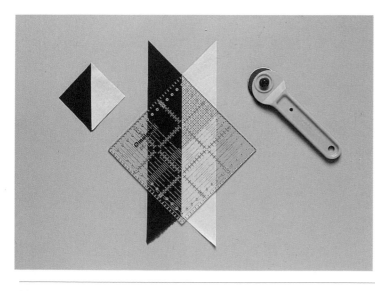

Cutting the 2-triangle squares from fabric formed by two strips will create some extra triangles, which could be used in a patchwork composition too. To calculate the width of the strips from which the 2-triangle squares are to be cut, add ⅝" (1.5 cm) to half of the diagonal of the square. If the diagonal is 1½" (4 cm), then the width of the strip will be 1⅜" (¾" + ⅝") or 3.5 cm (2 + 1.5 cm).

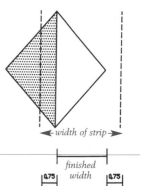

width of strip

0.75cm
⁵/₁₆"

finished width

0.75cm
⁵/₁₆"

# CUTTING QUARTER-SQUARE TRIANGLES

To make quarter-square triangles, all you need to do is cut a 2-triangle square along the diagonal perpendicular to the stitching. But you must calculate the size to include the additional seam allowances.

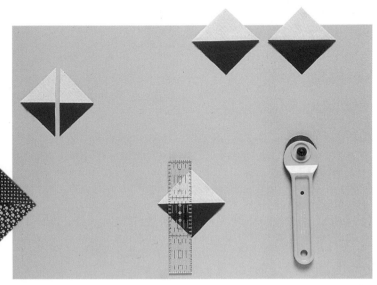

# USING FABRIC STRIPS ON THE STRAIGHT GRAIN

Making fabric strips on the straight grain is easier than making bias strips and uses less fabric, so this is the way to go if the piece allows for it.

The same patchwork patterns usually made with bias strips can be created with strips cut on the straight grain, if the following are true:

◆ If the pieces needed are not very big, and thus the piece sides on the bias won't be too stretchy;

◆ If the piece sides on the bias are to be machine-stitched before joining them with the others, which reduces elasticity;

◆ If the piece sides on the bias are joined to others on the straight grain, which would stabilize them;

◆ If the dense nature of the fabric keeps it from stretching;

◆ If the direction of the quilting will maintain the shapes of the pieces;

◆ If the article is not meant to be hung and is not too wide. Experience will help to guide you in such cases as to whether fabric cut in strips on the straight grain can be substituted for fabric cut in strips on the bias without causing problems.

*Decorated bag made with a Log Cabin square.*

# PIECING ON A TRANSLUCENT PAPER BASE

Although using a paper base to facilitate the sewing of blocks is not new, the system of using translucent paper that is drawn on is new. It allows you to pin the fabric on one side of the paper and stitch right through the paper, adding pieces as you go, using the paper pattern as a guide throughout, resulting in a very precise joining. Precision, as those who have done large patchwork quilts know, is indispensable, especially when joining many squares together.

This method is designed for straight patterns and lets you make perfectly put together blocks in periods of time that are much shorter than were needed for traditional methods. Compared to the English method, paper piecing saves time; compared to the traditional American method, it is more precise.

The ideal translucent paper is the kind that is used for technical drawing. It is consistent and translucent to the right degree and it can be torn off when the block is all stitched together. The basic phases are cutting and stitching.

*Opposite: Pieces for the Pinwheel design, created by a paper piecing method.*

# CUTTING

You can proceed in several ways, but we will consider only two. The first is recommended if you want to create a single block or a few. The second method should be used if the blocks are numerous and you can work in steps.

1st METHOD:
◆ To get templates, draw the patchwork pattern on paper that is sturdy enough, trace the pattern, number the sections that make up the pattern, and cut them out.
◆ Pin templates onto corresponding fabrics and cut pieces out of fabric, adding seam allowances all around.

2nd METHOD:
◆ Trace the patchwork pattern on translucent paper, including all the sections. Cut out the pieces in the corresponding fabrics with a rotary cutter, using the speed-cutting method (first preparing strips of fabric and then cutting out pieces in a series).

If you are not skilled enough yet in the paper piecing method, to leave wider seam allowances; the excess fabric, which eventually will be trimmed off, is important if you need to make any modifications.

# SEWING WITH PAPER PIECING

To stitch the patchwork pieces together, you need to:

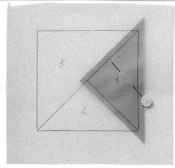

♦ Choose the patchwork design you want (from a book, magazine), draw it on graph paper, put it on the work surface, put a translucent sheet of paper over it, and trace the design, numbering the sections that make it up (the pieces). The drawn-on side is the back of the block.

♦ Put the paper on the work surface. On the work surface, lay out piece 2, right-side up, over the paper, positioning it precisely. Superimpose piece 1, right-side down. Hold up to the light to be sure they are positioned well.

♦ Pin the pieces parallel to the stitching line you will make next.

♦ Sew by machine with short stitches where piece 1 and 2 join, beginning and ending two or three stitches beyond the drawn line.

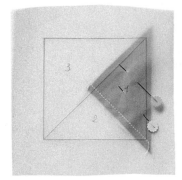

♦ Raise the foot of the machine, take out the work, cut the excess threads, remove pins, but leave paper attached.

♦ Open out piece 2 and press the stitching.

♦ On the work surface, place piece 3, right-side up; over it place the paper, positioned so piece 3 is lined up where it should be joined; pin, stitch, unfold, and flatten piece 3.

♦ After sewing all of the pieces in the order indicated by the numbers, tear off the paper, press, and trim around the square with the rotary cutter and see-through square.

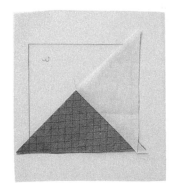

♦ Pay special attention to asymmetrical designs, remembering that the part that is seen as it is sewn will later be seen in reverse. For example, the letter L is seen backwards and facing left while being stitched; when turned to its right side, the piece will have the L facing to the right (see patterns, p. 108).

Working with the paper piecing method and with drawings on translucent paper, you can do figurative patterns and traditional ones like Log Cabin, Pineapple, Fence, Stars, Pinwheel, etc.

Using this work method, some designs should be executed in two or more parts; the drawing should be subdivided into two or more sections.

In the drawings in this book, a little dot on the line indicates the stitching to execute in parts; i.e., it indicates a section of the drawing.

# PATTERNS WITH MANY SECTIONS

To create blocks with many sections:
◆ Draw the block design on paper of any kind and draw the lines that will subdivide the sections.
◆ Trace the drawings of the different sections onto separate sheets of transparent paper, and number the parts in order of sewing.
◆ Cut the pieces out of fabric.
◆ Pin, stitch, and press the pieces of the first section, and then those of the second section, etc.
◆ Sew the sections of the block together, press, and neaten the edges of the whole block with cutter and see-through square.

Novices at this method should choose patterns with the following characteristics:
◆ Patterns in which the order of assembly is clearly indicated by numbers;
◆ Simple ones, made of half- or quarter-squares, of just a few pieces;
◆ Patterns with sewing lines that are parallel and perpendicular, without angled lines;
◆ Blocks of a single piece;
◆ Symmetrical patterns.

Save more complex designs for the second time around. Eventually you will be able to choose any pattern you like.

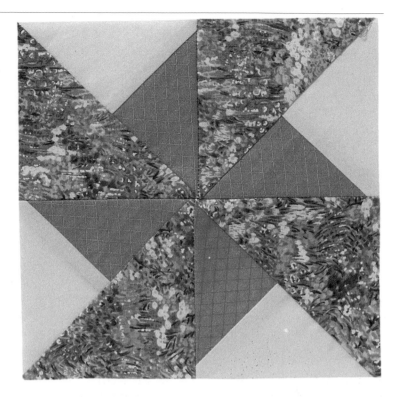

*Small toffee-shaped cushion decorated with an Ohio Star (G. Berti).*

95

# PATCHWORK DESIGN ASSEMBLY DRAWINGS

Pages 96–108 have reduced template drawings; numbers and dots indicate order of assembly and sections.

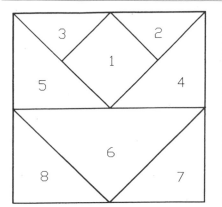

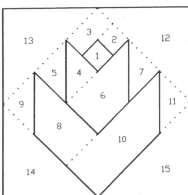

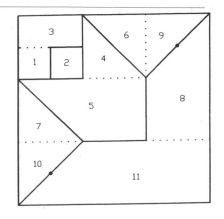

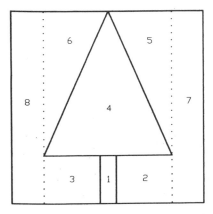

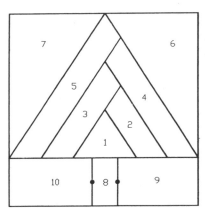

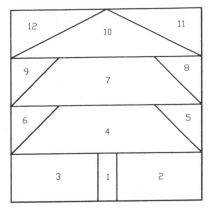

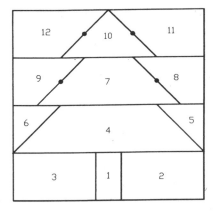

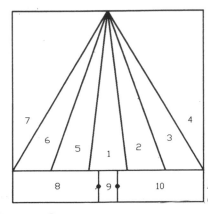

*Package decorated with Log Cabin square.*

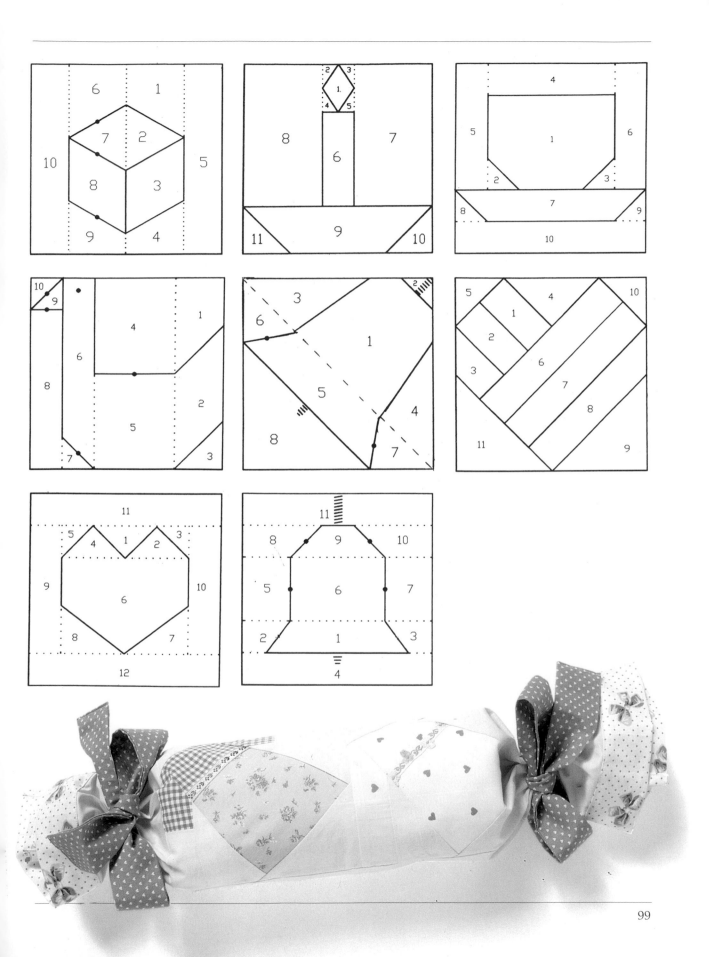

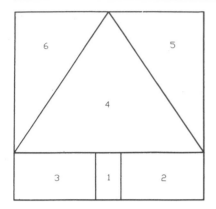

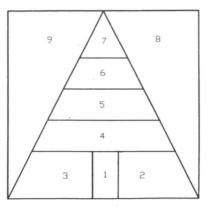

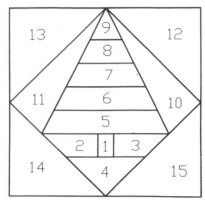

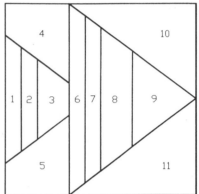

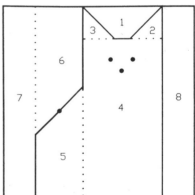

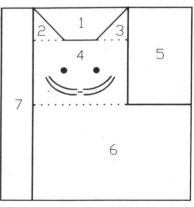

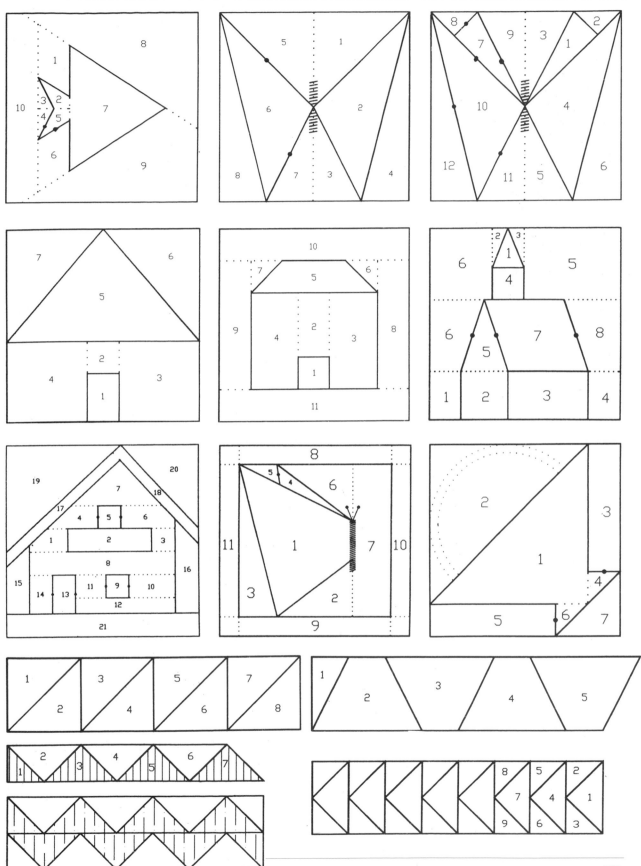

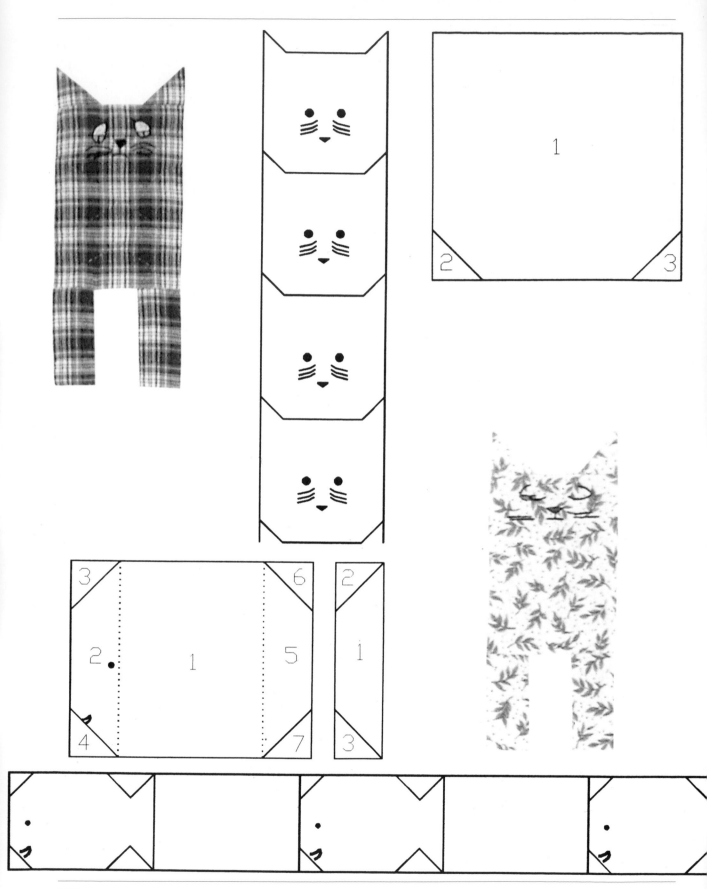

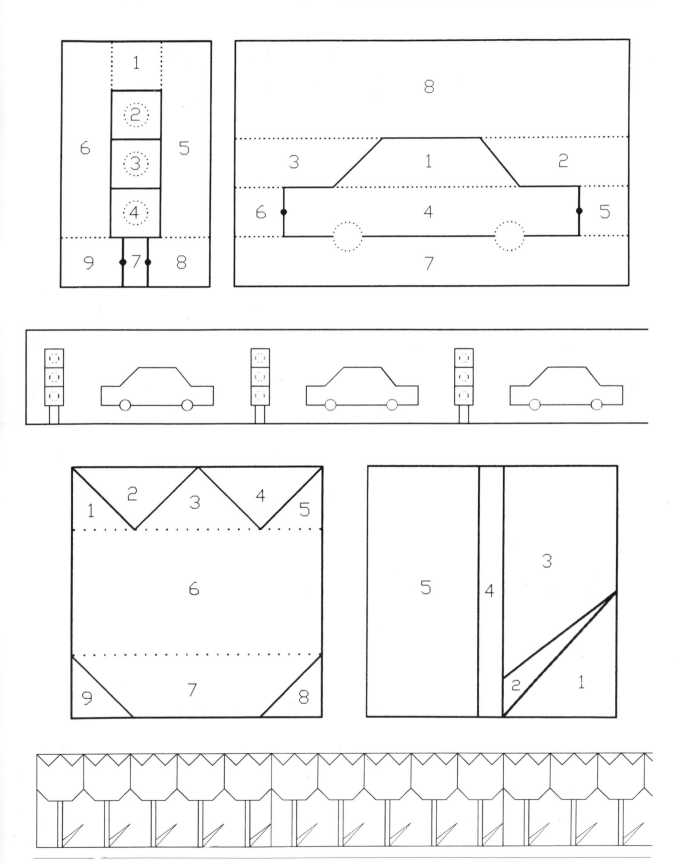

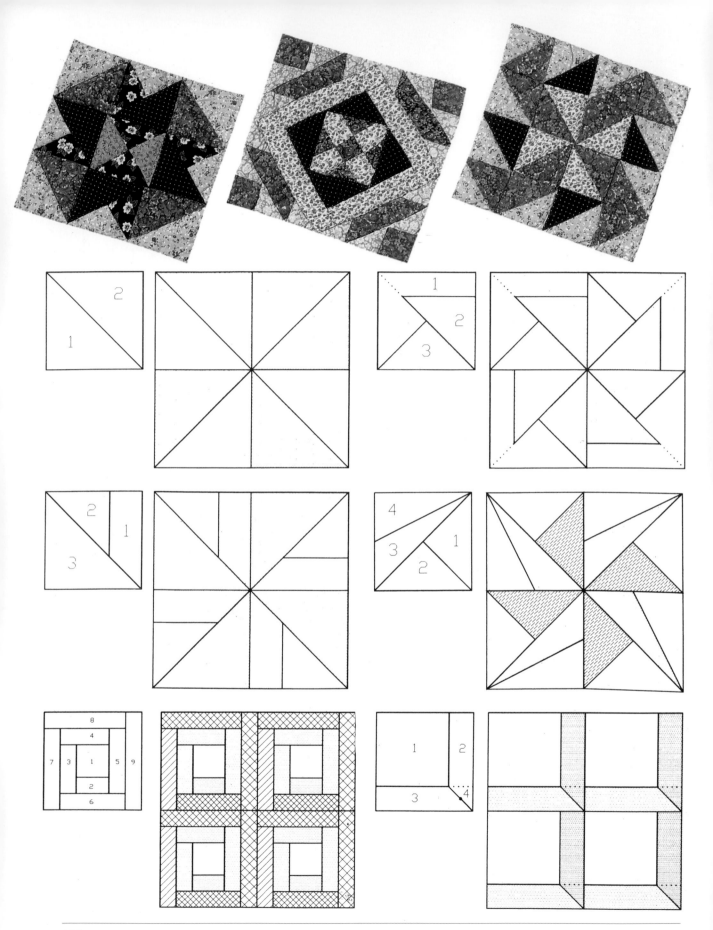

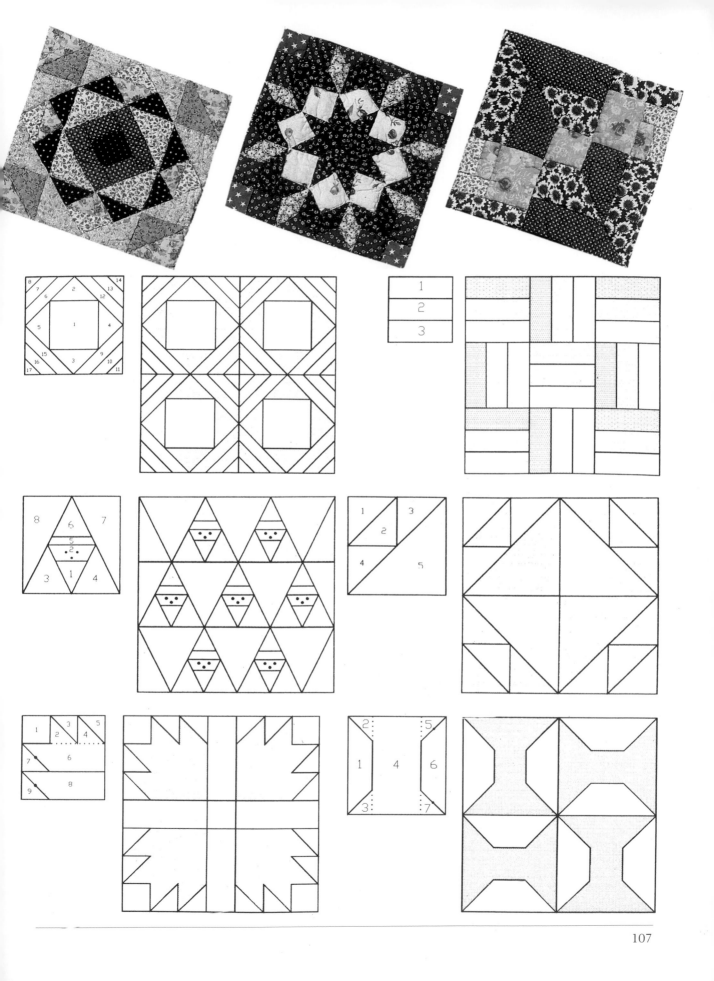

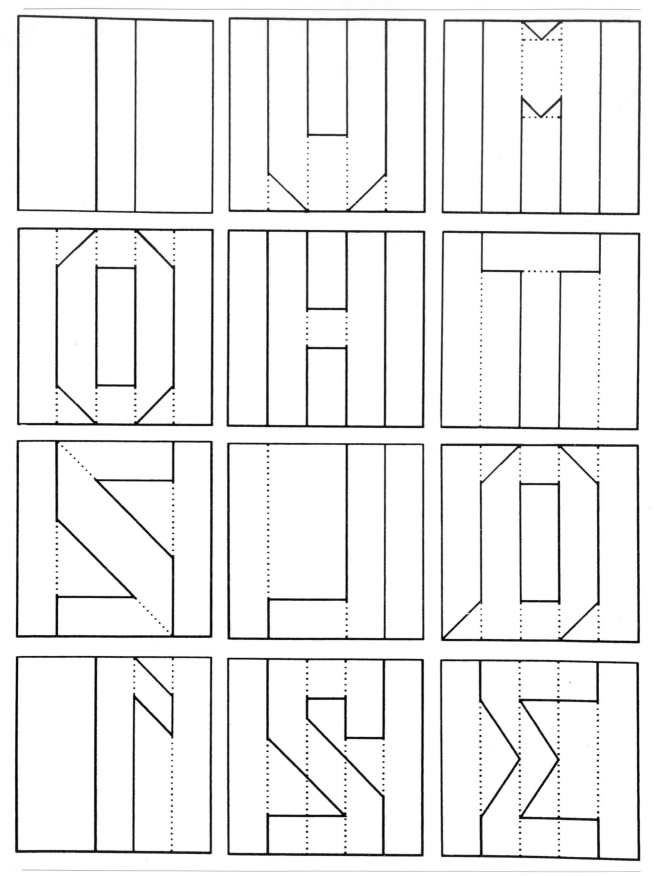

*Some letters and numbers are symmetrical and some are asymmetrical.*

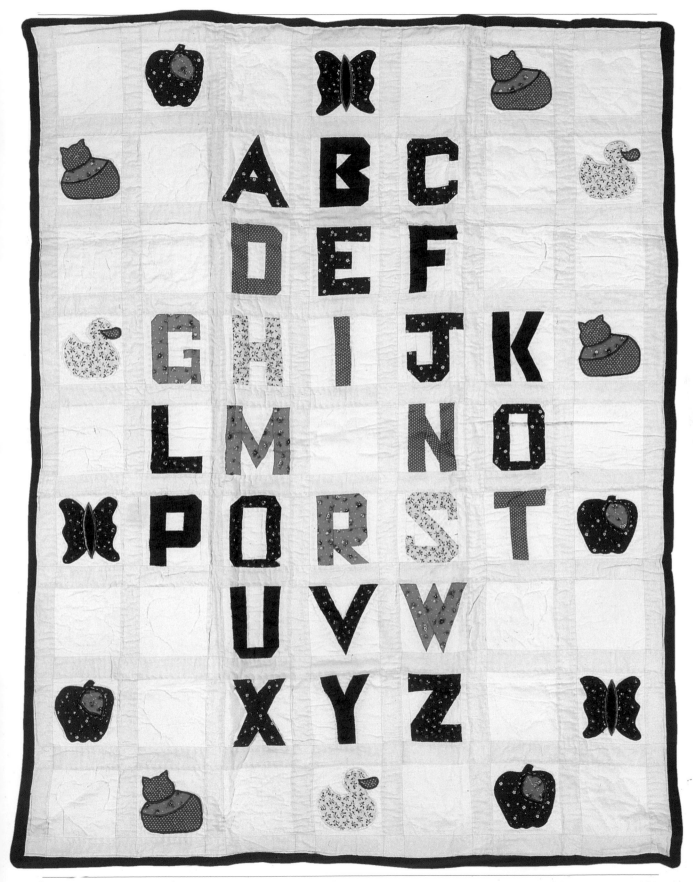

*Quilt by Coin.*

# PATCHWORK
# DESIGNS

# OVERVIEW OF PATCHWORK PATTERNS

The names of quilt designs, especially early American ones, are interesting. Every patchwork design, or at least every recurring design, has its own name, often a poetic one, which is sometimes descriptive or evocative, but always suggestive of the time period in which it was created. Every composition has its own particular symbolism, which reflects actual historical or social situations. For this reason, it is possible to date quilts quite accurately, based on their patchwork designs as well as the type of fabrics, colors, and prints used. It's possible to reconstruct a true and unique history of America through patchwork.

The name of a design often depends on the locality in which the work was created, and names changed as local conditions varied. The Lemoyne Star eventually became the Lemon Star; the design known as Duck's Foot in the Mud in Long Island was the Hand of Friendship in Philadelphia and the Bear's Paw in Ohio. The pattern originally called the Wedding Ring later was called the Crown of Thorns or the Windmill. Sometimes two different patterns have the same name, e.g., Road to California.

Generally the name is a clear reference to the pattern, as happens most of the time for designs from the natural world (leaves, fruit, wreaths, flowers, trees, countryside, etc.). At times, however, the reference is less direct, and we are confronted more with an idea than a figure, as with the Lady of the Lake, named to honor Walter Scott, author of a widely read book in the 1800s whose title was *The Lady of the Lake*. Delectable Mountains is another pattern that had literary inspiration, but here the design is more easily readable. With its sober colors (often white and green), it has the same feeling of peace evoked by a view of the mountains cloaked in green, described in John Bunyan's work *The Pilgrim's Progress,* very popular in the American colonies.

Some pattern names have a Biblical reference, e.g., Rose of Sharon or Jacob's Ladder. Many other patterns arose from early American family life because until the end of the 1800s most pioneer families lived on farms (only 2% lived in the city). Among these patterns we find: Goose in the Pond, Basket, Cake Stand, Fan, Spider Web, Birds in the Air (also known as Mosaic), Carpenter's Wheel or Dutch Rose, Dresden Plate, Honeybee, Shells, Flying Geese, and Corn and Beans. Some have very unusual names, like the Drunkard's Path, whose design suggests the idea of a winding path, or Robbing Peter to Pay Paul, where the pattern may be perceived in several ways.

Log Cabin quilts became popular in 1863 in the United States, quilt historians have discovered, when the Union army was raising money to finance the Civil War by raffling quilts. Because the president of the United States, Abraham Lincoln, grew up in a log cabin, the pattern may have become symbolic of loyalty to him. The Log Cabin pattern has been popular ever since. Depending on the way the Log Cabin blocks are arranged, or set, it may be known under a variety of names, including Barn Raising, Court House Steps, and Straight Furrows.

This book presents a certain number of patchwork designs. They are the most common ones, chosen because, in addition to their visual pleasure, mastering them will give you a greater ability to deal with more complex patterns later on.

Among the patchwork patterns used in the early pioneer times, the most common were: Bricks, Checkerboard, Octagons, Log Cabin, Pineapple, Square in a Square, 4-Patch, Double 4-Patch, 9-Patch, Double 9-Patch, 16-Patch, Christian Cross, and later on the Irish Chain. Irish Chain, known also as Puss in the Corner, was frequently done in England and in America. There are several variations: Double Irish Chain, Triple Irish Chain, and more complex ones called Multiple Irish Chains.

The early American designs generally were easy to do and used very small pieces of fabric, an essential factor in places of great poverty. Quilting stitches often enriched the composition of the quilts and compensated for the simplicity of their design.

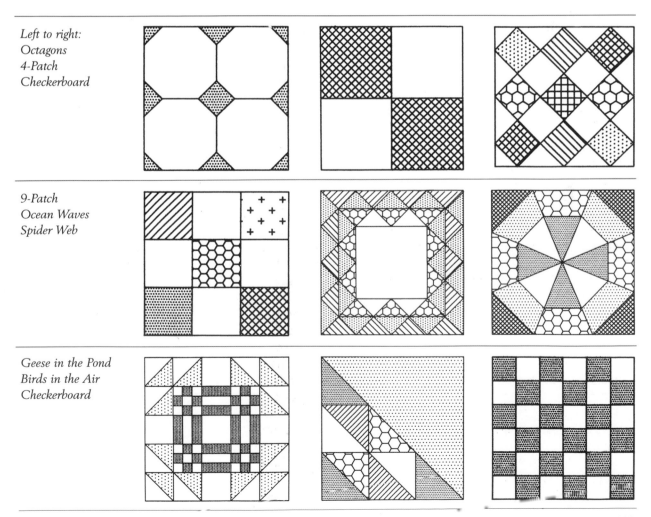

*Left to right:*
*Octagons*
*4-Patch*
*Checkerboard*

*9-Patch*
*Ocean Waves*
*Spider Web*

*Geese in the Pond*
*Birds in the Air*
*Checkerboard*

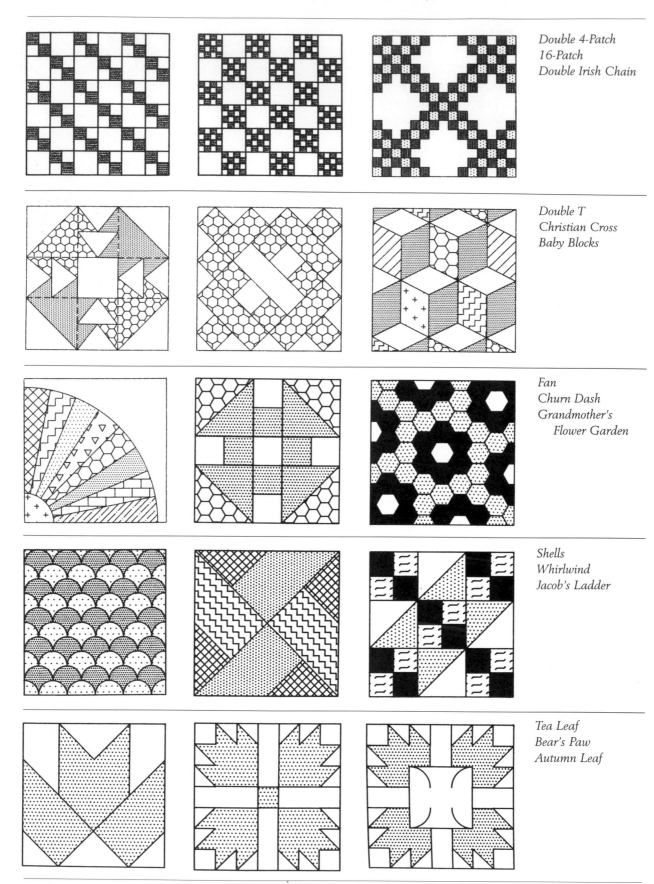

*Double 4-Patch*
*16-Patch*
*Double Irish Chain*

*Double T*
*Christian Cross*
*Baby Blocks*

*Fan*
*Churn Dash*
*Grandmother's*
   *Flower Garden*

*Shells*
*Whirlwind*
*Jacob's Ladder*

*Tea Leaf*
*Bear's Paw*
*Autumn Leaf*

*Road to California*
*Corn and Beans*
*Lady of the Lake*

*Dresden Plate*
*Pinwheel*
*Robbing Peter to*
*Pay Paul*

*Cactus Flower*
*Pine Tree*
*Cake Stand*
*Basket*

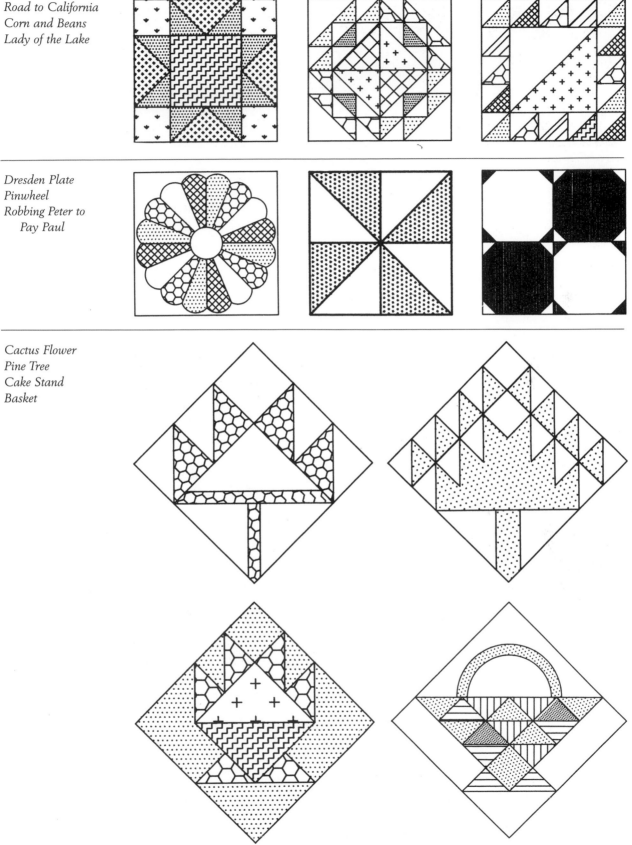

*Quilt of recent vintage, with Road to California blocks set at an angle, carried out in subdued colors (US).*

*Quilt with Ocean Waves pattern, in traditional white and blue (Ohio, about 1970).*

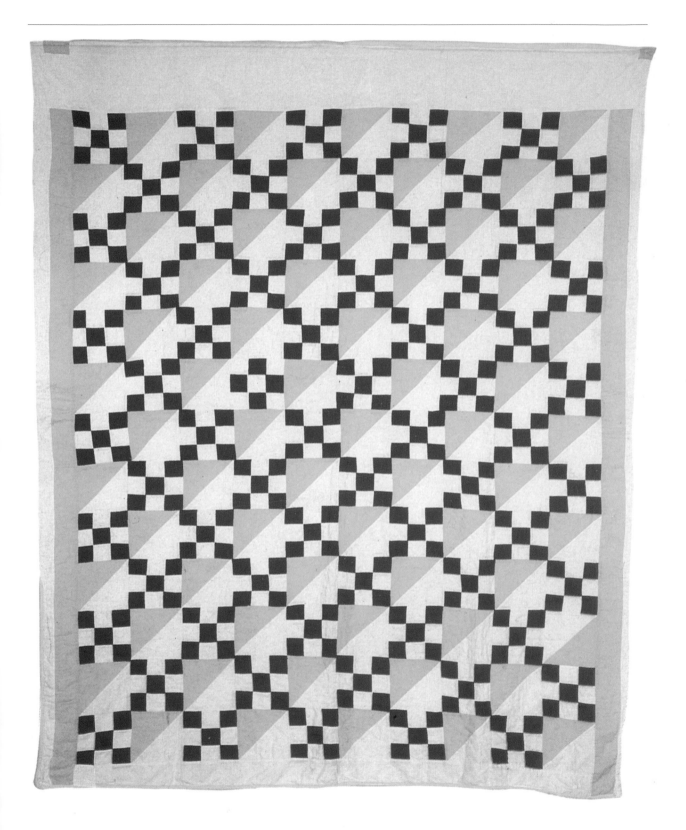

*Composition of 9-patch squares alternating with 2-triangle squares. This pattern also is called Road to California, even though it is a different design than the one on p. 116 (US, 1925–1950).*

*Opposite: Quilt in the Milky Way pattern, in pastel colors with straight and sawtooth borders, in delicate tones (US).*

*Two-color quilt with the Basket pattern; the inner border is saw-tooth, which empha-sizes the central section (US).*

*Opposite: Quilt with 9-Patch design in delicate colors, which also are used here in various borders (US).*

*Quilt in classic colors, ecru and red, with the Robbing Peter to Pay Paul design (US, about 1925).*

*Two-color quilt with the Christian Cross design, with a border of Flying Geese (US, about 1890).*

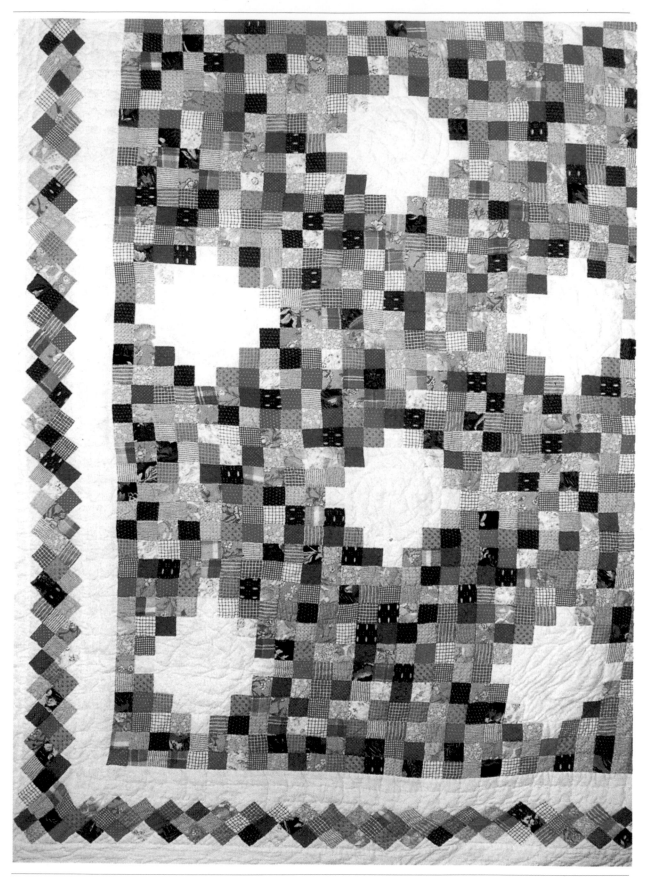

*Early American quilt in the Pinwheel design. Its wide lattice strips and borders are made of the same fabric (US, 1870).*

*Opposite: Quilt in Multiple Irish Chain pattern; the white part, which is the background of the chain, highlights the multicolored composition (US).*

*Below: Chips and Stones. A curious pattern, clearly of pioneer origin. The seven points of the star recall whetstone fragments (stones that men took with them to sharpen their hatchets), while the outer area represents branches (US).*

# LOG CABIN

The Log Cabin is undoubtedly the most famous of the innumerable patchwork designs that exist. Many think that it is of American origin. In reality, its origins grew from earlier traditions on both sides of the Atlantic. A well-advanced hypothesis by an English researcher indicates that a source of inspiration is to be found in the way land was subdivided and cultivated in England from ancient times to the 1600s.

The Log Cabin was done in England in 1700, but American quilters made it famous during pioneer times. From the 1800s, it was so intimately linked to the New World traditions that its American origins were taken for granted. The Log Cabin, perfectly suited to the pioneers' lifestyle, was always present in their rooms and therefore became the symbol of shelter from the natural elements and at the same time an example of civility in the wild New World.

The Log Cabin was suited to the lifestyle of the pioneers in terms of its graphic design as well as its simple work method, which meant it could be executed anywhere, even in the most limited and inhospitable of places, as was often the case in the early American colonies. Since it is possible to construct the Log Cabin on a base layer of fabric, you can use the most varied of fabrics; problems from this disparity are minimized or eliminated by having an underlying layer.

*Variations on the Log Cabin pattern.*

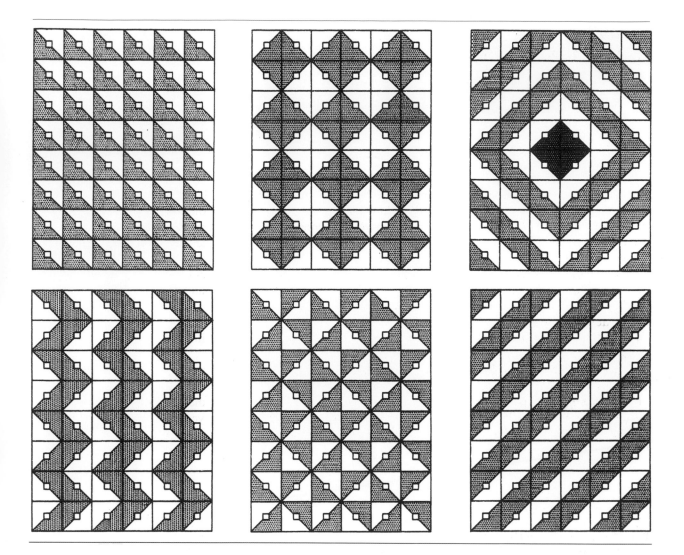

*Various settings of*
*Log Cabin blocks.*

In various places and times, the Log Cabin has been called by many different names: Roof Pattern, Canadian Logwood, and also Mummy Pattern, because it recalls the windings used in the tombs of ancient Egypt.

The current name is Log Cabin. With the square, usually red, in the center and strips of light colors on two sides and dark on the other two, it represents the inside of the house, with a fire in the center that lights up two walls and leaves the other two in darkness.

The Log Cabin, very easy to piece, is one of the most interesting patchwork designs, visually speaking. From the original pattern infinite variations were derived by altering of one or more compositional elements, such as: the final geometric shape (square, triangle, rectangle, diamond, hexagon, etc.); the position of the initial patch (in the center, off center, in a corner); and the layout of the strips, which may progress as spirals or in opposite parallel pairs, such as in the Court House Steps, or overlap to form the classic Pineapple Log Cabin.

The Log Cabin is very versatile, because it offers innumerable variations in the setting (layout) of the quilt blocks. In viewing the Log Cabin quilt it may be difficult to make out the individual quilt blocks, because the optical impression of the whole overpowers them.

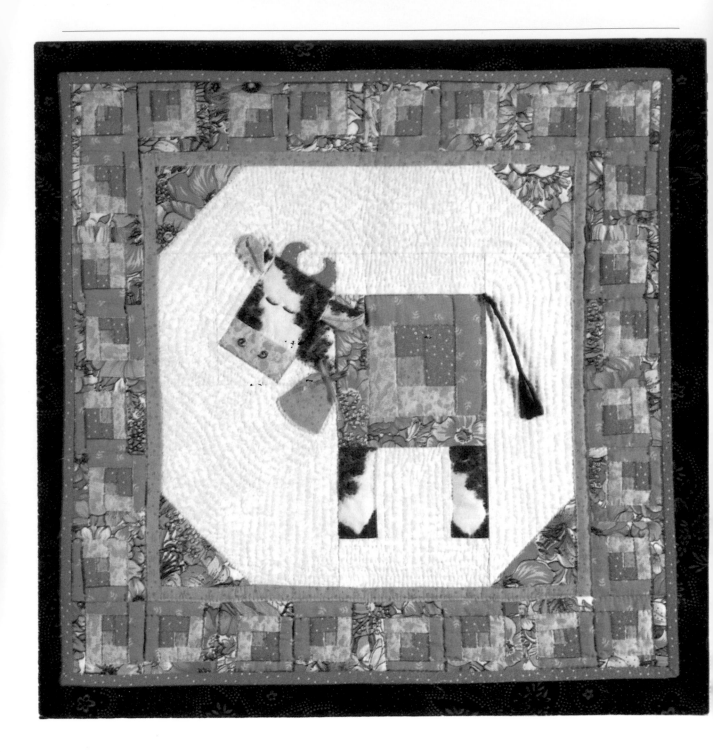

*Log Cabin squares form a
part of the central pattern
and decorative border.*

*Quilt with Log Cabin squares in a
Pinwheel setting.*

# STARS

Lemon Star, Ohio Star, Feathered Star, Radiant Star—the varieties of star patterns number in the hundreds. We might wonder why this figurative element was so immensely popular.

The star has always been an inspiration, as seen in decorations carried out by people all over the world. We find stars in the mosaics on Roman and Arab floors and in clothing, as well as in furniture decorations and other household items.

Stars have always inspired every form of craftsperson and artist, from those who sewed patchwork to painters and poets, who called stars the forget-me-nots of the angels, the windows of paradise, and the daisies of the sky.

In patchwork, stars can constitute a basic design element or a complementary one; they may appear individually or in groups; and they may be used in various combinations. They may have 4, 5, 6, 7 or 8 points and an infinite array of colors. The star is a very versatile design, and it has been one of the most popular patterns over the years. We can make a few guesses about the reasons for the popularity of stars among Americans who sewed.

Stars were a constant and meaningful presence in the lives of the sailors and navigators, who scrutinized them in the evening sky. They trusted them as their guides and consulted directions on their nautical maps. The importance of the stars was not ignored by the navigators' wives on the banks of the Atlantic, who awaited the return of their husbands.

The women of the first generation of pioneer Americans also navigated by the stars as they made their long journey across the sea from the mother country, coming to a dark, unknown destiny, illuminated only by hope and the light of the stars.

In the daily lives of these hard-working people, stars marked the passing of time and accompanied their work on the land, which depended a great deal on the weather. Other stars, waving in the wind on the American flag, expressed the longing for peace and unity of so many states.

The Amish, particularly sensitive to religious symbolism, put stars on many of their wonderful quilts to express their admiration for creation.

Today the star pattern is used on quilts of every country, and every artist brings to it his or her own personal interpretation. Among the many stars that have now become classic is the Lemon Star: it has 8 points and is made up of diamonds or rhomboids. It was introduced in America at the time of French colonization, and was named for Jean Baptiste Lemoyne, who in 1718 founded New Orleans, called Nouvelle Orléans at the time, in honor of the French regent, the Duke of Orleans. Lemoyne had a coat of arms with an 8-pointed star on it, from which the Lemoyne Star arose. Later the design became unpopular in America because of to its pro-French associations, perhaps the reason that the Lemoyne Star became the Lemon Star. Others believe it is only an unwitting mispronunciation or simply the Americanization of a French name.

*Star blocks alternate with a different geometric pattern make up this country style American quilt.*

The Lemon Star lends itself to being joined to so many other designs that it greatly enriches the whole. In many variations of the Lemon Star design, every diamond or rhomboid corresponding to a point is divided into 4, 9, or 16 parts or even many more, sometimes hundreds of tiny pieces. Every variation has its own name, such as Virginia Star, Bethlehem Star, Blazing Star, Eastern Star, and Radiant or Texas Star.

A quilt with these designs acted as a kind of status symbol for those sewing during the 1800s; it was appreciated not so much for its warmth, since it wasn't often used as a daily blanket, as for its aesthetic prestige. It was the masterpiece that every quilter strove to do. The stars, made up of many little patches, were frequently done because it was possible to make them with tiny pieces of fabric. In earlier times, these designs were sewn by hand, but they can also be done by machine. They are designs for expert quilters. The least bit of imperfection becomes a serious problem when repeated such a large number of times in the pieces.

Other very famous stars are the Ohio Star and the Road to California, which are quite similar and often are confused with each other.

Road to California evokes the adventures of the pioneers. In a diary of that time period, we read, for example, of a family who, after leaving the Atlantic coast, took one year to reach the Far West. It is easy to imagine scenes of rickety wagons and many people, exposed to the harsh night climate, sleeping in covered wagons under quilts. They were called utility quilts for good reason!

During all those long months, it was a relief to be able to enjoy the pleasure of doing patchwork. The pieces multiplied, the squares increased, and the dream of the quilt, which would be completed at the next stopover, perhaps at a quilting bee, lightened hearts and alleviated the hardships of endless travel.

The Ohio Star and the Road to California were the jumping off points for innumerable variations such as Missouri Star, Broken Star, Rising Star, and so on. Their names arose because of the different places and times of their composition.

*Opposite: The Ohio Star or Road to California, and variations.*

*Below: The Lemoyne or Lemon Star and its variations.*

*Elaborate quilt with Dutch Rose pattern. The rich patch-work composition is decorated with feathered quilting designs, in addition to the color gradations of the fabric.*

*Quilt with the Compass
Rose design (US, 1867).*

# GRANDMOTHER'S FLOWER GARDEN

*Opposite:
Velvet sofa cover
with hexagons in
bright and contrasting
colors, in a scattered
arrangement
(R. D. Sassi).*

The hexagon often was used in English patchwork, starting in the early 1700s. In Victorian times, very tiny hexagons of costly fabrics were made, and these made the quilts true gems.

The pattern most commonly composed with hexagons is Grandmother's Flower Garden, which enjoyed great popularity in America as well, especially after it became commonplace for the two countries to exchange the most noteworthy examples of their creations.

In the original pattern, we find a piece in the center, generally yellow (the flower bud), 6 equal-sized hexagons around it (the petals), at times another 12 equal-sized hexagons around them (more petals), and beyond these, many green hexagons signifying the grassy paths of the grandmother's garden. Setting the hexagons in diamond form, rather than in the hexagonal layout, also was common.

Quilts where the setting of the hexagons is not uniformly arranged and doesn't form any geometric shape are equally delightful. Where the size of the hexagons permits, quilting stitches, also in hexagonal designs, may enrich the completed work.

*Hexagons arranged
in petal (left) or
diamond setting
(right).*

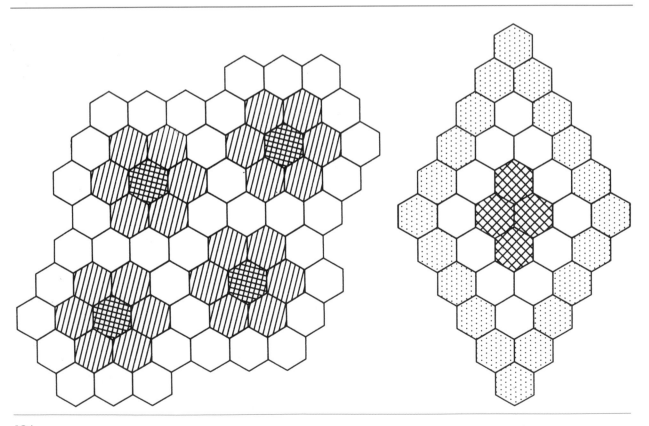

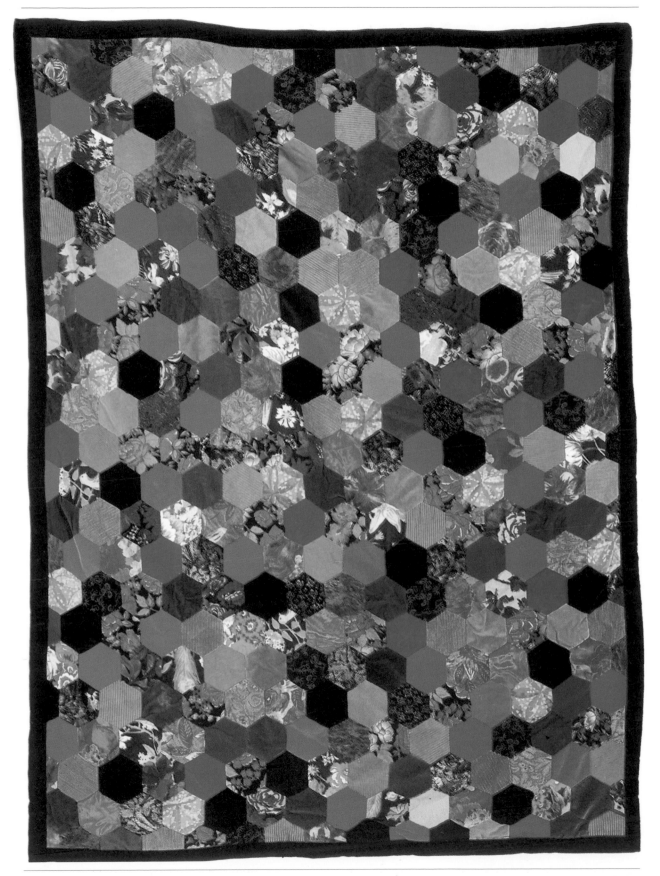

# BRIDAL OR WEDDING QUILTS

Patchwork arose and developed mainly within the family setting, so it is easy to understand why the Bridal Quilt has always been considered special. Quilts made to celebrate matrimonial knot-tying have always displayed the highest level of ingenuity, creativity, and skill.

Why did American women of the 1800s devote so much effort to creating quilts if not for the preparation of a hope chest? The American girl, initiated into quilting from the time she was little, began early to prepare the quilt tops that would later be quilted. It isn't known with certainty how many quilts generally were included in the bride's trousseau. One estimate puts the ideal number at 12. Girls who were particularly fortunate sometimes went beyond 12, which for most people remained a dream. One writer tells us of a trousseau that had more than 20 quilts, but then adds that the bride was uglier than ugly. The quilt tops were prepared well in advance and were batted, backed, and stitched at the last moment, so as not to take up a lot of room in the home or cause the parents to prematurely face the expense of finishing the quilts, the last effort of the family before marrying off their daughter. Furthermore, superstition forbad stitching the whole trousseau before the engagement was announced officially. Finishing the partially ready quilts and the creation of the Bridal Quilt were generally occasions for a quilting party, eagerly awaited by everybody.

What quilts were contained in the bride's trunk? No doubt an elegant quilt for use on special occasions. Perhaps for this reason these are the only kind that have reached us. Most likely, one with the Wedding Ring pattern or with the glorious Double Wedding Ring pattern and another with the Rose of Sharon pattern. Heart pattern quilts which, had they been used for a different reason, would have been thought to bring bad luck, were included, as were love knots, flowers, wreaths, and baskets, which, as symbols of abundance, augured good fortune. Finally, there was the dove, symbol of fidelity because this white, spotless bird only mates with a single companion during its lifetime, even if the companion dies.

*Opposite: The classic pattern for wedding quilts, the Double Wedding Ring, done in pale colors and edged with delicately colored scalloping.*

*Details of quilt with Wedding Ring design.*

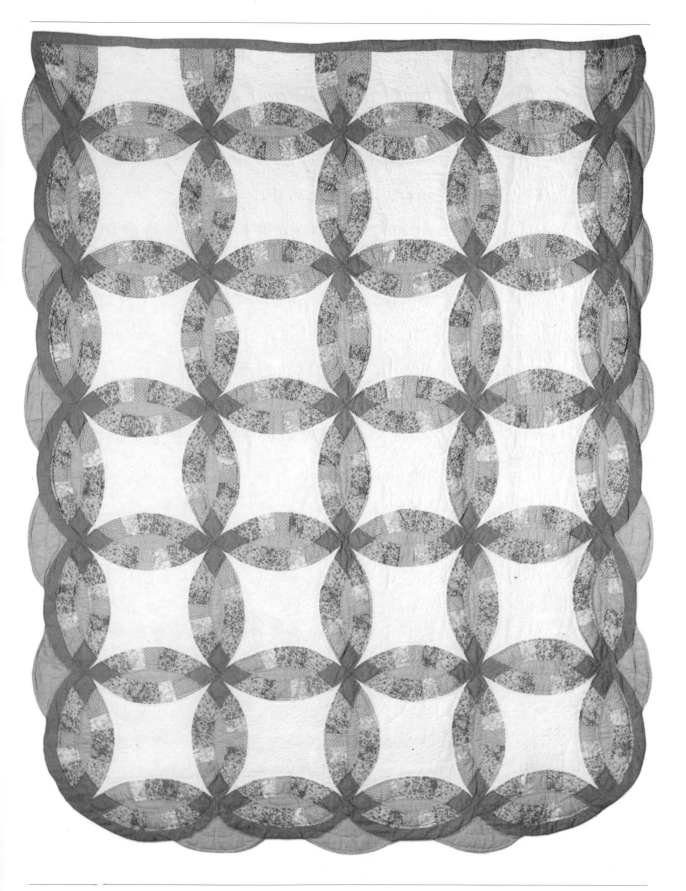

*Opposite: Richly worked quilt with piecing and appliqué of geometric and floral designs. Love knots, wreaths, and baskets, symbolic of good fortune, a must in every trousseau, embellish the squares. The quilting stitches, extended over the whole quilt, add nuances of light and darkness (US).*

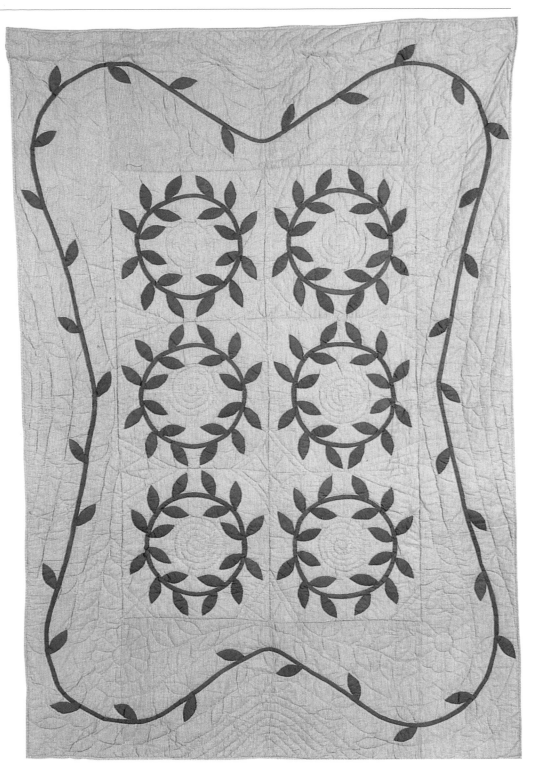

*Appliqué quilt with wreath patterns in the center. On the border there are loosely spaced leaves and a long, uninterrupted stem, in accordance with superstition. The basic design of the appliqués is enriched by the quilting overall (US).*

# CHRISTMAS QUILT

*Christmas wreath in wool.*

From the mid-1800s in America and even earlier in England, the Christmas Quilt helped to create the warm atmosphere of Christmas at home.

In the world of the pioneers, a bright Christmaslike cover was particularly delightful, in part because it compensated for the rigors of the season in modest homes. Every family possessed at least one quilt which, lovingly put away for the rest of the year, came out in all its glory for Christmas and was a much sought after inheritance.

Christmas quilts were generally done in white, green, and red, colors that symbolize Christmas. Green recalls holly and in the Christian liturgy symbolizes eternal life; red is the color of berries and symbolizes the passion of Christ; white is symbolic, in turn, of the purity bequeathed to humans by the Savior. White is also the color of the cloak of snow that always has been associated with nature during Christmastime. The appliquéd or pieced patterns most frequently employed in quilts and other quilted creations for Christmas have a symbolic value: the wreath (the circle symbolizes eternity), bells (joyous announcement of the coming of the Savior), candles (lights of hope in the dark world of humans), and stars (lights that guide people, as at the time they guided the Three Magi). The spruce tree, Santa Claus, sleds and reindeer, long stockings for gifts and toys, dolls, stuffed bears, little drums, and decorated boxes also appear often. Designs such as the Log Cabin and House, done in white, green and red, are classic, because they evoke a particularly pleasing element associated with Christmastime: the home.

*Stocking for gifts, made with the shell pattern.*

*Little tree decorated with hearts in classic Christmas colors.*

*Quilt with Double Wedding Ring design,*
*using traditional holiday colors.*

# OTHER TYPES OF QUILT

The ordinary and special occasions that were commemorated by the creation of quilts are numerous. There are friendship quilts, group quilts, freedom quilts (for coming of age), presentation quilts (gifts), commemorative quilts, album quilts, Bible quilts, and political quilts. Often the same piece may be classified in several categories. A freedom quilt, for example, can also be considered a group quilt or a friendship quilt. The freedom quilt was a gift traditionally given to a young man in America at the time of his 21st birthday, when he was emancipated from the family. It was generally made by friends and relatives and bore their words and names, written in ink or embroidered in the central part of the design or in other areas that were purposely laid out in light colors. Sometimes symbolic designs appeared, appliquéd or pieced, as well as words of luck and love from the man's mother.

The friendship quilt usually was a work done by the group, made to be given as a gift of welcome to a family that had come to settle in the area or to one that was going away to seek their fortune elsewhere. The friendship quilt frequently had blocks that were signed by their creators—a physical reminder of the support of the people and the community. It might be given to express a feeling of friendship on many other occasions also.

Another gift quilt in the American tradition is the album quilt, made up of squares done by many different people. It could also be made by a single person with the intention of commemorating important events in the life of a family, at times displaying the entire genealogical tree. A good number of old American album quilts have survived, because they were used exclusively for specific occasions and more often than not were hung on the walls.

The Mourning Quilt was created to commemorate a deceased person and generally included symbolic patterns linked to the person who had passed away. The Death Watch Quilt was made by one or more persons at the bedside of a dying person and often used fabrics that belonged to that person. Love and sensitivity to nature, very noticeable in Hawaiian culture, are demonstrated in the Hawaiian quilt, where appliqué, masterfully done, creates works of high aesthetic value.

*Preceding pages:*
*Page 142: Valuable example of Hawaiian work, in red and green on ecru background. The composition of squares is enhanced by sawtooth borders and restrained quilting.*

*Page 143: Album Quilt, richly worked in appliqué. The lattice strips and sawtooth border highlight the composition (US, about 1940).*

*Friendship Quilt, made in squares with the Chimney Sweep pattern (named because of the "hole" in the middle of the design), which offers space for the signatures of those who collaborated in making it. The lattice strips in pink delightfully set off the multicolored squares (US, about 1940).*

The patterns, inspired by flowers, fruit, and leaves, are generally done in bright colors of whole cloth, appliquéd to a light-colored background, which highlights the richness of the design and the clarity of the outline. The template for the Hawaiian appliqué pattern is made by folding a paper square several times and cutting it to obtain symmetrical sections.

## CRAZY QUILTING

Crazy Quilting was perhaps the first pattern that joined varied pieces of fabric to a base to keep them together. If this is the case, it has come a long way, bringing with it examples of spectacular quilts, especially those done at the end of the 1800s in Victorian England. At that time very elaborate and rich Crazy Quilting was done, which used valuable fabrics (often brocade, silk, or velvet), meticulous appliqués, and an abundance of embroidery in threads of every type, not only along the stitch lines of the patches, but also in the centers of the patches.

America made this style its own for a while, as it tried to emulate overseas elegance, but the Depression of the 1920s and 1930s resulted in simpler works, and even Crazy Quilting was done in simple cotton fabrics, losing its elegance.

*Friendship Quilt, made with fabric scraps of the period and signed by those who participated in its creation (US, about 1840).*

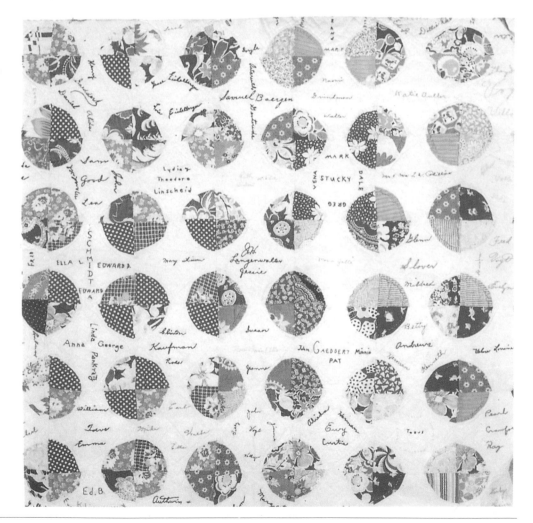

# AMISH QUILTS

Amish quilts have become world-famous. The Amish are a religious subgroup of Anabaptists of mostly Swiss and German origin. In the 1700s, during the time of the Protestant Reformation, the Amish came to the New World to escape religious persecution. The Amish lead a simple life that tries to avoid the seductions of the modern world. They do not use cars, trains, or buses, but rather walk or use a horse and carriage. They don't use electricity and are unfamiliar with such everyday diversions as the movies and television.

In their simple lives, they find serenity through their deep religious beliefs and have a special sensitivity to nature and colors. Their quilts were traditionally done with solid colors of fabric, since Amish religious teachings forbid fabric with patterns. The quilts are mostly made up of simple geometric shapes (rectangles, squares, and triangles) but are embellished with quilting stitches that are beautifully planned and executed. The most captivating characteristic of the Amish quilts is their wonderful use of color, which is achieved even though the fabrics they use are mostly the green, blue, brown, and black prevalent in Amish garments, from which the scraps come. Bright colors such as light blues, pinks, and reds also appear in their work.

# RECENT TRENDS IN QUILTING

In addition to traditional quilting, which repeats classic designs in a myriad of interpretations, a new way of understanding patchwork has developed. In America, in 1976, the term "art quilt" was used for the first time with reference to patchwork, to indicate that the fabrics used were like the palette of colors that compose a painting. Art quilts, figurative or

*Small Amish patchwork quilt has a geometric composition and simple quilted designs.*

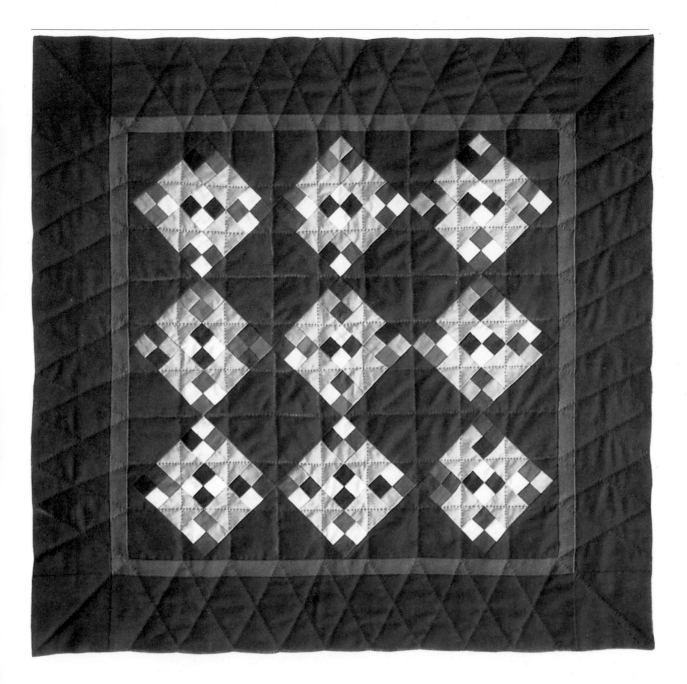

*Dark colors of the background and the border are characteristic of the Amish and highlight the patchwork squares (Rochester, Minnesota).*

abstract, are true and proper paintings and as such are valued and usually are not used as bed quilts but as panels or wall hangings.

In 1976, when quilts were still serving a predominantly practical function, an interest in quilts solely as art seemed revolutionary. At that time people might have wondered if this new tendency resulted only from by the desire to commemorate the Bicentennial of the founding of the United States with patchwork. It seemed visionary then to think that fabric could be used to create quilts that would one day hang in museums alongside paintings, but now, more than 25 years later, the idea of quilts as art has become an established reality.

Many artists, even those with academic backgrounds, at a certain point in their careers have rediscovered themselves through textiles, stimulated by fabrics of a wide range of lusters, opacities, transparencies, and weights.

*Florence at dusk has a peaceful feeling (pictorial quilt by A. Brenti).*

*Pictorial quilt has a rich representation of the natural environment (from Les Nouvelles du Patchwork magazine, Paris).*

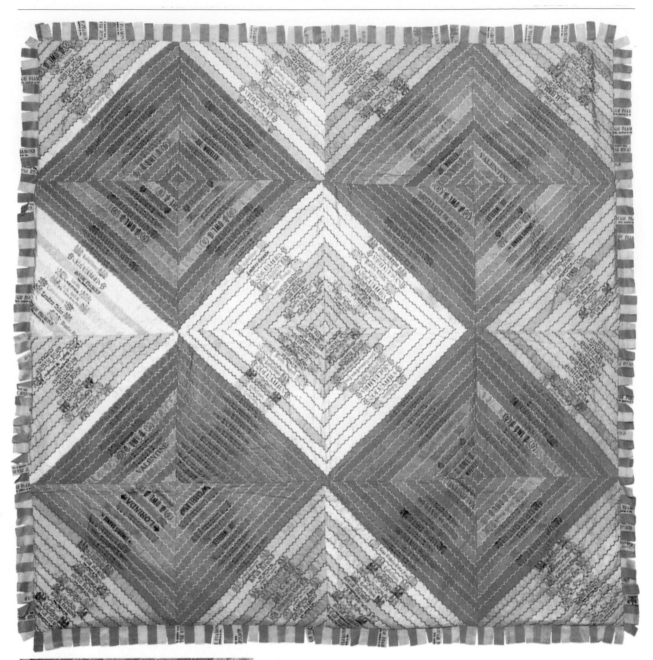

*Quilt from the 1800s
made with distinctive
remnant material: the
printed silk tape pieces
that decorated cigar
boxes.*

*On p. 151, Crazy
Quilt in the style of
England in the 1800s,
characterized by rich
decoration.*

# PROJECTS

# CUP-AND-SAUCER POTHOLDERS

## DIRECTIONS

◆ Add seam allowances to all cutting dimensions given below

◆ Prepare paper templates using the patterns on p. 372

◆ Cut the background fabric 8 × 8" (20 × 20 cm)

◆ Cut the fabric cup, saucer, and handle pieces, prepare the appliqués, and sew them to the background square to make the quilt top

◆ Cut the backing 10¼ × 10¼" (26 × 26 cm)

◆ Cut the batting 8 × 8" (20 × 20 cm)

◆ Pin together the three layers: quilt top, batting, and backing

◆ Baste and outline-quilt around appliqué.

◆ Fold the edges of the backing to the front of the piece to form the border and stitch in place

◆ Create and apply the bow and a loop for hanging from plaid fabric

◆ Make the second potholder in the same way.

**TECHNIQUES**
*Appliqué, outline quilting*

**PATTERNS**
*Cup and saucer*

**SIZE**
*8 × 8" (20 × 20 cm)*

**MATERIALS**
• *Print fabric for the cup*
• *Solid-color fabric for background*
• *Plaid for backing, border, bow, and loop* .
• *Batting*

# CUP-AND-SAUCER PANEL

## DIRECTIONS

**TECHNIQUES**
*Appliqué, quilting*

**PATTERNS**
*Cup and saucer*

**SIZE**
*31½ × 41¼" (80 × 105 cm)*

**MATERIALS**
• *Print fabrics in various colors for cups and saucers*
• *Pink plaid for background*
• *Red print for 1st border*
• *Ecru print for 2nd border*
• *Batting*
• *Backing fabric*

◆ Add seam allowances to all cutting dimensions given below
◆ Prepare paper templates using the patterns on p. 372
◆ Cut out the fabric pieces and prepare the appliqués
◆ Cut the background fabric 26 × 34" (66 × 86 cm) and appliqué the cups and saucers to it
◆ Cut the first border 1½" (3.5 cm) wide and sew onto the background

◆ Cut the second border 5" (12 cm) wide, which includes 2½" (6 cm) width plus and an additional 2½" (6 cm) for finishing, and sew it on
◆ Cut the batting and backing 33½ × 41¼" (85 × 105 cm)
◆ Pin together the three layers: quilt top, batting, and backing
◆ Baste and quilt the layers
◆ Trim the batting. Finish by folding and stitching the excess of outer border to back.

# HEARTS WALL HANGING

## DIRECTIONS

◆ Add seam allowances to all cutting dimensions given below

◆ Prepare paper templates using the heart pattern on p. 373 and cut out 12 hearts from fabric

◆ Cut 12 background squares 7 × 7" (18 × 18 cm)

◆ Cut the lattice strips, 2" (5 cm) wide

◆ Cut 6 light blue lattice squares 2 × 2" (5 × 5 cm)

◆ Cut the outer borders 4½" (11½ cm) wide, which includes 2½" (6½ cm) plus 2" (5 cm) to finish edge

◆ Cut batting and backing 39¼ × 30¼" (100 × 77 cm)

◆ Prepare the appliqués and appliqué one to the center of every background square

◆ Pin and stitch the background squares and adjoining lattice strips in horizontal rows (see #1, p. 373)

◆ Stitch together the lattice strips and light blue lattice squares in 2 horizontal rows (see #1, p. 373)

◆ Stitch the horizontal rows together to form the quilt top (see #2, p. 373)

◆ Stitch on the border (see #3 and #4, p. 373)

◆ Pin the three layers: top, batting, and backing

◆ Baste and quilt the layers together, using outline quilting around hearts.

◆ Trim batting. Finish the sides by folding part of border to the back and stitching it in place.

**TECHNIQUES**
*Appliqué, American piecing, quilting*

**PATTERN**
*Heart*

**SIZE**
*Block: 7 × 7"
(18 × 18 cm)
Wall-hanging: 39¼ ×
30¼" (100 × 77 cm)*

**MATERIALS**
• *Prints and solid fabrics in several colors for hearts*
• *Ecru for background squares*
• *Ecru print for lattice strips*
• *Light blue dotted fabric for border and lattice squares*
• *Batting*
• *Backing fabric*

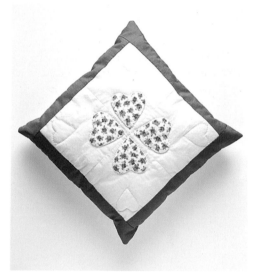

Baby carriage cover.

Above right:
Potholders with
hearts.

Center right: Pillow
with hearts.

Below: Cat pillows.

Below right: Bathrobe and bib
plus baby sack with hearts.

# QUILT WITH HEART WREATHS

## DIRECTIONS

◆ Add seam allowances to all cutting dimensions given below
◆ Prepare paper templates using heart pattern on p. 374
◆ Cut background squares 11¾ × 11¾" (30 × 30 cm)
◆ Cut out fabric hearts and prepare the appliqués
◆ Appliqué 10 hearts in a wreath in every square (see p. 374 for layout)
◆ Stitch the squares together in horizontal rows

◆ Stitch the rows together to form the quilt top
◆ Draw the quilting designs on the quilt
◆ Cut the batting and backing 71 × 94½" (180 × 240 cm)
◆ Pin together the three layers: quilt top, batting, and backing
◆ Baste and quilt the layers; trim batting
◆ Finish the sides with satin blanket binding or borders of white fabric.

**TECHNIQUES**
*Piecing, appliqué, quilting*

**PATTERN**
*Heart*

**SIZE**
*Block: 11¾ × 11¾" (30 × 30 cm)*
*Quilt: 71 × 94½" (180 × 240 cm)*

**MATERIALS**
• *Several colorful prints for hearts*
• *White fabric for background*
• *Batting*
• *Backing fabric*
• *Satin binding*

# LITTLE BEAR APPLIQUÉ

**TECHNIQUES**
*Appliqué, piecing (for tote)*

**PATTERN**
*Little bear*

**SIZE**
*Block: 8 × 8"
(20 × 20 cm)*

**MATERIALS**
• *Colorful prints and solids for appliqués*
• *Solid color (or small print) for background square*

## DIRECTIONS

◆ Add seam allowances to all appliqué pieces and blocks
◆ Cut the fabric squares and paper templates for bear, using patterns on p. 375

◆ Prepare appliqués and sew to background square
◆ Stitch finished block to garment or bag.

*The same little bear pattern can be appliquéd to a T-shirt or a tote bag (bag layout on p. 375).*

# LITTLE QUILT WITH SQUARES

## DIRECTIONS

◆ Add seam allowances to all cutting dimensions given below

◆ Cut 25 squares 4 × 4" (10 × 10 cm) out of print fabrics

◆ Stitch the squares together in horizontal rows

◆ Stitch rows together to form the quilt top (see diagrams, p. 376)

◆ Cut the first border 1½" (3.5 cm) wide and the second one ¾" (2 cm) wide

◆ Stitch on first border and second border,

◆ Cut the ruffle 4" wide (10 cm) and fold it in half; stitch to the second border

◆ Cut the batting and backing about 22 × 22" (56 × 56 cm)

◆ Pin together the three layers: quilt top, batting, and backing

◆ Baste and quilt layers together

◆ Square up the sides and stitch backing to the ruffle with hemstitch.

**TECHNIQUES**
*American piecing, quilting*

**PATTERN**
*Square*

**SIZE**
*Square: 4 × 4"
(10 × 10 cm)
Quilt: 22 × 22"
(56 × 56 cm)*

**MATERIALS**
• *Three colorful prints for squares*
• *Solid fabrics in pale rose and green for borders*
• *Bright pink fabric for ruffle*
• *Batting*
• *Backing fabric*

*Above: Little wall hanging of brightly colored squares.*

*Upper right: Satchel bag with ribbon decoration.*

*Right: Bright squares for a toy tote.*

*Below: Small tote bag, decorated with grosgrain ribbon.*

*Lower right: Carriage blanket.*

# SHELLS SQUARE

## DIRECTIONS

◆ Add seam allowances to all cutting dimensions given below
◆ Prepare paper templates using the pattern on p. 377
◆ Cut the fabric pieces and prepare 18 appliqués
◆ Cut the base fabric 9½" × 8" (24 × 20 cm)
◆ Cut 5 squares 3 × 3" (7.5 × 7.5 cm) out of prints, join 3 to form a horizontal strip
◆ Appliqué the strip to the upper part of the base rectangle (see p. 377 for diagrams)

◆ Appliqué 4 shells on the strip of squares to form the first line at the top
◆ Appliqué 3 more shells to form a second row
◆ Appliqué 4 shells to form a third row and so on, until you cover all of the base fabric
◆ Trim the sides of the square, cutting off the extra parts of the shells that extend beyond the rectangle
◆ Cut a border 2" wide (5 cm) and stitch to the square. Frame square and hang.

**TECHNIQUE**
*Appliqué*

**PATTERN**
*Shell*

**SIZE**
*Shell: 3 × 3"
(7.5 × 7.5 cm)
Quilt: 13 × 11¾"
(33 × 30 cm)*

**MATERIALS**
• *Several print fabrics for the shells, squares, and border*
• *Plain fabric for the base rectangle*
• *Picture frame*

*Baby quilt with Shell pattern in a*
*wide range of blue-and-white fabrics.*

# SUNBONNET SUE QUILT

## DIRECTIONS

◆ Add seam allowances to all cutting dimensions given below

◆ Prepare paper templates using the patterns on pp. 378 to 379

◆ Cut the appliqué pieces from fabric and prepare them; 5 boys and 4 girls

◆ Cut the background fabric 17¾ × 31½" (45 × 80 cm)

◆ Appliqué the figures to the background in numbered order as shown on pp. 378 to 379

◆ Cut the first border 1½" (4 cm) wide, the second one 1½" (4 cm) wide, and third one 4¾" (12 cm) wide, which includes 2¾" plus an additional 2" (5 cm) to bind. Stitch the borders on

◆ Cut the batting and backing 29½ × 45¼" (75 × 115 cm)

◆ Pin together the three layers: top, batting, and backing

◆ Baste and quilt the layers

◆ Trim batting and finish sides by folding outer border to back and hemstitching in place.

**TECHNIQUES**
*Appliqué, quilting*

**PATTERNS**
*Sunbonnet Sue*
*Farmer Fred*

**SIZE**
*29½ × 45¼"*
*(75 × 115 cm)*

**MATERIALS**
• *Small white print for background and 2nd border*
• *Green print and red print for borders*
• *Prints and solids for appliqués*
• *Batting*
• *Backing fabric*

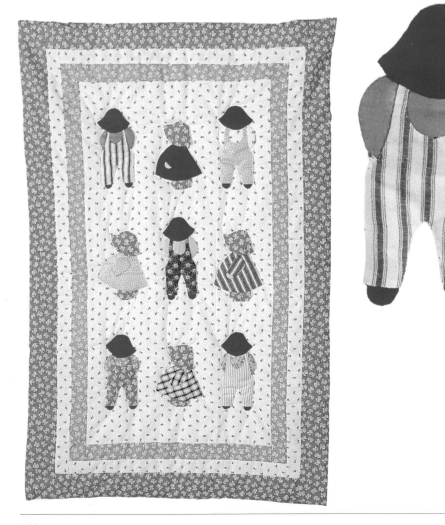

# AFRICAN GIRLS PANEL

## DIRECTIONS

### TECHNIQUES
*Appliqué, American piecing, quilting*

### PATTERN
*African girl*

### SIZE
*Block: 7⅞ × 7⅞" (20 × 20 cm)*
*Panel: 47¼ × 37¾" (120 × 96 cm)*

### MATERIALS
• *Many colorful fabrics for the clothing*
• *Brown fabrics for the body*
• *Ecru fabric for background squares*
• *Brown checked fabric for lattice strips and border*
• *Green fabric for lattice squares*
• *Batting*
• *Backing fabric*
• *Embroidery thread in white and black*

◆ Add seam allowances to all cutting dimensions given below
◆ Prepare paper templates using the patterns on p. 380
◆ Cut out the appliqué pieces and prepare the appliqués
◆ Cut 20 background squares 7⅞ × 7⅞" (20 × 20 cm)
◆ Appliqué an African girl in the center of every background square
◆ Embroider eyes and mouth
◆ Cut the checked lattice strips 1½" (4 cm) wide, and cut green squares 1½ × 1½" (4 × 4 cm)
◆ Sew 5 background squares and 4 lattice strips to form a horizontal row (see construction diagrams, p. 380). Make 4 rows

◆ Sew 5 horizontal lattice strips and 4 green squares together (see p. 380) to make a pieced lattice strip. Make 3 more the same way
◆ Stitch the rows and pieced lattice strips together to form the quilt top
◆ Cut and sew on the border 2¾" (7 cm) wide; it includes a ¾" (2 cm) border plus extra for finishing
◆ Cut the batting and backing, about 47¼ × 37¾" (120 × 96 cm)
◆ Pin the quilt top, batting, and backing together
◆ Baste and quilt the layers together
◆ Trim the batting, fold outer border to the back, and hemstitch in place.

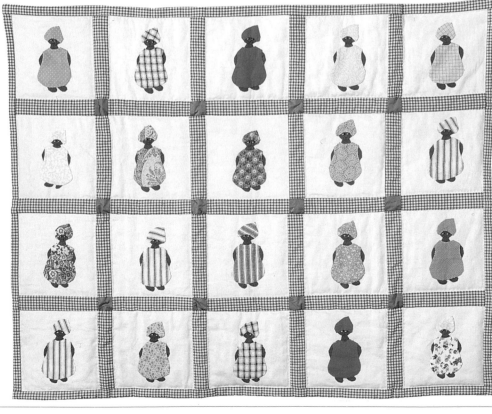

165

# CHECKERBOARD

## DIRECTIONS

◆ Add seam allowances to all cutting dimensions given below

◆ Cut a square of green felt cloth 18 × 18" (46 × 46 cm)

◆ Cut 32 squares 1⅜ × 1⅜" (3.5 × 3.5 cm) of red print fabric and 32 squares of green print fabric

◆ Stitch them in horizontal rows of 8 squares and then stitch the rows together to form the checkerboard (assembly diagrams on p. 381)

◆ Turn under the seam allowances of the quilt top and stitch, centered, to the green felt square

◆ Fold the green felt cloth edges to the back part of the wood square and glue in place

◆ To finish, glue a square of cardboard to the back.

**TECHNIQUE**
*American piecing*

**PATTERN**
*Checkerboard*

**SIZE**
*Board: 15¾ × 15¾"*
*(40 × 40 cm)*

**MATERIALS**
• *Red print fabric*
• *Green print fabric*
• *Solid green felt*
• *Square of wood 15¾ × 15¾" (40 × 40 cm)*
• *Cardboard for back*

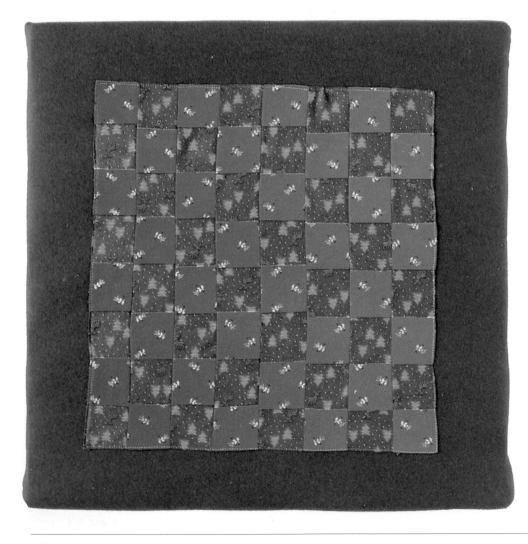

# IRISH CHAIN QUILT

## DIRECTIONS

**TECHNIQUES**
*American piecing, quilting*

**PATTERN**
*Irish Chain*

**SIZE**
*49½ × 49½" (126 × 126 cm)*

**MATERIALS**
• *White fabric for large whole-cloth squares, little squares, and outer border*
• *Pink fabric for the first border*
• *Batting*
• *Backing fabric*

◆ Add seam allowances to all cutting dimensions given below

◆ The pattern is made up of 9-patch blocks, alternating with whole-cloth blocks (see p. 382)

◆ Cut 5 little squares ¾ × ¾" (2 × 2 cm) out of fabrics of one color and 4 out of white fabric

◆ Stitch little squares three at a time in horizontal strips, and then join strips to form the 9-patch square (see 3, p. 382)

◆ Cut white squares 2⅜ × 2⅜" (6 × 6 cm) and stitch them to the 9-patch squares, first in horizontal rows and then vertically, to form double 9-patch blocks (see 4, p. 382)

◆ Cut large white squares 7 × 7" (18 × 18 cm) and stitch them to the double 9-patch blocks in horizontal rows; then stitch together the rows to form a quilt top with the Irish Chain pattern (see 5, p. 382)

◆ Cut the pink first border strips 3½" (9 cm) wide. Make pieced 9-patch squares for border corners and stitch on to top and bottom borders

◆ Cut the second border 6" (15 cm) wide, which is 3½" (9 cm) plus 2" (5 cm) to finish the border. Stitch the second border to the first one

◆ Cut the batting and backing about 49⅝ × 49⅝" (126 × 126 cm)

◆ Pin the three layers: quilt top, batting, and backing

◆ Baste and quilt the layers together

◆ Finish sides by folding outer border to the back; hemstitch in place.

# 9-PATCH CHECKERBOARD QUILT

## DIRECTIONS

◆ Add seam allowances to all cutting dimensions given below

◆ Cut squares 1⁹⁄₁₆ × 1⁹⁄₁₆" (4 × 4 cm) of print fabrics in many colors

◆ Join the squares by twos to form 4-patch squares (see 1 to 3, p. 383)

◆ Cut squares 3⅛ × 3⅛" (8 × 8 cm) out of medium blue print fabric and stitch them to the 4-patch squares, first in horizontal rows and then vertically, to form 9-patch blocks (see 4, p. 383) that are themselves pieced

◆ Cut large squares 9½ × 9½" (24 × 24 cm) out of dark blue print fabric; stitch them to the pieced 9-patch blocks in horizontal rows; stitch the rows together to form the quilt top (5 and 6, p. 383)

◆ Cut the batting and backing, about 85 × 94½" (216 × 240 cm), the size of the quilt top

◆ Pin, baste, and quilt together the quilt top, batting, and backing

◆ Trim batting. Finish edges with blanket binding or bias-cut strips.

**TECHNIQUES**
*American piecing, quilting*

**PATTERN**
*9-Patch in checkerboard*

**SIZE**
*Block: 9½ × 9½"*
*(24 × 24 cm)*
*Quilt: 85 × 94½"*
*(216 × 240 cm)*

**MATERIALS**
• *Print fabric with medium blue background*
• *Print fabrics in many colors*
• *Print fabric with dark blue background for whole-cloth blocks*
• *Batting*
• *Backing fabric*
• *Blanket binding or bias-cut fabric for edges*

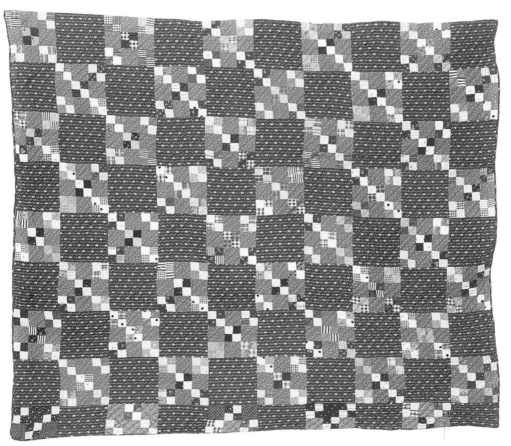

# 16-PATCH SQUARE QUILT

## DIRECTIONS

**TECHNIQUES**
*American piecing, quilting*

**PATTERN**
*16-Patch square*

**SIZE**
*Block: 9½ × 9½"
(24 × 24 cm)
Quilt: 99¼ × 113¼"
(252 × 288 cm)*

**MATERIALS**
*• Fabrics of various colors and patterns for the pieced squares
• Light blue fabric for lattice strips
• Pink fabric for lattice squares
• Dark red fabric for first border
• Beige fabric for second border
• Batting
• Backing fabric*

◆ Add seam allowances to all cutting dimensions given below
◆ Cut squares 2⅜ × 2⅜" (6 × 6 cm) for the 16-patch blocks out of a variety of fabrics
◆ Cut lattice strips 4¾" (12 cm) wide from light blue fabric
◆ Cut pink squares 4¾ × 4¾" (12 × 12 cm) for the lattice squares
◆ Stitch the 2⅜ × 2⅜" (6 × 6 cm) squares together in groups of 4 to form horizontal strips (see p. 384 for construction diagrams)
◆ Stitch four 4-square strips together to form a 16-patch square. Make other 16-patch squares the same way
◆ Stitch the pink lattice squares and blue lattice strips into horizontal bands
◆ Stitch the lattice strips and pieced squares together in horizontal rows
◆ Stitch the block rows and lattice bands together to form the quilt top
◆ Cut the first border 2⅜" (6 cm) wide and the second one 9" (23 cm) wide, which includes 2" (5 cm) for finishing
◆ Stitch on the borders
◆ Cut batting and backing each about 99¼ × 113¼" (252 × 288 cm)
◆ Pin together the top, batting, and backing
◆ Baste and quilt
◆ Trim batting. Fold the excess outer border to back and hemstitch it in place.

# LITTLE BAG WITH DIAMONDS

## DIRECTIONS

◆ Add seam allowances to all cutting dimensions given below
◆ Cut 36 squares 3½ × 3½" (9 × 9 cm), 12 of each fabric
◆ Stitch the squares in 6 rows of 6 squares (see p. 385)
◆ Stitch the rows together (see p. 385) and trim the sides off the outer squares

◆ Sew the diagonal ends together, and sew one straight side closed to form the little bag
◆ Cut two lining pieces. Stitch them closed on bottom and sides
◆ Stitch the lining and bag together at the top
◆ Stitch a track for the cord and insert cord.

**TECHNIQUE**
*American piecing*

**PATTERN**
*Diamond*

**SIZE**
*Squares: 3½ × 3½"*
*(9 × 9 cm)*
*Bag: 10¼ × 15¾"*
*(26 × 40 cm)*

**MATERIALS**
• *Fabrics of three colors (A, B, C) for the squares*
• *Fabric for lining*
• *Cord for the tie*

# FAN QUILT

## DIRECTIONS

**TECHNIQUES**
*American piecing, quilting*

**PATTERN**
*Fan*

**SIZE**
*Block: 7⅞ × 7⅞"
(20 × 20 cm)
Quilt: 70⅛ × 79½"
(180 × 202 cm)*

**MATERIALS**
• *Prints in 4 colors for the fans and second and third borders*
• *White fabric for background and first border*
• *Batting*
• *Backing fabric*

◆ Add seam allowances to all cutting dimensions given below
◆ Make the templates using patterns on p. 386. B is the background pattern (cut on folded paper)
◆ Cut the quilt block fabric pieces
◆ Stitch together the pieces to form the Fan blocks (see diagrams 1 to 3 on p. 387)
◆ Stitch together the Fan blocks to form horizontal rows
◆ Stitch the rows together to form the quilt top center

◆ Cut the 1st border 2⅜" (6 cm) wide, the 2nd one 6⁵⁄₁₆" (16 cm) wide, and the 3rd one 7" (18 cm) wide
◆ Stitch on the borders
◆ Draw the quilting pattern on the quilt top
◆ Cut the batting and backing 70⅞ × 79½" (180 × 202 cm)
◆ Pin together the quilt top, batting, and backing
◆ Baste the layers and quilt
◆ Finish the edges.

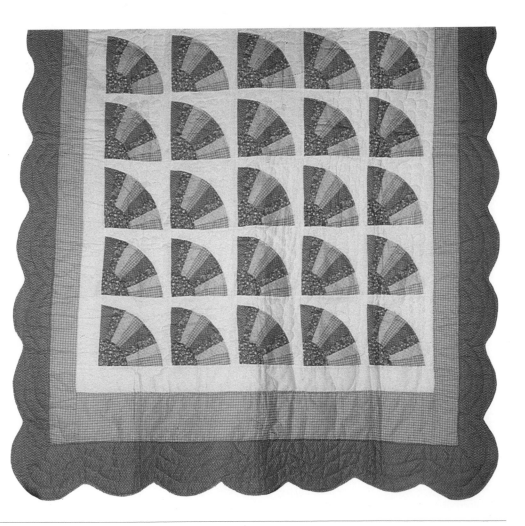

*Details of Fan Quilt with scalloped border on three sides.*

# BIRDS IN THE AIR PANEL

## DIRECTIONS

◆ Add seam allowances to all cutting dimensions given below

◆ Cut 56 right triangles 4 × 4 × 5½" (10 × 10 × 14 cm) in bright colors and 56 others in a lighter color

◆ Stitch a triangle in a bright color to a light one to form a 4 × 4" (10 × 10 cm) square

◆ Stitch 8 squares together to form each horizontal row (see p. 388)

◆ Stitch the rows together to form the quilt top center

◆ Cut the first border 1⁹⁄₁₆" (4 cm) wide in red; the second one 2⅜" (6 cm) wide in gray; and the third border 2¾" (7 cm) wide in red. The third one includes ¾" (2 cm) for the border and 2" (5 cm) for finishing

◆ Stitch on the borders

◆ Cut the batting and backing about 34⅝ × 31½" (88 × 80 cm)

◆ Pin together the three layers: quilt top, batting, and backing

◆ Quilt with outline quilting

◆ Trim batting, fold part of the outer border to the back, and hemstitch in place.

(see p. 388)

**TECHNIQUES**
*American piecing, quilting*

**PATTERN**
*Birds in the Air*

**SIZE**
*Block: 4 × 4"*
*(10 × 10 cm)*
*Quilt: 34½ × 31½"*
*(88 × 80 cm)*

**MATERIALS**
• *Prints in bright colors for half of the triangles*
• *Prints in a lighter color for half of the triangles*
• *Red print and gray print fabrics for the borders*
• *Batting*
• *Backing fabric*

172

# BIRDS IN THE AIR QUILT

## DIRECTIONS

**TECHNIQUES**
*American piecing, quilting*

**PATTERN**
*Birds in the Air*

**SIZE**
*71 × 94½" (180 × 240 cm)*

**MATERIALS**
• *White, gray, and black fabrics*
• *Thin white ribbon for binding*
• *Batting*
• *Backing fabric*

◆ Add seam allowances to all cutting dimensions given below

◆ Cut right triangles 6 × 6 × 8¼" (15 × 15 × 21 cm) in white, black, and gray

◆ Stitch together the triangles in twos to form the squares (see diagrams, p. 389)

◆ Stitch together the squares to form the horizontal rows

◆ Stitch together the rows to form the quilt top

◆ Cut the batting and backing about 71 × 94½" (180 × 240 cm)

◆ Pin together the three layers: quilt top, batting, and backing

◆ Baste and quilt on the stitch lines

◆ Bind the edges with thin ribbon.

# VELVET STRIP-PIECED PANEL

## DIRECTIONS

◆ Add seam allowances to all cutting dimensions given below

◆ Cut strips 1⁹⁄₁₆" (4 cm) wide from many colorful fabrics

◆ Stitch the strips together in groups of 6 or more, arranging the colors in a harmonious way

◆ From the strip fabric you made, cut right triangles 6¹¹⁄₁₆ × 6¹¹⁄₁₆ × 9½" (17 × 17 × 24 cm) with long sides on assembled edge of strips (see 2, p. 390)

◆ Stitch the triangles together by twos to form squares

◆ Stitch 5 squares into a row (see 5, p. 390)

◆ Stitch the rows together to form the quilt top center

◆ Cut and stitch the first border 1⁹⁄₁₆" (4 cm) wide to the quilt top

◆ Cut the second border 3½" (9 cm) wide, which includes 2" (5 cm) to finish edge, and stitch to quilt top

◆ Cut the batting and backing 39¾ × 39¾" (101 × 101 cm)

◆ Pin, baste, and quilt the three layers: quilt top, batting, and backing

◆ Trim batting. Fold the excess outer border to the back and hemstitch in place.

(see 2, p. 390)
(see 5, p. 390)

**TECHNIQUES**
*American piecing, strip piecing*

**SIZE**
*Block: 6¾ × 6¾"*
*(17 × 17 cm)*
*Quilt: 39¾ × 39¾"*
*(101 × 101 cm)*

**MATERIALS**
• *Velvet prints in many colors for strips and first border*
• *Solid-color velvet for the second border*
• *Batting*
• *Backing fabric*

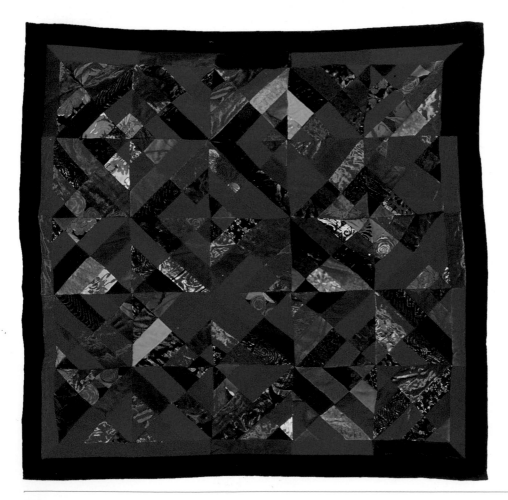

# STRIP-PIECED TEA COZY

## DIRECTIONS

(see p. 391)

**TECHNIQUES**
*Strip piecing, quilting*

**SIZE**
*9¾ × 13¾"*
*(25 × 35 cm)*

**MATERIALS**
• *Prints in many colors for the strips*
• *Batting*
• *Backing fabric*
• *Blue bias tape or ribbon*

◆ Add seam allowances to all cutting dimensions given below
◆ Cut strips of different widths and stitch together
◆ From the pieced fabric, cut 2 rectangles (see p. 391) that are 9¾ × 13¾" (25 × 35 cm)
◆ Cut the batting and backing 9¾ × 13¾" (25 × 35 cm) for each of the two parts

◆ Pin and stitch together the three layers of front and back separately: pieced top, batting, and backing
◆ Stitch the front and back together on the sides and top, leaving an opening for the handle and the spout of the teapot
◆ Finish off the sides, and tie the tea cozy with blue ribbon to use.

*Colorful placemats in pieced fabric with heart appliqués.*

*Right: A cute knapsack for a youngster.*

# STRIP-PIECED TULIPS

## DIRECTIONS

◆ Add seam allowances to all cutting dimensions given below
◆ Cut fabric strips of different widths and stitch together to form pieced fabric
◆ Prepare templates for the appliqué using the patterns on p. 391 (given in 2 sizes)

◆ From pieced fabric, cut out appliqué pieces; lay out the templates with the arrows aligned on straight grain of fabric
◆ Stitch together three petals for each tulip
◆ Appliqué as desired.

**TECHNIQUES**
*Strip-piecing, appliqué*

**PATTERN**
*Tulip*

**SIZE**
*Tulip: 5 × 4"*
*(13 × 10 cm)*

**MATERIALS**
• *Prints in various colors*

*Tablecloth with appliqués of squares in the corners and strip-pieced tulips in the middle.*

# DOUBLE IRISH CHAIN QUILT
## (STRIP PIECED)

## DIRECTIONS

**TECHNIQUES**
*Strip piecing, quilting*

**PATTERN**
*Double Irish Chain*

**SIZE**
*Block: 8¼ × 8¼" (21 × 21 cm)*
*Quilt: 62⅜ × 56⁵⁄₁₆"*
*(158 × 143 cm)*

**MATERIALS**
• *Fabrics in light blue, blue, and black for the quilt blocks and borders*
• *Batting*
• *Backing fabric*

◆ Add seam allowances to all cutting dimensions given below

FOR BLOCK A
◆ Cut strips 1¼" (3 cm) wide of light blue (LB), blue (B), and black (K) fabric
◆ Stitch together the strips in groups of five as follows: Group 1: K, LB, B, LB, K. Group 2: LB, K, LB, K, LB. Group 3: B, LB, K, LB, B, to form 3 groups of strip-pieced fabric (see p. 392, top)
◆ With a rotary cutter, cut down across the pieced fabrics to get strips that are 1³⁄₁₆ × 6" (3 × 15 cm) wide
◆ Stitch the strips together in groups of 5 to form block A (see 1 and 2, p. 392)

FOR BLOCK B (spacer block)
◆ Cut light blue squares 1³⁄₁₆ × 1³⁄₁₆" (3 × 3 cm) and blue ones 3½ × 3½" (9 × 9 cm), and 1³⁄₁₆ × 3½" (3 × 9 cm) blue rectangles
◆ Stitch the pieces horizontally in rows and then vertically to form block B (see 3 and 4 on p. 392)
◆ Stitch blocks together, alternating blocks A and B, to form a row (see 5, p. 392)
◆ Stitch the rows together to form the quilt top center (see 6 and 7, p. 392)
◆ Cut the first border 1³⁄₁₆" (3 cm) wide; the second border 6" (15 cm) wide; and the third border 2⅜" (6 cm) wide, which includes 2" (5 cm) to finish. Stitch borders to quilt center
◆ Draw the quilting patterns on quilt top
◆ Cut batting and backing 62⅜ × 56⁵⁄₁₆" (158 × 143 cm)
◆ Pin the quilt top, batting, and backing together
◆ Baste and quilt
◆ Trim batting. Fold extra width of outer border to back; hemstitch in place.

# LOG CABIN POTHOLDERS

## DIRECTIONS

◆ Add seam allowances to all cutting dimensions given below

◆ See full-size pattern on p. 393. Refer to photo for colors

◆ Make templates and cut the pieces from fabric as follows:

piece 1: ¾ × ¾" (2 × 2 cm)
piece 2: ¾ × ¾" (2 × 2 cm)
piece 3: 1⁹⁄₁₆ × ¾" (4 × 2 cm)
piece 4: 1⁹⁄₁₆ × ¾" (4 × 2 cm)
piece 5: 2⅜ × ¾" (6 × 2 cm)
piece 6: 2⅜ × ¾" (6 × 2 cm)

piece 7: 3⅛ × ¾" (8 × 2 cm)
piece 8: 3⅛ × ¾" (8 × 2 cm)
piece 9: 4 × ¾" (10 × 2 cm)

◆ Stitch together the Log Cabin block by hand or by machine, with or without base fabric (see section on Log Cabin, p. 124)

◆ Cut the batting and backing 4 × 4" (10 × 10 cm)

◆ Stitch together the three layers: pieced block, batting, and backing

◆ Hem with bias binding and add loop.

**TECHNIQUE**
*American piecing*

**PATTERN**
*Log Cabin*

**SIZE**
*Block: 4 × 4"*
*(10 × 10 cm)*

**MATERIALS**
• *Prints in many colors for the pieces*
• *Backing fabric*
• *Base fabric for attaching the pieces*
• *Batting*
• *Bias binding for edge and loop*

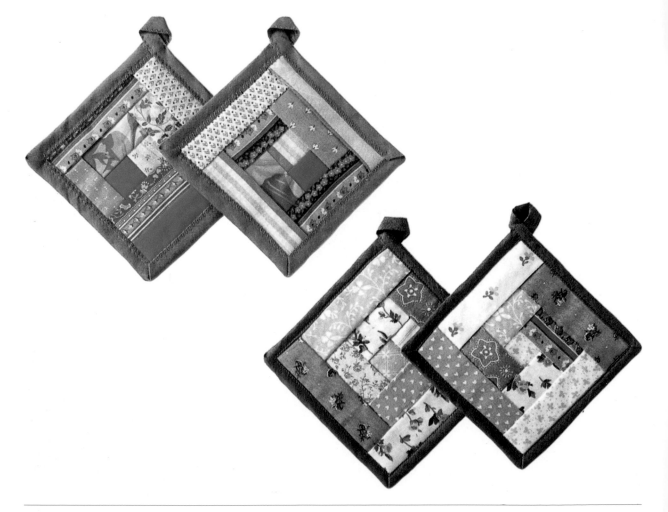

*Potholders and apron with the Log Cabin design.*

*Bib with the Log Cabin pattern.*

*Velvet tote with Log Cabin squares.*

# T-SHIRT WITH RECTANGULAR LOG CABIN

## DIRECTIONS

◆ Add seam allowances to all cutting dimensions given below
◆ Cut the pieces and make the Log Cabin block (see p. 393 for pattern) on base fabric:
piece 1: 1⁹⁄₁₆ × 1⁹⁄₁₆" (4 × 4 cm)
piece 2: 1⁹⁄₁₆ × ¾" (4 × 2 cm)
piece 3: 2⅜ × ¾" (6 × 2 cm)
piece 4: 2⅜ × ¾" (6 × 2 cm)
piece 5: 3⅛ × ¾" (8 × 2 cm)
piece 6: 3⅛ × ¾" (8 × 2 cm)
piece 7: 4 × ¾" (10 × 2 cm)
piece 8: 4 × ¾" (10 × 2 cm)
piece 9: 4¾ × ¾" (12 × 2 cm)
piece 10: 4¾ × ¾" (12 × 2 cm)
piece 11: 4¾ × ¾" (12 × 2 cm)
◆ Fold under seam allowances of Log Cabin block and appliqué onto the T-shirt with machine-appliqué.

see p. 393 for pattern

### TECHNIQUES
*American piecing, appliqué*

### PATTERN
*Rectangular Log Cabin*

### SIZE
*6⁵⁄₁₆ × 4¾" (16 × 12 cm)*

### MATERIALS
• *Prints and solids in a variety of colors*
• *T-shirt*
• *Base fabric for block*

# LOG CABIN PLACEMAT

## DIRECTIONS

**TECHNIQUE**
*American piecing*

**PATTERN**
*Rectangular Log Cabin*

**SIZE**
*Block: 15¼ × 11"
(40 × 28 cm)*

**MATERIALS**
• *Prints and solids in a variety of colors*
• *Checked fabric for background*
• *Base fabric for attaching pieces*

◆ Add seam allowances to all cutting dimensions given below

◆ Cut the fabric pieces and make the rectangular Log Cabin block (see p. 124 for Log Cabin information). Piece sizes are as follows (see p. 393 for diagram):

piece 1: 1⁹⁄₁₆ × 1⁹⁄₁₆" (4 × 4 cm)
piece 2: 1⁹⁄₁₆ × 1³⁄₁₆" (4 × 3 cm)
piece 3: 2¾ × 1³⁄₁₆" (7 × 3 cm)
piece 4: 2¾ × 1³⁄₁₆" (7 × 3 cm)
piece 5: 4 × 1³⁄₁₆" (10 × 3 cm)
piece 6: 4 × 1³⁄₁₆" (10 × 3 cm)
piece 7: 5 × 1³⁄₁₆" (13 × 3 cm)
piece 8: 5 × 1³⁄₁₆" (13 × 3 cm)
piece 9: 6⁵⁄₁₆ × 1³⁄₁₆" (16 × 3 cm)

piece 10: 6⁵⁄₁₆ × 1³⁄₁₆" (16 × 3 cm)
piece 11: 7½ × 1³⁄₁₆" (19 × 3 cm)
piece 12: 7½ × 1³⁄₁₆" (19 × 3 cm)
piece 13: 8¹¹⁄₁₆ × 1³⁄₁₆" (22 × 3 cm)
piece 14: 8¹¹⁄₁₆ × 1³⁄₁₆" (22 × 3 cm)
piece 15: 9¹³⁄₁₆ × 1³⁄₁₆" (25 × 3 cm)
piece 16: 9¹³⁄₁₆ × 1³⁄₁₆" (25 × 3 cm)
pieces 17, 18, 19, 20, and 21: 11 × 1³⁄₁₆" (28 × 3 cm)

◆ After the block is pieced, cut a backing that is 1" (2.5 cm) larger than the block all around.

◆ Fold the backing excess to front to form border; stitch in place.

# LOG CABIN INFANT CARRIER

## DIRECTIONS

To create the infant carrier:

◆ Add seam allowances to all cutting dimensions given below

◆ Make the Log Cabin blocks with strips of many varied fabrics of 1" (2.5 cm) width, as follows (see p. 394 for diagrams):

piece 1: 1¾ × 1¾" (4.5 × 4.5 cm)
piece 2: 1¾ × 1" (4.5 × 2.5 cm)
piece 3: 2¾ × 1" (7 × 2.5 cm)
piece 4: 2¾ × 1" (7 × 2.5 cm)
piece 5: 3¾ × 1" (9.5 × 2.5 cm)
piece 6: 3¾ × 1" (9.5 × 2.5 cm)
piece 7: 4¾ × 1" (12 × 2.5 cm)
piece 8: 4¾ × 1" (12 × 2.5 cm)
piece 9: 5¹¹⁄₁₆ × 1" (14.5 × 2.5 cm)
piece 10: 5¹¹⁄₁₆ × 1" (14.5 × 2.5 cm)
piece 11: 6¹¹⁄₁₆ × 1" (17 × 2.5 cm)
piece 12: 6¹¹⁄₁₆ × 1" (17 × 2.5 cm)
piece 13: 7¹¹⁄₁₆ × 1" (19.5 × 2.5 cm)

◆ See p. 124 for details of making Log Cabin block

◆ Appliqué Log Cabin block (after folding seam allowances under) to the background fabric, which is 35½ × 23⅝" (90 × 60 cm)

◆ Cut batting 35½ × 23⅝" (90 × 60 cm) and backing 39⅜ × 27½" (100 × 70 cm)

◆ Put the quilt top, batting, and backing together; baste and quilt them

◆ Fold and stitch backing edges to front to form borders 1½" (4 cm) wide, inserting thin strips for ties (previously prepared) to strengthen and close the infant carrier.

**TECHNIQUES**
*American piecing and appliqué*

**PATTERN**
*Log Cabin*

**SIZE**
*Block: 7¾ × 7¾"
(19.5 × 19.5 cm)
Carrier: 35½ × 23⅝"
(90 × 60 cm)*

**MATERIALS**
• *Various colorful fabrics for Log Cabin blocks*
• *Pink print for background*
• *Light blue print for backing and ties*
• *Batting*
• *Base fabric for attaching pieces*

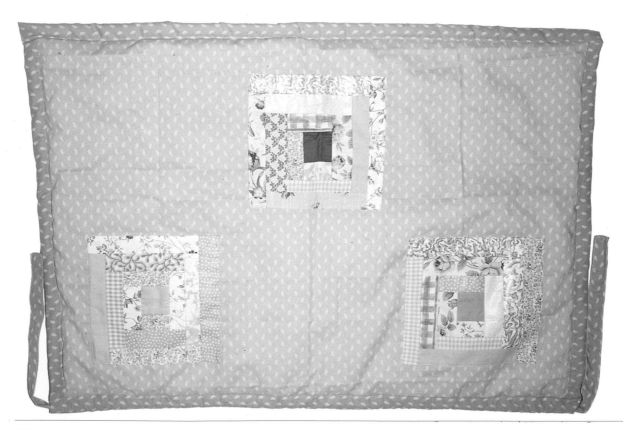

*Infant carriers in lively colors.*

# LOG CABIN QUILT

## DIRECTIONS

◆ Add seam allowances to all cutting dimensions given below

◆ Cut pieces according to the diagram on p. 395 and make the Log Cabin squares, planning fabrics for two dark sides of each square and two light ones:

piece 1: 1⁹⁄₁₆ × 1⁹⁄₁₆" (4 × 4 cm)
piece 2: 1⁹⁄₁₆ × 1⁹⁄₁₆" (4 × 4 cm)
piece 3: 3⅛ × 1⁹⁄₁₆" (8 × 4 cm)
piece 4: 3⅛ × 1⁹⁄₁₆" (8 × 4 cm)
piece 5: 4¾ × 1⁹⁄₁₆" (12 × 4 cm)
piece 6: 4¾ × 1⁹⁄₁₆" (12 × 4 cm)
piece 7: 6⁵⁄₁₆ × 1⁹⁄₁₆" (16 × 4 cm)
piece 8: 6⁵⁄₁₆ × 1⁹⁄₁₆" (16 × 4 cm)
piece 9: 7⅞ × 1⁹⁄₁₆" (20 × 4 cm)
piece 10: 7⅞ × 1⁹⁄₁₆" (20 × 4 cm)
piece 11: 9½ × 1⁹⁄₁₆" (24 × 4 cm)
piece 12: 9½ × 1⁹⁄₁₆" (24 × 4 cm)
piece 13: 11 × 1⁹⁄₁₆" (28 × 4 cm)

◆ Lay out blocks on work surface to make the pattern (Barn Raising); see 4, p. 395

◆ Sew Log Cabin blocks together in groups of 4 to form rows

◆ Sew the rows together to form the quilt top center

◆ Cut first border 4" (10 cm) wide, second border 2" (5 cm) wide, and third border 8" (20 cm) wide, which includes 6" (15 cm) plus 2" (5 cm) to finish; stitch on borders

◆ Trace quilting designs onto the borders, etc.

◆ Cut batting and backing about 67¾ × 100" (172 × 254 cm)

◆ Pin together the three layers: quilt top, batting, and backing

◆ Baste and quilt

◆ Trim the sides, turn excess of outer border to the back of the piece, and hemstitch in place.

**TECHNIQUES**
*American piecing, quilting*

**PATTERN**
*Log Cabin*

**SIZE**
*Block: 11 × 11"
(28 × 28 cm)
Quilt: 67¾ × 100"
(172 × 254 cm)*

**MATERIALS**
• *Solids and prints of 13 different kinds for the squares and borders (half light, half dark)*
• *Batting*
• *Backing fabric*

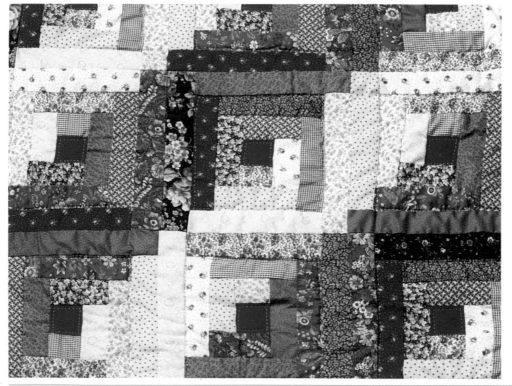

*Closeup of a Log Cabin quilt in which the block setting, Straight Furrows, forms dark bands that contrast with light ones.*

*Opposite: Log Cabin quilt with blocks in Barn Raising setting.*

# PLACEMAT WITH HEXAGONS

## DIRECTIONS

◆ Add seam allowances to all cutting dimensions given below
◆ Prepare paper patterns using the template on p. 396
◆ Cut the fabric pieces
◆ Cut the background 19¾" × 13¾" (50 × 35 cm)
◆ Cut the backing 25½ × 19¾" (65 × 50 cm)

◆ Prepare hexagons and assemble Grandmother's Flower Garden pattern using English method (see p. 134)
◆ Appliqué the assembled pieces to the background
◆ Put the quilt top and backing together
◆ Fold backing edges to front and stitch in place to form border.

**TECHNIQUES**
*English piecing, appliqué*

**PATTERN**
*Grandmother's Flower Garden*

**SIZE**
*19¾ × 13¾" (50 × 35 cm)*

**MATERIALS**
• *Solids and prints for the hexagons*
• *Fabric for the background*
• *Checked fabric for backing*

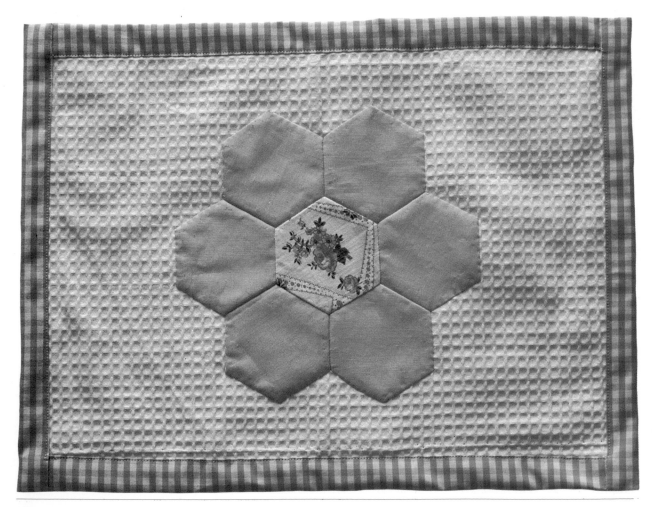

# HEXAGONS QUILT

## DIRECTIONS

**TECHNIQUES**
*English piecing,
quilting*

**PATTERN**
*Grandmother's Flower
Garden*

**SIZE**
*Quilt: your choice*

**MATERIALS**
• *Prints and solids for
hexagons of the
flowers*
• *White fabric for the
surrounding hexagons
and binding*
• *Batting*
• *Backing fabric*

◆ Add seam allowances to all cutting
dimensions given below
◆ Prepare paper templates using the pattern
on p. 397 (see English method, p. 60)
◆ Cut the fabric pieces
◆ Prepare pieces and make Grandmother's
Flower Garden with two circles of petals
around center (see p. 397)
◆ Stitch the surrounding white hexagons to
the flowers to form the quilt top
◆ Cut the batting and backing a few inches
(5 or 7 cm) wider and taller than the quilt
top
◆ Pin together the three layers: top, batting,
and backing
◆ Baste and quilt
◆ Trim sides and bind with strips of white
fabric.

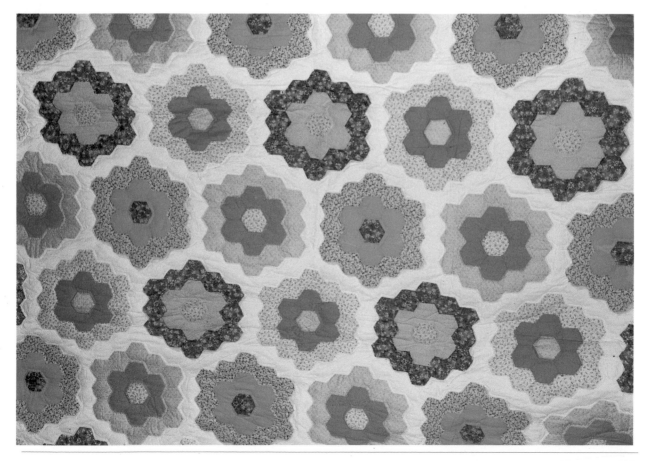

# BOW TIE POTHOLDERS

## DIRECTIONS

◆ Add seam allowances to all cutting dimensions given below
◆ Prepare paper templates using the patterns on p. 398
◆ Cut and prepare the fabric pieces for the block (see English method, p. 60)
◆ Make the Bow Tie block (see 1 to 4, p. 398)
◆ Cut and stitch on border 3¼" wide (8 cm), which includes 1³⁄₁₆" (3 cm) plus 2" (5 cm) to finish

◆ Cut the batting and backing 6⁵⁄₁₆ × 6⁵⁄₁₆" (16 × 16 cm)
◆ Pin and quilt together the three layers: quilt top, batting, and backing
◆ Fold and hemstitch the excess border to back of piece
◆ Make the second potholder and add loops to both.

**TECHNIQUES**
*English piecing, quilting*

**PATTERN**
*Bow Tie*

**SIZE**
*6⁵⁄₁₆ × 6⁵⁄₁₆" (16 × 16 cm)*

**MATERIALS**
• *Fabrics in three different patterns*
• *Batting*

# BOW TIE PILLOW

## TECHNIQUES
*English and American piecing, quilting*

## PATTERN
*Bow Tie*

## SIZE
*Bow Tie block: 4 × 4"
(10 × 10 cm)
Pillow: 15 × 15"
(38 × 38 cm)*

## MATERIALS
• *Colorful prints for
Bow Tie blocks*
• *Ecru fabric for back-
ground, borders, and
back of pillow*
• *Lining for the
pillow top*
• *Low-loft batting*
• *Stuffing for pillow*

## DIRECTIONS

◆ Add seam allowances to all cutting dimensions given below

◆ Make 4 Bow Tie squares, using the pattern on p. 398 (steps 1 to 5)

◆ Stitch together the Bow Tie squares and the background pieces to form the pillow top (see p. 398)

◆ Cut the border 2" (5 cm) wide and stitch it on

◆ Trace the drawings for quilting on the pillow top

◆ Cut batting and lining 15 × 15" (38 × 38 cm); assemble pillow top, batting, and lining

◆ Baste and quilt the three layers

◆ Cut the back part of the pillow 15 × 15" (38 × 38 cm), and stitch on, right sides facing, leaving an opening of about 4" (10 cm); turn right-side out

◆ Insert the stuffing

◆ Hand-stitch the side opening closed.

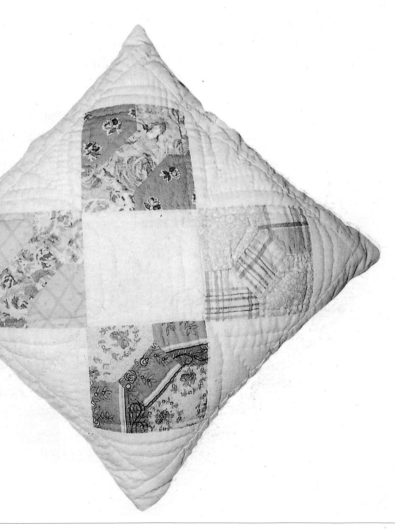

# BOW TIE QUILT

## DIRECTIONS

◆ Add seam allowances to all cutting dimensions given below
◆ Create the Bow Tie blocks using the patterns and instructions on p. 398, steps 1 to 4
◆ Lay out blocks on a work surface in a pleasing pattern
◆ Stitch the blocks together to form horizontal rows
◆ Stitch the rows together to form the quilt center

◆ Add borders if you wish
◆ Cut the batting and backing a few inches (5 or 7 cm) larger than the quilt top
◆ Baste and quilt the quilt top, batting, and backing together; trim batting
◆ Bring excess backing to front; hemstitch in place to finish.

The Bow Tie pattern can also be made by an easier method; see diagrams 5 and 6 on p. 398.

**TECHNIQUES**
*English and American piecing*

**PATTERN**
*Bow Tie*

**SIZE**
*Bow Tie Square: 4 × 4"*
*(10 × 10 cm)*

**MATERIALS**
• *Many colorful prints for Bow Tie blocks*
• *Batting*
• *Backing fabric*
• *Fabric for borders (optional)*

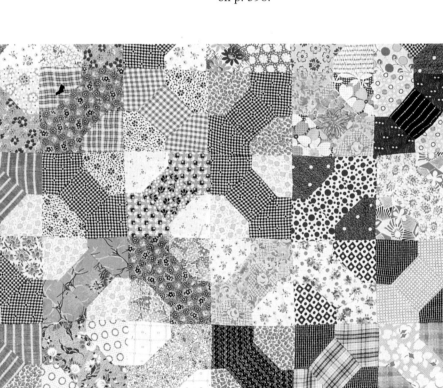

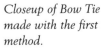

*Closeup of Bow Tie made with the first method.*

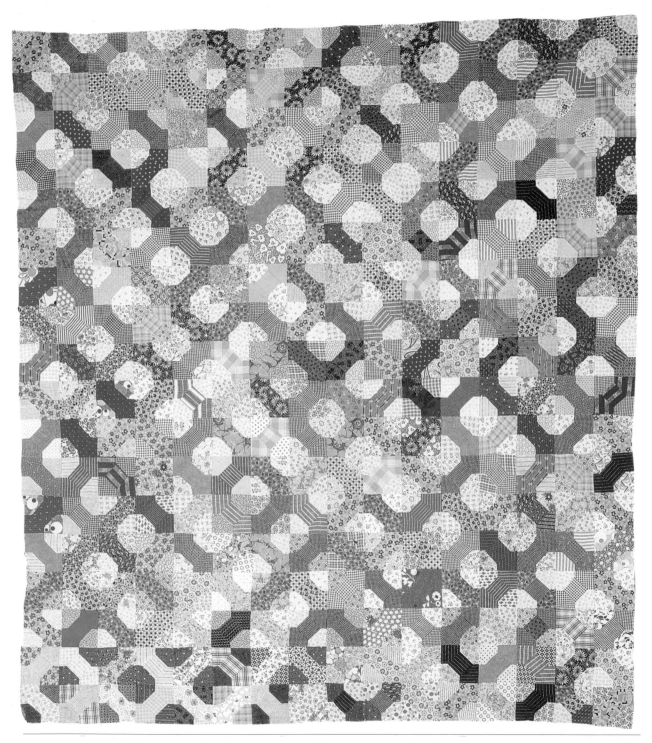

# LITTLE SPOOLS BAG

## DIRECTIONS

◆ Add seam allowances to all cutting dimensions given below
◆ Prepare paper templates from patterns on p. 400 to make 3 spool blocks
◆ Cut and prepare the Spool fabric pieces (see English method, p. 60)
◆ Stitch the pieces together to form the Spool blocks (see p. 400)
◆ Stitch pieced blocks to whole-cloth ones to form two vertical strips of 3 blocks each

◆ Stitch the strips together in a rectangle
◆ Cut fabric for the little bag 26¾ × 23⅝" (68 × 60 cm)
◆ Appliqué the Spools rectangle to front of little bag
◆ Sew the side and the bottom of the bag closed
◆ Finish off the upper part and close with ribbon.

### TECHNIQUES
*English and American piecing, appliqué*

### PATTERN
*Spool*

### SIZE
*Block: 4¾" × 4¾" (12 × 12 cm)*
*Bag: 13⅜ × 23⅝" (34 × 60 cm)*

### MATERIALS
• *Colorful fabric for the bag and thread*
• *Ecru fabric for spools*
• *Light blue fabric for the whole-cloth squares*
• *Ribbon*

*Opposite: Quilt with the Spool pattern, decorated with saw-tooth edges on squares.*

# HOUSES WALL HANGING

## DIRECTIONS

- ◆ Add seam allowances to all cutting dimensions given below
- ◆ Prepare paper templates using the pattern on p. 401
- ◆ Cut fabric pieces for patchwork design
- ◆ Cut the white-print side strips 2" (5 cm) wide and the white center strip between the house rows 5½" (14 cm) wide
- ◆ Prepare the house pieces and sew them together, first in horizontal bands; then sew the bands together to finish the house block (see diagrams, p. 401).
- ◆ Cut 2 A rectangles the same size as the house blocks, 4¾ × 4" (12 × 10 cm), of white background fabric to go between the houses vertically. Cut 4 B rectangles 4¾ × 2" (12 × 5 cm) from the white fabric for

above the top houses and below the bottom houses.
- ◆ Stitch the house blocks and A and B white rectangles into columns (see 2, p. 401)
- ◆ Stitch pieced house columns and background strips to form the center of quilt
- ◆ Cut the first border ⅜" (1 cm) wide; the second one 2" (5 cm) wide; and the third one 2¾" (7 cm) wide, of which 2" (5 cm) is for finishing. Sew on the borders
- ◆ Cut the batting and backing 21⅝ × 23⅝" (55 × 60 cm)
- ◆ Pin the three layers together: quilt top, batting, and backing
- ◆ Baste and quilt the layers
- ◆ Trim batting; fold excess outer border to back; hemstitch in place.

**TECHNIQUES**
*English piecing, quilting*

**PATTERN**
*House*

**SIZE**
*Block: 4¾ × 4"
(12 × 10 cm)
Quilt: 21½ × 23½"
(55 × 60 cm)*

**MATERIALS**
• *Several colorful prints for the house blocks*
• *White print for background*
• *Red checked fabric for border*
• *Green print for borders and backing*
• *Batting*

*Pillow with little house pattern. There are many little house patterns. This is another example.*

194

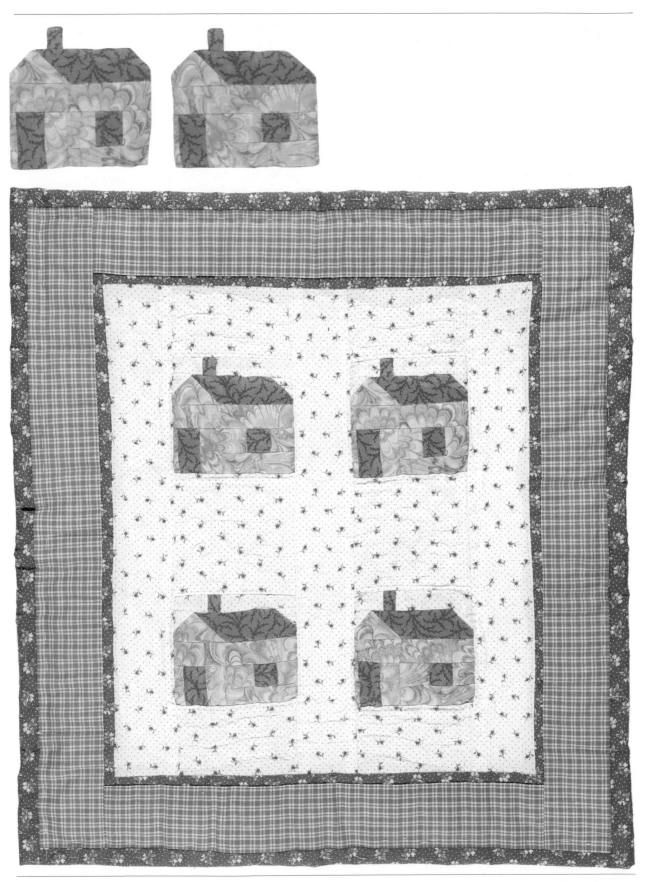

# OHIO STAR TRAY LINER

## DIRECTIONS

◆ Add seam allowances to all cutting dimensions given below

◆ Prepare paper templates from patterns on pp. 402 to 403

◆ Cut the fabric pieces for the Ohio Star block

◆ Sew the Ohio Star block (see p. 403)

◆ Cut strips of pink fabric 1½" (4 cm) wide for the border

◆ Stitch on the pink border

◆ Cut white strips 2" (5 cm) wide for the side borders and stitch on

◆ Cut the ruffle 4" (10 cm) wide. Fold ruffle in half on its length and stitch to the quilt top

◆ Cut the batting and the backing 17¼ × 12½" (44 × 32 cm)

◆ Draw quilting patterns on the quilt top

◆ Pin the three layers: top, batting, and backing

◆ Baste and quilt

◆ Turn under the backing edges and secure with hemstitching.

**TECHNIQUES**
*English piecing, quilting*

**PATTERN**
*Ohio Star*

**SIZE**
*Block: 9½ × 9½"*
*(24 × 24 cm)*
*Tray cover: 17¼ × 12½"*
*(44 × 32 cm)*

**MATERIALS**
• *Red print fabric for the star*
• *Pink print for border, ruffle, and backing*
• *White fabric for background*
• *Batting*

# OHIO STAR PILLOW

## DIRECTIONS

◆ Prepare paper templates from patterns on pp. 402 to 403

**TECHNIQUE**
*English piecing*

**PATTERN**
*Ohio Star*

**SIZE**
*Block: 9½ × 9½"
(24 × 24 cm)
Pillow: 14¼ × 14¼"
(36 × 36 cm)*

**MATERIALS**
*• Several print fabrics in blue for background
• Pink prints and checks for the star, border, ruffle, and pillow back
• Stuffing for the pillow*

◆ Add seam allowances to all cutting dimensions given below
◆ Prepare paper templates from patterns on pp. 402 to 403
◆ Cut the fabric pieces for the Ohio Star block
◆ Sew the Ohio Star block (see p. 403 for assembly)
◆ Cut border strips 2⅜" (6 cm) wide and the ruffle 2⅜" (6 cm) wide
◆ Stitch the border to the block
◆ Stitch the ruffle to the pillow front
◆ Cut the pillow back
◆ Stitch together the pillow front and back part, right sides facing, leaving a side opening for stuffing; turn right-side out
◆ Stuff the pillow and stitch the opening closed.

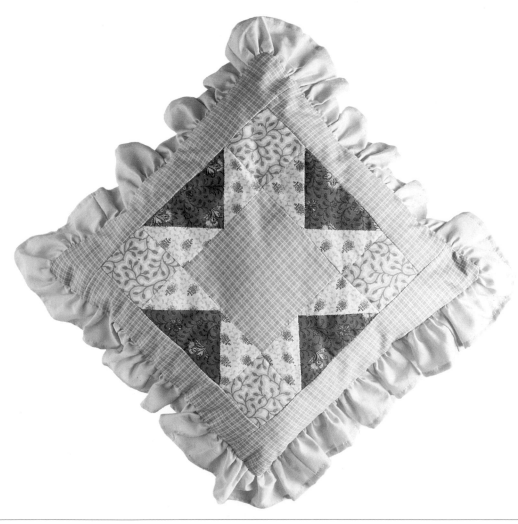

# VIRGINIA STAR QUILT

## DIRECTIONS

◆ Add seam allowances to all cutting dimensions given below

◆ Prepare paper templates using the patterns on p. 404

◆ Cut the fabric pieces for the stars and prepare using the English method

◆ Sew the Virginia Star blocks (see p. 405)

◆ Cut the lattice strips 3⅛" (8 cm) wide; the lattice squares 3⅛ × 3⅛" (8 × 8 cm); the ecru side strips 4" (10 cm) wide; and the ecru strip at bottom 6" (15 cm) wide

◆ Stitch Virginia Star blocks and lattice strips together to make a horizontal row

◆ Stitch the lattice strips and lattice squares together to form horizontal bands below the Star blocks

◆ Stitch the rows and bands together to form the quilt center

◆ Cut and stitch together the ecru and colored right triangles (the triangles are 4 × 2¾ × 2¾" or 10 × 7 × 7 cm) to form sawtooth strip for the bottom border

◆ Cut and stitch together ecru and colored 2 × 2" (5 × 5 cm) squares to make 6 pieced strips for the borders for 3 sides

◆ Stitch 2 pieced border strips, one above the other, to form the square border

◆ Stitch on the borders to the quilt center

◆ Cut the batting and backing, about 73¼ × 105½" (186 × 268 cm)

◆ Pin together the three layers: top, batting, and backing

◆ Baste and quilt the layers

◆ Finish the sides with ecru bias tape or strips of fabric.

**TECHNIQUES**
*English and American piecing, quilting*

**PATTERN**
*Virginia Star*

**SIZE**
*Block: 15 × 15"*
*(38 × 38 cm)*
*Quilt: 73¼ × 105½"*
*(186 × 268 cm)*

**MATERIALS**
• Many colorful print fabrics for the stars, borders, and lattice squares
• Ecru fabrics in solid colors and small prints for the stars, background pieces, solid borders and lattice strips
• Batting
• Backing fabric
• Bias binding or bias strips in ecru

*Quilt tote is made with the same fabrics and star pattern.*

# VIRGINIA STAR PILLOW

## DIRECTIONS

◆ Add seam allowances to all cutting dimensions given below
◆ Prepare paper templates using the patterns on p. 406
◆ Cut the pattern pieces from fabric
◆ Prepare the Star block pieces according to the English method and stitch together in the Virginia Star (see p. 407)
◆ Cut strips for the ruffle 4" (10 cm) wide
◆ Cut the lining for the pillow front, the pillow back, and the batting 15¾ × 15¾" (40 × 40 cm)

◆ Draw the quilting patterns on the pieced pillow front
◆ Pin, baste, and quilt the three layers: pillow front, batting, and lining
◆ Stitch on the ruffle, folded in half, and the lace to the pillow front
◆ With right sides of fabric facing, stitch together the front and back of the pillow, leaving an opening of about 4" (10 cm) for stuffing; turn right-side out
◆ Stuff with batting and stitch the side closed.

**TECHNIQUES**
*English or American piecing*

**PATTERN**
*Virginia Star*

**SIZE**
*15¾ × 15¾"*
*(40 × 40 cm)*

**MATERIALS**
• *Colored fabrics for the star, ruffle, and back of the pillow*
• *Plain fabric for lining*
• *Ecru fabric for background of star*
• *Lace*
• *Low-loft batting for pillow front*
• *Stuffing for pillow*

# TRAPEZOIDS WALL HANGING

## DIRECTIONS

**TECHNIQUES**
*English piecing, quilting*

**PATTERNS**
*Trapezoids*
*Triangles*

**SIZE**
*47¼ × 46½"*
*(120 × 118 cm)*

**MATERIALS**
• *Velvet in many colors and patterns for the "Y"s*
• *Black velvet for the border and "Y"s*
• *Batting*
• *Backing fabric*

◆ Add seam allowances to all cutting dimensions given below
◆ Prepare paper templates using the patterns on p. 408
◆ Cut and prepare the velvet pieces by the English method
◆ Lay out the pieces on the work surface to form "Y"s, arranging the colors in a pleasing way (see p. 408)
◆ Create the "Y"s and whipstitch them together in groups of six (5 around a central "Y")

◆ Whipstitch the groups together to form the quilt top
◆ Cut and stitch extra trapezoids and triangles on the sides to make a rectangular quilt
◆ Cut the borders 1½" (4 cm) wide and stitch on
◆ Pin, baste, and quilt the three layers: top, batting, and backing
◆ To finish, fold part of border to the back; hemstitch in place.

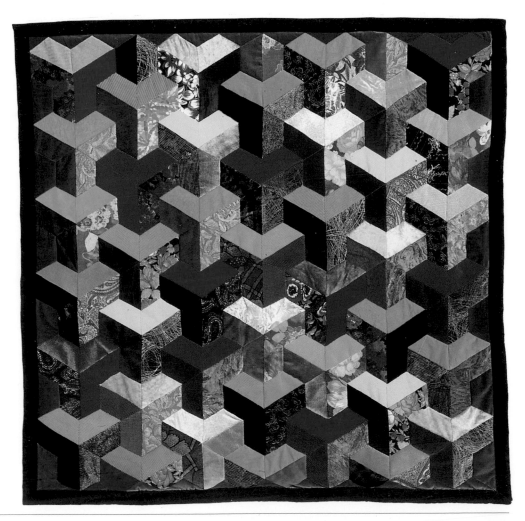

*Quilt by R. D. Sassi.*

# BABY BLOCKS WALL HANGING

## DIRECTIONS

◆ Add seam allowances to all cutting dimensions given below
◆ Prepare paper templates using the patterns on p. 409
◆ Cut the fabric pieces
◆ Prepare the pieces by the English method, and stitch together to form cubes (see p. 409)
◆ Stitch the cubes together in horizontal rows
◆ Stitch the rows together to form the quilt top

◆ Cut and stitch on the triangles to complete the edges
◆ Cut the border strips 6¼" (11 cm) wide from red fabric, which includes 2" (5 cm) width for finishing
◆ Stitch on the border
◆ Cut the batting and backing about 53 × 43¼" (135 × 110 cm)
◆ Pin, baste, and quilt the quilt top, batting, and backing together
◆ Fold the excess border to back and hem-stitch in place.

**TECHNIQUES**
*English piecing, quilting*

**PATTERN**
*Baby Blocks*

**SIZE**
*53 × 43¼"*
*(135 × 110 cm)*

**MATERIALS**
• *Variety of prints and solid-color fabrics for diamonds in cubes and side triangles*
• *Red fabric for border*
• *Batting*
• *Backing fabric*

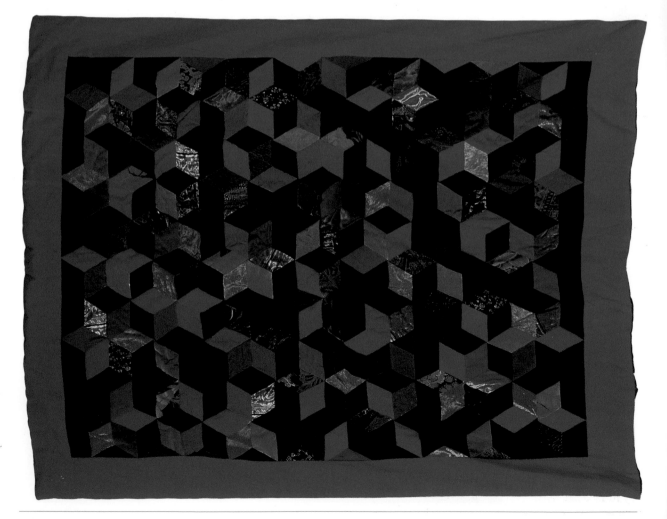

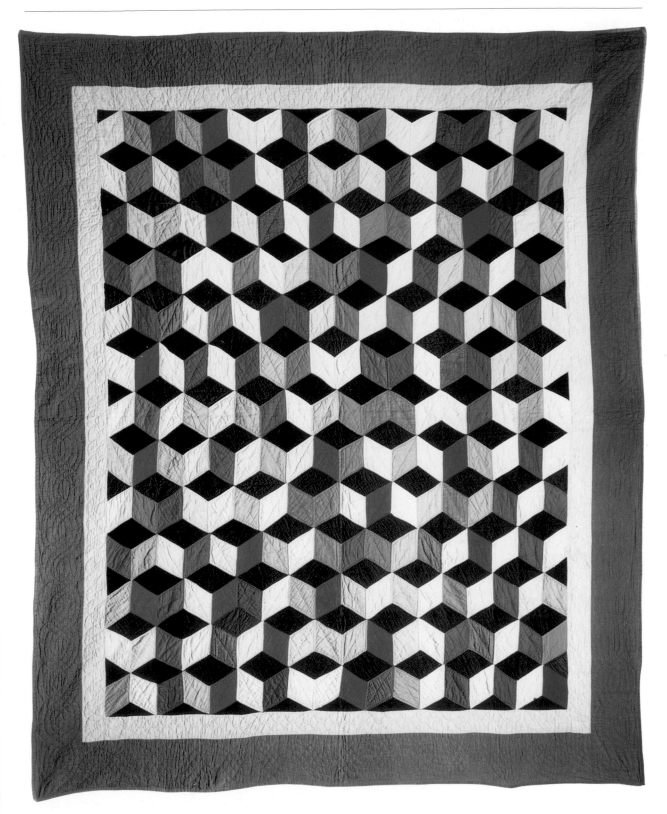

Opposite: Panel with multi-colored blocks and red border by R. D. Sassi.

Above: Baby Blocks quilt, highlighted by quilting patterns.

# DRESDEN PLATE QUILT

## DIRECTIONS

◆ Add seam allowances to all cutting dimensions given below

◆ Prepare paper templates using the patterns on p. 410 (to make quilt shown on p. 205)

◆ Cut the fabric pieces for the Dresden Plate blocks

◆ Prepare the fabric pieces by the English method and stitch them together to form the Dresden Plate blocks

◆ Cut the lattice strips 2" (5 cm) wide and lattice squares 2 × 2" (5 × 5 cm)

◆ Stitch together 4 Dresden Plate blocks and 5 lattice strips to make a row

◆ Stitch 4 lattice strips and 5 lattice squares in a horizontal band

◆ Stitch the bands and rows together to make the quilt center

◆ Cut the first border 4" (10 cm) wide and the third border 4¾" (12 cm) wide, which includes 2" (5 cm) for finishing

◆ Make the second (pieced) border, 2¾" (7 cm) wide from squares and triangles

◆ Stitch on the borders to the quilt top

◆ Draw the quilting patterns on the quilt top

◆ Cut the batting and backing about 68 × 80" (173 × 203 cm)

◆ Pin, baste, and quilt the quilt top, batting, and backing

◆ Fold part of the outer border to the back; hemstitch in place.

**TECHNIQUES**
*English piecing, quilting*

**PATTERN**
*Dresden Plate*

**SIZE**
*Block: 9¾ × 9¾"*
*(25 × 25 cm)*
*Quilt: 68 × 80"*
*(173 × 233 cm)*

**MATERIALS**
• *Variety of colorful prints for Dresden Plate blocks and borders*
• *Ecru fabric for the lattice strips and border*
• *Batting*
• *Backing fabric*

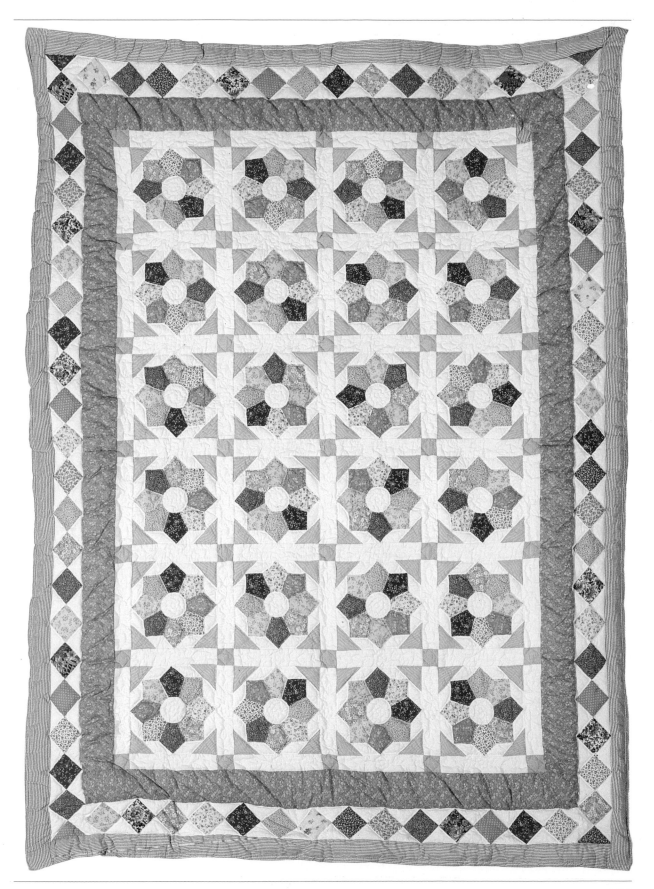

# LEAF SQUARE

**TECHNIQUES**
*Speed piecing, quilting*

**PATTERN**
*Leaf*

**SIZE**
*9½ × 9½" (24 × 24 cm) or 11¾ × 11¾"*
*(30 × 30 cm) with border*

**MATERIALS**
* *Red print fabric for pattern*
* *Light blue print fabric for the pattern, background, backing, and 1st border*
* *Green fabric for the stem*
* *Red checked fabric for the 2nd border*
* *Large light blue print for border squares*
* *Low-loft batting*

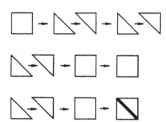 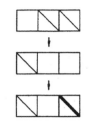 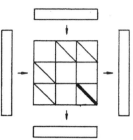 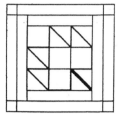

# DIRECTIONS

◆ Add seam allowances to all cutting dimensions given below

◆ From the red and light blue print fabrics, cut  2⅜ × 2⅜" (6 × 6 cm) squares and 2⅜ × 2⅜ × 3⅜" (6 × 6 × 8.5 cm) right triangles for the pattern and background

◆ From the green fabric cut a strip ⅜" (1 cm) wide for the stem, fold under seam allowances, and appliqué it diagonally onto a background square

◆ Stitch together the squares and triangles to form horizontal rows (see diagrams above)

◆ Stitch the rows together to form the Leaf block

◆ From the blue print fabric, cut the first border 1³⁄₁₆" (3 cm) wide and stitch onto the pieced block

◆ Cut red checked strips 1³⁄₁₆" (3 cm) wide and blue squares 1³⁄₁₆" × 1³⁄₁₆" (3 × 3 cm) for the second border; make borders

◆ Stitch on the second border

◆ Cut the batting and backing 11¾ × 11¾" (30 × 30 cm)

◆ Pin, baste, and quilt the Leaf block top, batting, and backing together

◆ Neaten edges and turn excess of border to back; hemstitch in place.

*Potholders with Leaf pattern.*

# SUNSHINE AND SHADOW SQUARE

**TECHNIQUE**
*Speed cutting and piecing*

**PATTERN**
*Sunshine and Shadow*

**SIZE**
*9½ × 9½" (24 × 24 cm); 11¾ × 11¾" (30 × 30)
with border*

**MATERIALS**
- *Print fabrics in several colors for the pattern*
- *Red-and-white checked fabric for the border*
- *Large light blue print for border squares*

# DIRECTIONS

◆ Add seam allowances to all cutting dimensions given below

◆ From the print fabrics, cut 1" (2.5 cm) wide strips and cut 1 × 1" (2.5 × 2.5 cm) squares from the strips

◆ Lay out the squares on the work surface, arranging the colors to form the Trip Around the World pattern shown

◆ Stitch the squares together to form horizontal rows (see diagrams below)

◆ Stitch the rows together to form the pattern

◆ Cut border strips 1³⁄₁₆" (3 cm) wide from red checked fabric; cut 1³⁄₁₆ × 1³⁄₁₆" (3 × 3 cm) blue border squares

◆ Assemble borders and stitch to the pieced square. Finish edges.

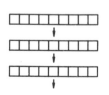

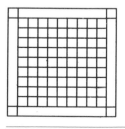

*Oven mitt and potholders with square patterns.*

# CHURN DASH SQUARE

## TECHNIQUES
*Speed techniques*

## PATTERN
*Churn Dash*

## SIZE
*Square: 9½ × 9½" (24 × 24 cm); 11¾ × 11¾"*
*(30 × 30 cm) with border*

## MATERIALS
*• Red-and-white checked fabric for the Churn*
*Dash pattern*
*• Light blue print pattern for the background*
*• Large blue print pattern for the border*
*• Gray or ecru fabric for the border squares*

# DIRECTIONS

◆ Add seam allowances to all cutting dimensions given below

◆ From background fabric and red checked fabric, cut rectangles 3⅛ × 1⁹⁄₁₆" (8 × 4 cm), right triangles 3⅓ × 3⅛ × 4½" (8 × 8 × 11.3 cm) and a square 3⅛ × 3⅛" (8 × 8 cm); see photo

◆ Stitch triangles together, and stitch rectangles together, to form squares 3⅛ × 3⅛" (8 × 8 cm); see diagrams

◆ Stitch the squares as shown to form horizontal rows

◆ Stitch the rows together to form the Churn Dash square

◆ Cut border strips 1³⁄₁₆" (3 cm) wide and cut squares 1³⁄₁₆ × 1³⁄₁₆" (3 × 3 cm) for the border; piece borders

◆ Stitch the borders to the pieced square; neaten edges.

*Potholders have the Churn Dash pattern with figurative design in the center.*

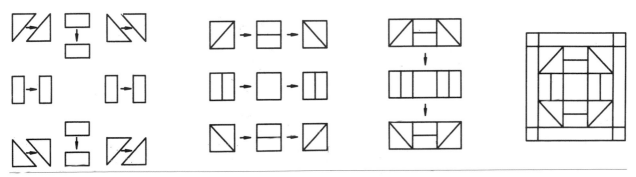

# INTERLOCKED SQUARES SQUARE

**TECHNIQUES**
*Speed techniques*

**PATTERN**
*Interlocked Squares*

**SIZE**
*9½ × 9½" (24 × 24 cm); 11¾ × 11¾" (30 × 30 cm)*
*with border*

**MATERIALS**
• *Fabric in three shades of light blue for the pattern*
• *Red-and-white checked fabric for the border*
• *Large light blue print for the border squares*

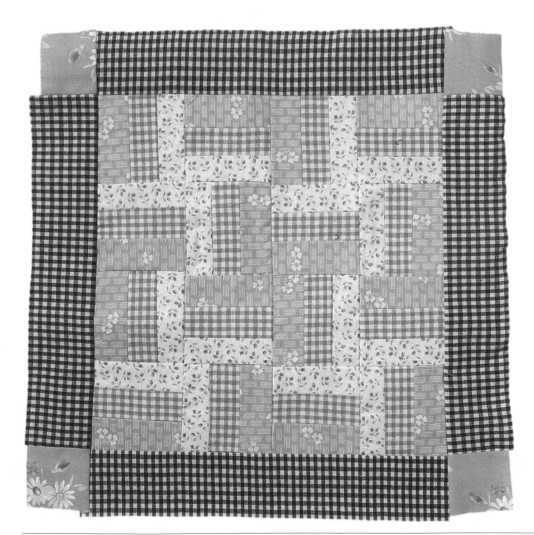

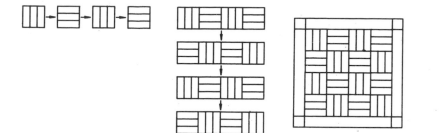

*Terry cloth bag decorated with the Interlocked Squares pattern.*

# DIRECTIONS

◆ Add seam allowances to all cutting dimensions given below
◆ From the fabrics in three tones of light blue, cut the strips ¾" (2 cm) wide and stitch them together to form strip-pieced fabric (see above)
◆ From the pieced fabric, cut 2⅜ × 2⅜" (6 × 6 cm) squares and stitch 4 together to form a horizontal row. Make 4 rows
◆ Stitch the rows together to form the central square
◆ Cut 1³⁄₁₆" (3 cm) wide red checked strips and 1³⁄₁₆ × 1³⁄₁₆" (3 × 3 cm) blue squares for the border. Piece the borders
◆ Stitch the borders to the central square; neaten edges.

# LITTLE BOAT SQUARE

**TECHNIQUES**
*Speed techniques*

**PATTERN**
*Boat*

**SIZE**
*9½ × 9½" (24 × 24 cm); 11¾ × 11¾" (30 × 30 cm)*
*with border*

**MATERIALS**
• *Red print for the boat*
• *Light blue print for the background*
• *Red-and-white checked fabric for sails*
• *Blue-and-white prints for the border*
*and border squares*

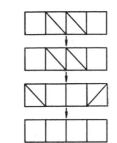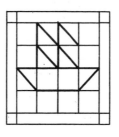

*Apron with Little Boat pattern.*

## DIRECTIONS

◆ Add seam allowances to all cutting dimensions given below

◆ From the red print and light blue background print fabrics, cut the 2⅜ × 2⅜" (6 × 6 cm) squares and right triangles 2⅜ × 2⅜ × 3⁵⁄₁₆" (6 × 6 × 8.5 cm) for the pattern and background; see diagrams above

◆ Stitch the triangles and squares to form horizontal rows

◆ Stitch the rows together to form the Boat block

◆ Cut 1³⁄₁₆" (3 cm) wide strips and 1³⁄₁₆ × 1³⁄₁₆" (3 × 3 cm) squares from the blue-and-white print fabrics for the border and border squares. Piece the borders

◆ Stitch the borders to the Boat block; neaten edges.

# TRIANGLES SQUARE

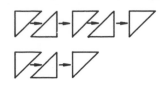

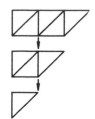

## TECHNIQUES
*Speed techniques*

## PATTERN
*2-triangle squares*

## SIZE
*9½ × 9½" (24 × 24 cm); 11¾ × 11¾" (30 × 30 cm)
with border*

## MATERIALS
• *Prints in several patterns and colors for the
central square*
• *Red-and-white checked fabric for border*
• *Large light blue print for border squares*

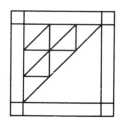

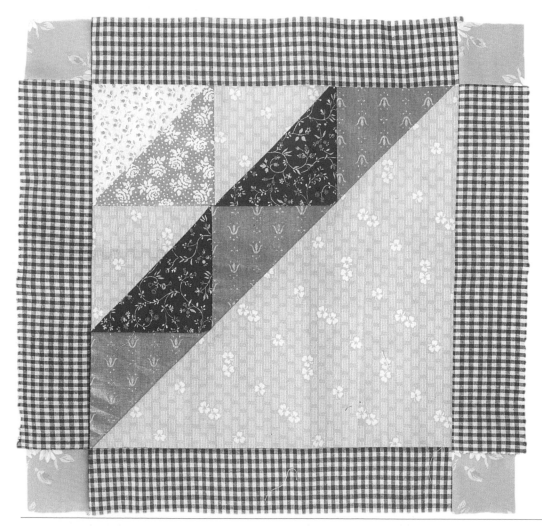

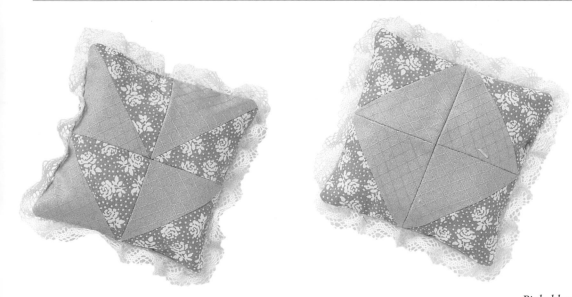

*Pinholders and placemat
with triangle patterns.
Placemat design is called
Battlegrounds.*

# DIRECTIONS

◆ Add seam allowances to all cutting
dimensions given below
◆ To make square on p. 216, cut 9 small
right triangles 3⅛ × 3⅛ × 4⁷⁄₁₆" (8 × 8 ×
11.3 cm) and one large right triangle 9½
× 9½ × 13⁷⁄₁₆" (24 ×
24 × 34 cm)
◆ Stitch the small
triangles together to
form horizontal
bands (see p. 216)
◆ Stitch the bands
together to form a
right triangle 9½ ×
9½ × 13⁷⁄₁₆" (24 × 24
× 34 cm)
◆ Stitch the pieced
triangle to the large
triangle to form the
central square
◆ Cut red checked
border strips 1³⁄₁₆"
(3 cm) wide and
blue 1³⁄₁₆ × 1³⁄₁₆"
(3 × 3 cm) squares
for the border. Piece
the borders
◆ Stitch the borders
to the pieced square;
neaten edges.

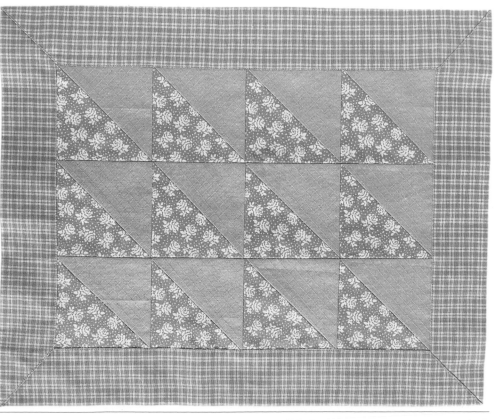

# SQUARE IN A SQUARE

**TECHNIQUES**
*Speed techniques*

**PATTERN**
*Amish Square in a Square*

**SIZE**
*9½ × 9½" (24 × 24 cm); 11¾ × 11¾" (30 × 30 cm)
with border*

**MATERIALS**
• *Checked and print fabrics for the pattern*
• *Checked fabric for border*
• *Large blue print for border squares*

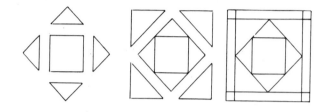

*Apron and potholders with the Square in a Square pattern.*

# DIRECTIONS

◆ Add seam allowances to all cutting dimensions given below

◆ From the light blue checked fabric, cut a square 4¾ × 4¾" (12 × 12 cm)

◆ From the red print fabric, cut right triangles 3⅜ × 3⅜ × 4¾" (8.5 × 8.5 × 12 cm)

◆ Stitch the red print triangles to the sides of the blue checked square to form a larger square 6¹¹⁄₁₆ × 6¹¹⁄₁₆" (17 × 17 cm)

◆ From the small light blue print fabric, cut right triangles 4¾ × 4¾ × 6¹¹⁄₁₆" (12 × 12 × 17 cm)

◆ Stitch the light blue print triangles to the sides of the red pieced square to form the final square

◆ Cut red checked border strips 1³⁄₁₆" (3 cm) wide and cut blue print border squares 1³⁄₁₆ × 1³⁄₁₆" (3 × 3 cm). Piece the borders

◆ Stitch the borders to the square; neaten edges.

# BASKET SQUARE

**TECHNIQUES**
*Speed cutting and piecing*

**PATTERN**
*Basket*

**SIZE**
*9½ × 9½" (24 × 24 cm); 11¾ × 11¾" (30 × 30 cm)
with border*

**MATERIALS**
- *Prints in red, light blue, and blue for the pattern and background*
- *Red-and-white checked fabric for the border*
- *Large light blue print for the border squares*

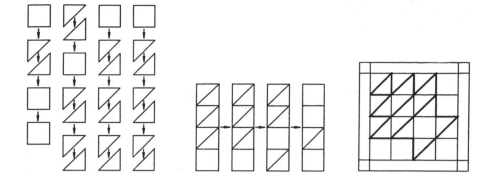

# DIRECTIONS

◆ Add seam allowances to all cutting dimensions given below
◆ Cut 2⅜ × 2⅜" (6 × 6 cm) squares and right triangles 2⅜ × 2⅜ × 3⁵⁄₁₆" (6 × 6 × 8.5 cm)
◆ Stitch the triangles together and join with the whole-cloth squares to form vertical strips (see diagrams above)
◆ Stitch the strips together to form the pieced basket block
◆ Cut checked strips 1³⁄₁₆" (3 cm) wide and blue print squares 1³⁄₁₆ × 1³⁄₁₆" (3 × 3 cm) for the borders. Piece the borders
◆ Stitch the borders to the pieced blocks; neaten edges.

*Apron with Basket pattern.*

# LOG CABIN SQUARE

**TECHNIQUES**
*American method, paper piecing*

**PATTERN**
*Log Cabin*

**SIZE**
*9½ × 9½" (24 × 24 cm); 11¾ × 11¾"*
*(30 × 30 cm) with border*

**MATERIALS**
• *Many different patterns of red and blue fabric*
*for the Log Cabin pattern*
• *Red-and-white checked fabric for border*
• *Large light blue print fabric for border squares*

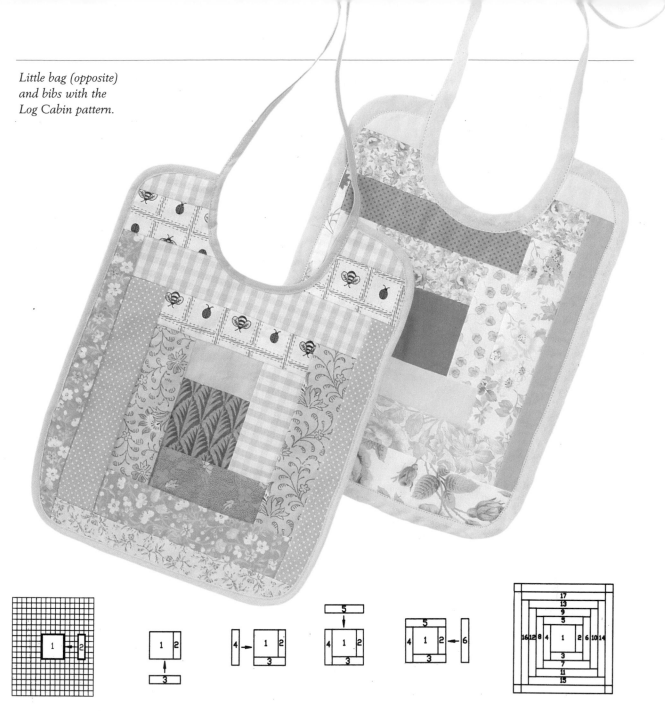

*Little bag (opposite) and bibs with the Log Cabin pattern.*

# DIRECTIONS

◆ Add seam allowances to all cutting dimensions given below

◆ See Log Cabin instructions on 124

◆ From the darkest red fabric cut a square for piece 1 that is 1⁹⁄₁₆ × 1⁹⁄₁₆" (4 × 4 cm)

◆ From many other red and blue fabrics, cut strips 1" (2.5 cm) wide

◆ Pin piece 1 to the center of a piece of graph paper; superimpose a strip of fabric so its long side lines up with the square's side

◆ Sew the seam allowances of the strip and square

together, fold open, press, and cut off the strip's excess length, creating piece 2

◆ Pin a strip to the adjacent sides of pieces 1 and 2 and proceed as you did earlier to stitch on piece 3

◆ Continue in this way to stitch on all of the pieces

◆ Remove the paper that served as a guide for sewing the strips. Once you have mastered this pattern, you can eliminate the paper guide

◆ Cut checked strips 1³⁄₁₆" (3 cm) and squares 1³⁄₁₆ × 1³⁄₁₆" (3 × 3 cm) for the borders. Piece the borders

◆ Join the borders to the Log Cabin block; neaten edges.

# PINWHEEL SQUARE

**TECHNIQUE**
*Speed piecing*

**PATTERN**
*Pinwheel*

**SIZE**
*9½ × 9½" (24 × 24 cm); 11¾ × 11¾" (30 × 30 cm)
with border*

**MATERIALS**
• *Prints and solid-colored fabrics for the pattern*
• *Red-and-white checked fabric for the border*
• *Large light blue print for the border*

*Pincushions with
triangle designs.*

*Potholders with*
*Pinwheel designs.*

# DIRECTIONS

◆ Add seam allowances to all cutting dimensions given below

◆ Cut right triangles 2⅜ × 2⅜ × 3⁵⁄₁₆" (6 × 6 × 8.5 cm) and stitch together to form 2-triangle squares

◆ Stitch the squares together in two rows (see photo and diagrams below)

◆ Stitch the rows together to form the Pinwheel block

◆ Cut red checked strips 1³⁄₁₆" (3 cm) wide and blue print squares 1³⁄₁₆ × 1³⁄₁₆" (3 × 3 cm) for border

◆ Piece the borders, stitch to the Pinwheel square, and trim if necessary.

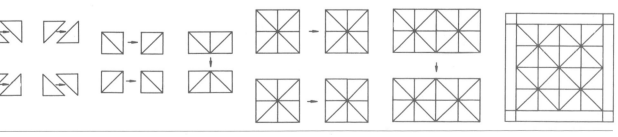

# EVENING STAR SQUARE

**TECHNIQUE**
*Speed piecing*

**PATTERN**
*Evening Star*

**SIZE**
*9½ × 9½" (24 × 24 cm); 11¾ × 11¾" (30 × 30 cm)
with border*

**MATERIALS**
*• Red and light blue prints for the pattern and
background*
*• Red-and-white checked fabric for border*
*• Large light blue print for border squares*

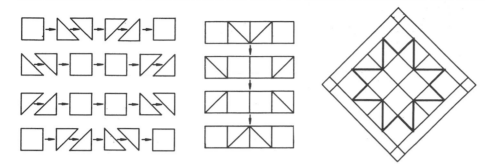

*Below: Virginia Star (see p. 198).*

## DIRECTIONS

◆ Add seam allowances to all cutting dimensions given below

◆ Cut 2⅜ × 2⅜" (6 × 6 cm) squares and 2⅜ × 2⅜" × 3⁵⁄₁₆" (6 × 6 × 8.5 cm) right triangles, and stitch them to form horizontal rows (see diagrams above)

◆ Stitch the rows together to form the Star block

◆ Cut red checked strips 1³⁄₁₆" (3 cm) wide and blue squares 1³⁄₁₆" × 1³⁄₁₆" (3 × 3 cm) for the border

◆ Stitch the border to the Evening Star block; trim if necessary.

*Tray liner with Star pattern.*

# HEART SQUARE

**TECHNIQUES**
*Speed stitching, appliqué*

**PATTERN**
*Heart*

**SIZE**
*9½ × 9½" (24 × 24 cm); 11¾ × 11¾" (30 × 30 cm)*
*with border*

**MATERIALS**
• *Light blue print fabrics for the background*
*square*
• *Red print fabric for appliqué*
• *Red-and-white checked fabric for border*
*squares and heart*
• *Colorful print fabric for border*

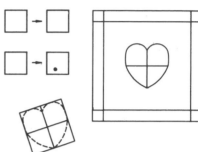

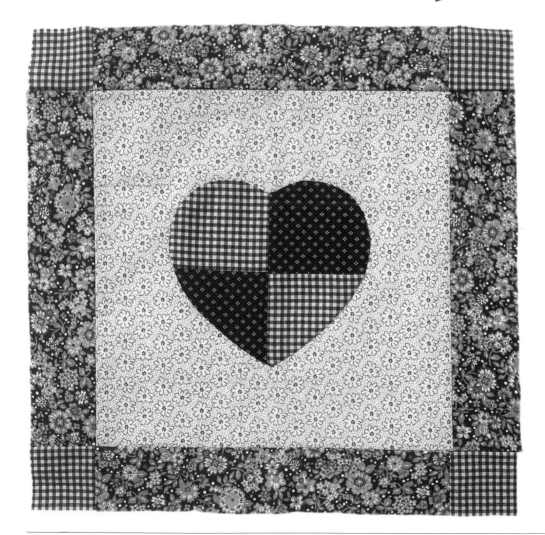

*Appliqué in the form
of a heart done in
Crazy Quilting style.*

## DIRECTIONS

◆ Add seam allowances to all cutting dimensions given

◆ From the light blue print fabric, cut the background square 9½ × 9½" (24 × 24 cm)

◆ From the red fabrics, cut four 3½ × 3½" (9 × 9 cm) squares and stitch them together to form a square (see diagrams)

◆ Cut a paper template for the heart (pattern on p. 374)

◆ From the pieced red fabric square, cut out and prepare the heart patch for appliqué

◆ Hemstitch the appliqué to the center of the background square

◆ Cut strips 1³⁄₁₆" (3 cm) wide and squares 1³⁄₁₆ × 1³⁄₁₆" (3 × 3 cm) for the border and stitch together

◆ Join the borders to the background square; trim if necessary.

*Hot pad decorated
with hearts in appliqué
(A. Alessandri).*

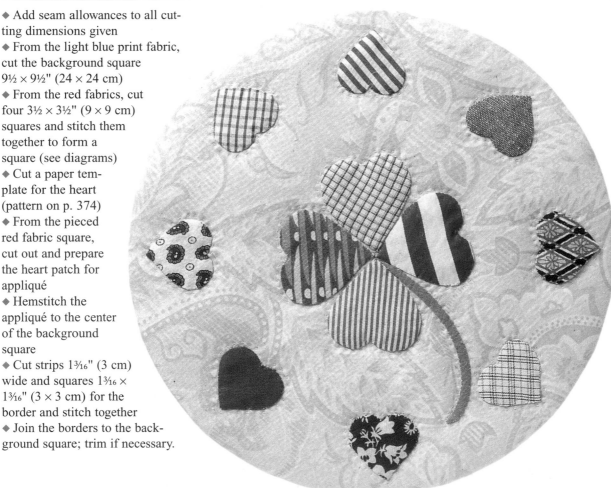

# MINI ALBUM QUILT

### TECHNIQUES
*Speed piecing, quilting*

### PATTERN
*Several*

### SIZE
*Square: 9½ × 9½" (24 × 24 cm)*
*Quilt: 43¼ × 52¾" (110 × 134 cm)*

### MATERIALS
• *Many blue and red prints for the squares*
• *Red checked fabric for lattice strips and first border*
• *Blue print fabric for the lattice squares and second border*
• *Red fabric for the third border*
• *Batting*
• *Backing fabric*

## DIRECTIONS

◆ Add seam allowances to all cutting dimensions given below

◆ Make the 12 blocks (use patterns on pp. 206 to 228). Adjust patterns if needed so blocks are all the same size

◆ Cut the lattice strips 1½" (4 cm) wide from red checked fabric

◆ Stitch 3 squares and 2 short lattice strips together to make a horizontal row

◆ Stitch the pieced rows and long lattice strips together to form the quilt top

◆ Cut small blue squares 2⅜ × 2⅜" (6 × 6 cm) for the lattice squares; turn under their seam allowances and hemstitch in place

◆ Cut the first border 1⁹⁄₁₆" (4 cm) wide of red checked fabric and stitch on

◆ Cut the second border 3½" (9 cm) wide of blue print and stitch on

◆ Cut the third border of red fabric 4⅜" (11 cm) wide, which includes 2⅜" (6 cm) for border and 2" (5 cm) to finish

◆ Draw the quilting pattern on the fabric

◆ Cut the batting and backing 43¼ × 54⅜" (110 × 138 cm)

◆ Pin the three layers: quilt top, batting, and backing

◆ Baste and quilt

◆ To finish, fold the excess third border to the back and hemstitch in place.

*Opposite: From Disegno di Modo Verceria (G. Berti).*

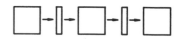
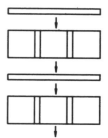
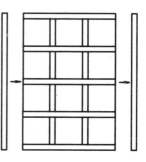

# ONE-PATCH QUILT

**TECHNIQUES**
*Speed piecing, quilting*

**PATTERN**
*One-Patch*

**SIZE**
*39⅜ × 47¼" (100 × 120 cm)*

**MATERIALS**
- *Many colors and patterns for the squares*
- *Green print for first border*
- *Checked fabric for second border*
- *Batting*
- *Backing fabric*

## DIRECTIONS

◆ Add seam allowances to all cutting dimensions given below

◆ Cut 4 × 4" (10 × 10 cm) squares of many fabrics

◆ Lay out the squares on the work surface; arrange colors and patterns harmoniously

◆ Stitch the squares together in horizontal rows

◆ Stitch the rows together to form the quilt top center

◆ Cut the first border 1³⁄₁₆" (3 cm) wide and the second one 2" (5 cm) wide; stitch on

◆ Cut the batting 41 × 49" (104 × 124 cm)

◆ Cut the backing 43¼ × 51¼" (110 × 130 cm), which also includes the third border

◆ Assemble the three layers (quilt top, batting, and backing). Pin, baste and quilt, using adhesive tape as a guide for stitching rows, which is removed after stitching the row

◆ To finish, fold the excess backing to the front to form the third border; stitch in place.

# HOUSES QUILT

**TECHNIQUES**
*American and English piecing, quilting*

**PATTERN**
*House*

**SIZE**
*Block: 6 × 6" (15 × 15 cm)*
*Quilt: 44½ × 67" (113 × 170 cm)*

**MATERIALS**
• *Many colors of prints for the House blocks, including green print for strips*
• *Black print fabric for lattice strips and border*
• *Yellow fabric for lattice squares*
• *Batting*
• *Checked backing fabric*

## DIRECTIONS

◆ Add seam allowances to all cutting dimensions given below
◆ Make Houses blocks, using the English method (pattern pieces on p. 414)
◆ Cut the lattice strips 1⁹⁄₁₆" (4 cm) wide
◆ Stitch the House squares and lattice strips together to form horizontal rows (p. 415)
◆ Stitch the rows and lattice strips together to form the quilt top
◆ Cut yellow squares 1 × 1" (2.5 × 2.5 cm), turn under the seam allowances, and hemstitch to the intersections of the lattice
◆ Cut and stitch on the border 6¼" (16 cm) wide from black print fabric
◆ Cut the batting and backing about 47½ × 70" (121 × 178 cm), which includes edging
◆ Put together, baste, and quilt the three layers: quilt top, batting, backing
◆ Trim batting; bring the excess backing to the front; hemstitch in place.

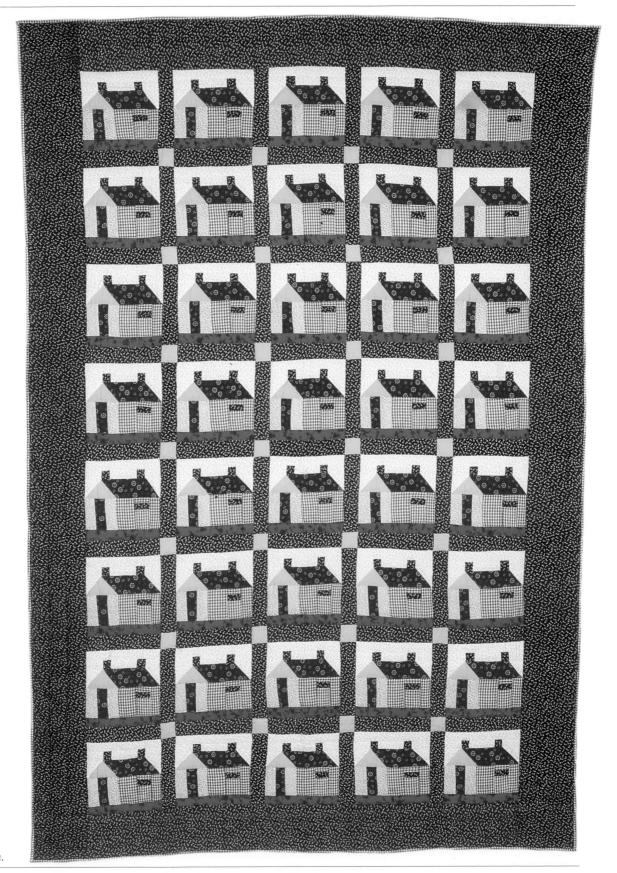

*Quilt by Coin.*

# INDIAN PRINT QUILT

## TECHNIQUES
*Speed quilting, quilting*

## PATTERN
*Whole-cloth blocks*

## SIZE
*82¾ × 96" (210 × 244 cm)*

## MATERIALS
• *Colorful print (such as chintz) in warm tones for the squares*
• *Yellow fabric for the lattice strips and first border*
• *Red fabric for the second border*
• *Batting*
• *Backing fabric*

## DIRECTIONS

◆ Add seam allowances to all cutting dimensions given

◆ Cut 5 × 5" (13 × 13 cm) squares from the print fabric
◆ Cut out lattice strips 1½" (4 cm) wide from the yellow fabric
◆ Stitch together the squares and lattice strips to form horizontal rows (see p. 413)
◆ Stitch the lattice strips and rows together to form the quilt center
◆ Cut the yellow first border 1½" (4 cm) wide and stitch on
◆ Cut the red second border 2⅜" (6 cm) wide, which includes 2" (5 cm) to finish
◆ Cut the batting and backing about 82¾ × 96" (210 × 244 cm)
◆ Put the 3 layers together: quilt top, batting, and backing. Baste and quilt the three layers
◆ Fold the excess border to the back of the piece; hemstitch in place.

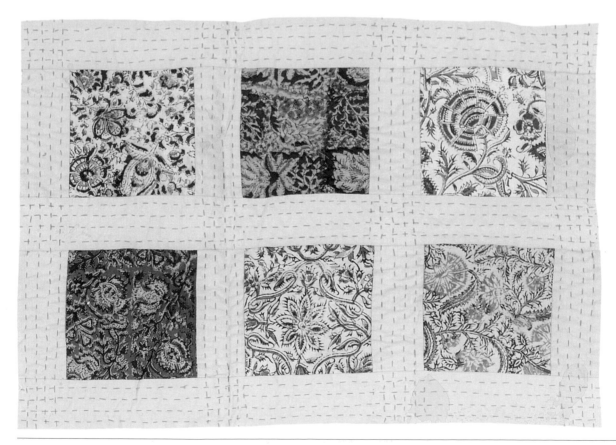

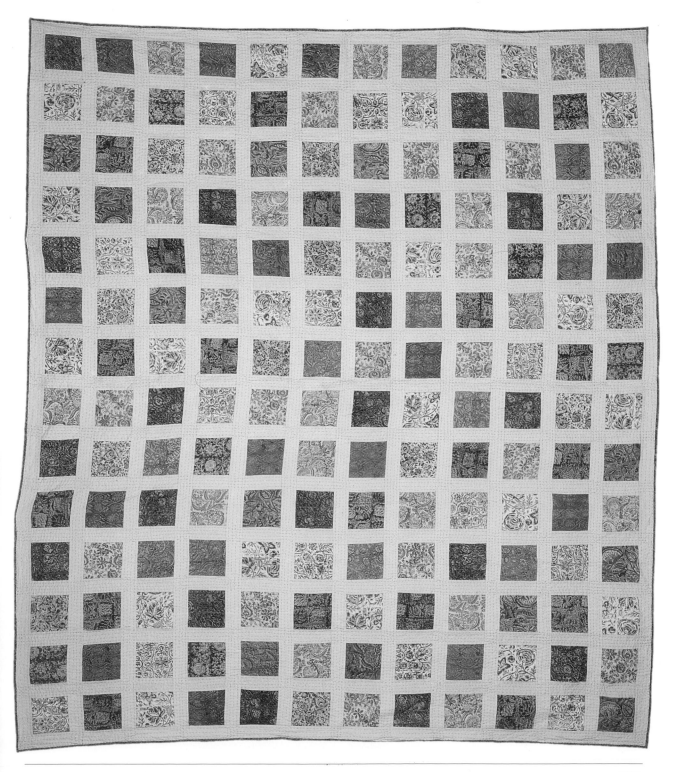

# SCRAP QUILT

**TECHNIQUES**
*Speed piecing, quilting*

**PATTERN**
*Triangle squares*

**SIZE**
*43¾ × 80¼" (111 × 205 cm)*

**MATERIALS**
• *Many colors and prints of scraps
(the quilt shown used men's shirt fabric)*
• *Mauve fabric for first border*
• *Backing fabric*
• *Batting*

# DIRECTIONS

◆ Add seam allowances to all cutting dimensions given below

◆ From scraps, cut 4 × 4" (10 × 10 cm) squares to make half-square triangles 4 × 4 × 5½" (10 × 10 × 14 cm); cut quarter-square triangles 2¾ × 2¾ × 3⅞" (7 × 7 × 10 cm)

◆ Lay out the pieces on the work surface; arrange them harmoniously

◆ Stitch together some of the triangles to form the squares (see p. 416)

◆ Stitch the pieced squares and triangles together to form rows, set at an angle

◆ Stitch the rows together to form the quilt center

◆ Cut and stitch on the first border, 1¾" (4.5 cm) wide

◆ Cut the batting 43⁵⁄₁₆ × 80¾" (110 × 205 cm) and backing 46½ × 83½" (118 × 212 cm)

◆ Join the three layers: quilt top, batting, and backing. Pin, baste and quilt

◆ Fold the excess backing to the front of the piece; hemstitch in place to form the second border ⅝" (1.5 cm) wide.

*Quilt by F. Morini.*

# 9-PATCH QUILT

**TECHNIQUES**
*Speed piecing, quilting*

**PATTERN**
*9-Patch*

**SIZE**
*Block: 6 × 6" (15 × 15 cm)*
*Quilt: 46½ × 64¼" (118 × 163 cm)*

**MATERIALS**
• *Many colors and patterns of fabric for the squares*
• *Checked fabric for first border*
• *Large colorful print for second border*
• *Batting*
• *Backing fabric*

*Opposite:*
*Quilt by Coin.*

## DIRECTIONS

◆ Add seam allowances to all cutting dimensions given

◆ Cut 2 × 2" (5 × 5 cm) squares for 9-Patch blocks

◆ Lay out the pieces on the work surface to form 9-Patch blocks in a pleasing design. Stitch together in horizontal rows of 3 pieces (see p. 417)

◆ Stitch together 3 rows of 3 pieces each to form the 9-Patch blocks

◆ Stitch the blocks together in rows, and then stitch the rows together

◆ Cut the first border 1⁹⁄₁₆" (4 cm) wide and stitch on

◆ Cut the second border 6" (15 cm) wide, which includes 2" (5 cm) to finish, and stitch it on

◆ Cut batting and backing 46½ × 64¼" (118 × 163 cm)

◆ Pin together and baste the three layers: quilt top, batting, backing

◆ Fold the 2nd border to back; hemstitch.

# ALL EARS CAT QUILT

**TECHNIQUES**
*Speed piecing, quilting*

**PATTERN**
*Cats*

**SIZE**
*Block: 4¾ × 6" (12 × 15 cm)*
*Quilt: 43¼ × 54" (110 × 137 cm)*

**MATERIALS**
• *Many colors and prints for the cats*
• *White fabric for the background, whole-cloth blocks, and first border*
• *Red checked fabric for the second border and corner squares*
• *Batting*
• *Backing fabric*
• *Embroidery thread*

*Opposite:*
*Quilt by Coin.*

## DIRECTIONS

◆ Add seam allowances to all cutting dimensions given below
◆ Copy the pattern templates (see p. 418). Make the Cat blocks using the English method (see p. 60)
◆ Cut the whole-cloth blocks 4¾ × 6" (12 × 15 cm) from white fabric and stitch them to the pieced blocks to form horizontal rows
◆ Stitch the rows together to form the quilt center
◆ Cut the inner side borders 4¾" (12 cm) wide from white fabric; stitch them to the quilt center
◆ Cut the inner top and bottom

borders 6" (15 cm) wide, and cut 4 red checked rectangles 4¾ × 6" (12 × 15 cm). Stitch 2 rectangles and a border piece together; then stitch the top border to the quilt. Repeat for bottom border
◆ Cut second (outer) border 2⅜" (6 cm) wide fom red checked fabric, which includes 2" (5 cm) to finish; stitch it on
◆ Embroider the cat faces
◆ Assemble the layers (quilt top, batting, and backing); pin, baste, and quilt
◆ To finish, fold excess 2nd border to the back and hemstitch in place.

# TRIANGLES PILLOW SHAM

**TECHNIQUE**
*Speed piecing*

**PATTERN**
*Triangles*

**SIZE**
*27½ × 19¾" (70 × 50 cm)*

**MATERIALS**
• *Many colors and patterns of fabric for the triangles, some light and some dark*
• *Blue-green fabric for the border and backing*

*Triangle bands quilt by Bassetti. On opposite page: Pillow sham by Bassetti.*

244

# DIRECTIONS

◆ Add seam allowances to all cutting dimensions given below

◆ Cut right triangles 3⅜ × 3⅜ × 4¾" (8.5 × 8.5 × 12 cm) from colorful fabrics and lay them out on the work surface so they form alternating bands of dark and light colors; cut small triangles for corners

◆ Stitch the triangles together in angled rows as shown on p. 420

◆ Stitch the rows together to form the quilt center

◆ Cut the top and bottom blue-green borders 2³⁄₁₆" (5.5 cm) wide and the side borders 4⁵⁄₁₆" (11 cm) wide; stitch on

◆ Cut the back of the pillow sham 33½ × 19½" (85 × 50 cm), which includes an extra side part that gets folded in after you insert the pillow

◆ Pin together the pillow sham top and backing, right sides together, and stitch together along three sides. Hem the fourth sides and turn the sham right-side out.

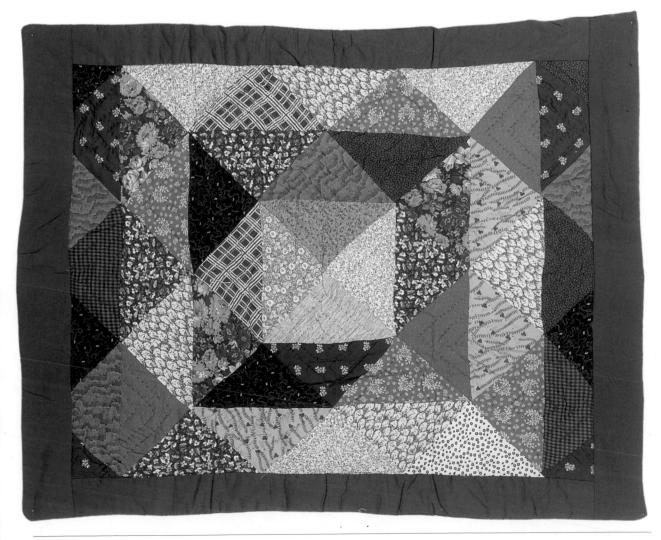

# FLYING GEESE PILLOW SHAM

**TECHNIQUE**
*Speed piecing*

**PATTERN**
*Flying Geese*

**SIZE**
*27½ × 19¾" (70 × 50 cm)*

**MATERIALS**
• *Prints for triangles*
• *White fabric for pieced block and border*
• *Red print fabric for border*
• *Blue fabric for backing and borders*

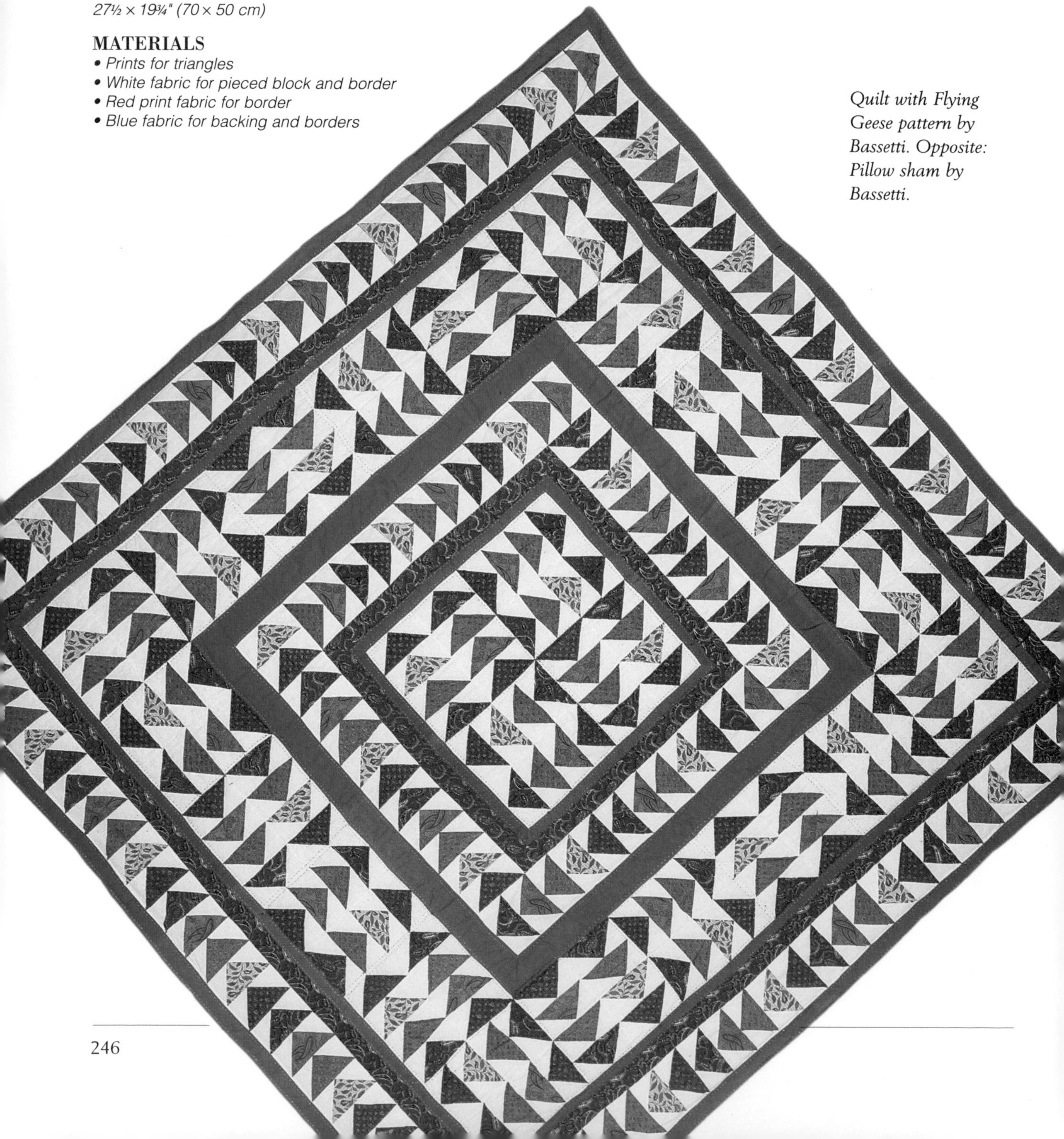

*Quilt with Flying Geese pattern by Bassetti. Opposite: Pillow sham by Bassetti.*

# DIRECTIONS

◆ Add seam allowances to all cutting dimensions given below

◆ Cut print fabric right triangles 2¾ × 2¾ × 3⅞" (7 × 7 × 10 cm) and white right triangles 2 × 2 × 2¾" (5 × 5 × 7 cm)

◆ Stitch two white triangles to every colored one to form rectangles 4 × 2" (10 × 5 cm); see p. 421

◆ Stitch the pieced rectangles together to form vertical columns

◆ Stitch the columns together to form the pieced center block

◆ Cut 4 or 5 borders at widths you like and stitch them one by one to the pieced quilt center; the pillow sham dimensions should be 27½ × 19¾" (70 × 50 cm)

◆ Cut the back for the pillow sham, but make it 6" (15 cm) wider than the pillow sham front, in order to include the side part that gets turned in over the pillow

◆ Assemble the sham top and back, right sides facing, and stitch together along three sides

◆ Finish off the fourth sides with hems; turn the sham right-side out.

# OHIO STAR QUILT

**TECHNIQUES**
*Speed piecing, quilting*

**PATTERN**
*Ohio Star*

**SIZE**
*Block: 9½ × 9½" (24 × 24 cm)*
*Quilt: 63 × 63" (160 × 160 cm)*

**MATERIALS**
• *Several patterns and colors of fabric for stars, backgrounds, and borders*
• *Ecru fabric for background, stars, and borders*
• *Batting*
• *Backing fabric*

# DIRECTIONS

◆ Add seam allowances to all cutting dimensions given below

◆ To make the Stars with the Square-in-a-Square pattern in their center: Cut 3⅜ × 3¼" (8.5 × 8.3 cm) rectangles and 2⅜ × 2⅜ × 3⅜" (6 × 6 × 8.5 cm) right triangles in ecru. Cut 2⅜ × 2⅜ × 3⅜" (6 × 6 × 8.5 cm) right triangles and 2⅜ × 2⅜ (6 × 6 cm) squares in colorful fabrics

◆ For the Stars with whole-cloth squares in the center: Cut 2⅜ × 2⅜" (6 × 6 cm) squares and 2⅜ × 2⅜ × 3⅜" (6 × 6 × 8.5 cm) right triangles in ecru. Cut 4¾ × 4¾" (12 × 12 cm) squares and 2⅜ × 2⅜ × 3⁵⁄₁₆" (6 × 6 × 8.5 cm) right triangles in colorful fabrics

◆ Stitch the squares and triangles to form horizontal rows (see p. 403 for piecing Ohio Star block)

◆ Stitch the rows together to form the Ohio Star blocks

◆ Arrange the Star blocks on the work surface. Stitch 5 to make a row

◆ Stitch the rows together to make the quilt top

◆ Cut and stitch on: The first border (ecru) 1⁹⁄₁₆" (4 cm) wide; the second border (print) 2" (5 cm) wide; the third border (ecru) 2⅜" (6 cm) wide; and the fourth border (print) 4" (10 cm) wide, which includes 2" (5 cm) to finish

◆ Cut the batting and backing about 63 × 63" (160 × 160 cm)

◆ Assemble the three layers (quilt top, batting, and backing); baste and quilt

◆ To finish, fold outer border to the back; hemstitch in place.

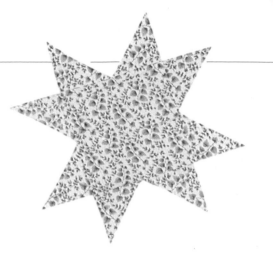

*Quilt by Bassetti.*

# TREE-OF-LIFE QUILT

### TECHNIQUES
*Speed piecing, quilting*

### PATTERN
*Tree of Life*

### SIZE
*Block: 13 × 13" (33 × 33 cm)*
*Quilt: 43¼ × 60" (110 × 152 cm)*

### MATERIALS
• *Solid white fabric for tree and background*
• *Blue dotted fabric for tree and backing*
• *Blue print fabric for tree and border*
• *Batting*

*Opposite: Tree-of-Life*
*quilt by G. Truffa.*

# DIRECTIONS

◆ Add seam allowances to all cutting dimensions
To create the Tree-of-Life blocks:
◆ From the blue print, cut 2 × 2" (5 × 5 cm) squares and
3½ × 3½ × 5" (9 × 9 × 12.7 cm) right triangles
◆ From the dotted blue fabric, cut 2 × 2 × 2¾" (5 × 5 ×
7 cm) right triangles and 1³⁄₁₆" (3 cm) wide strips for
the trunks
◆ From the white, cut 5 × 5 × 7¼" (13 × 13 × 18.4 cm)
right triangles and 7⅞ × 7⅞" (20 × 20 cm) squares
◆ Cut white squares 13 × 13" (33 × 33 cm)
◆ Cut 2 opposite corners off the 7⅞" (20 cm) white
squares, getting rid of two 3½ × 3½ × 5" (9 × 9 ×
12.7 cm) triangles on each square. Sew the blue strip
for the trunk on the remains of the square. Turn under
the trunk's seam allowances. Where the two white triangles were cut off, stitch two print triangles 3½ × 3½ × 5"
(9 × 9 × 12.7 cm) to re-form a square 7⅞ × 7⅞"
(20 × 20 cm).

For the upper part of the tree:
◆ Stitch a white and a dotted blue triangle together on a
long side to form a 2 × 2" (5 × 5 cm) square
◆ Stitch together the squares and triangles in rows;
then stitch the rows together
◆ Stitch the upper part of the tree to the lower one con-
taining the trunk, to form the 13 × 13" (33 × 33 cm)
Tree block
To assemble the quilt top:
◆ Stitch the pieced blocks to those that are whole-cloth,
in angled rows; stitch the rows together
◆ Cut the blue print fabric border 1½" (4 cm) wide and
stitch on
◆ Cut the batting 43¼ × 60" (110 × 152 cm) and the
backing 46½ × 63" (118 × 160 cm)
◆ Assemble the three layers (quilt top, batting, and
backing); baste and quilt them. To finish, trim batting;
turn the excess backing to the quilt front to form a border; hemstitch in place.

# STRIP-PIECED TABLECLOTH

**TECHNIQUE**
*Speed piecing*

**SIZE**
*51¼ × 51¼" (130 × 130 cm)*

**MATERIALS**
• *Fabric in many patterns in several shades of rust and ecru*
• *Backing fabric (striped in model)*

*Opposite: Strip-pieced tablecloth by G. Berti.*

## DIRECTIONS

◆ Add seam allowances to all cutting dimensions given below
◆ See p. 70 for general strip-piecing instructions
To create the tablecloth:
◆ Cut strips of varying widths from ¾" to 2¾" (2 to 7 cm); stitch the strips into fabric and cut them to form 4 trapezoids whose short parallel side is 8¾" (22 cm) and long parallel side is 51³⁄₁₆" (130 cm); see diagram on p. 422
◆ Cut a square 8¾ × 8¾" (22 × 22 cm) for the center

◆ Stitch the 4 trapezoids to the 4 sides of the square on their shortest sides
◆ Stitch the angled sides of the trapezoids together
◆ Cut the backing about 51¼ × 51¼" (130 × 130 cm)
◆ Put the top and backing together, right sides facing, and sew the sides, leaving an opening to turn the tablecloth right-side out; then turn
◆ Stitch closed the seam left open, press, and stitch along the outside to flatten the tablecloth.

# FOUR SEASONS BABY BLANKET

*By G. Berti.*

**TECHNIQUES**
*American piecing, appliqué*

**PATTERNS**
*Sunbonnet Sue*

**SIZE**
*Central square: 8¾ × 8¾" (22 × 22 cm)*
*Blanket: 23½ × 29" (60 × 74 cm)*

**MATERIALS**
• *Several prints and solids for the appliqué and border*
• *White fabric for the appliqué background square*
• *Pink fabric for the blanket top*
• *Backing fabric*
• *Edging lace*
• *Insertion lace*
• *Ribbon*
• *Batting*

# DIRECTIONS

◆ Add seam allowances to all cutting dimensions given below
◆ Cut the pink fabric for the blanket top 23½ × 29" (60 × 74 cm)
◆ Cut and prepare the Sunbonnet Sue appliqué using the French method (see p. 425 for patterns)
◆ Cut the white base square 6¾ × 6¾" (17 × 17 cm) and appliqué the little girl to it
◆ Cut the multicolored squares 2 × 2" (5 × 5 cm) and stitch them together to form bands
◆ Stitch the pieced bands to the white square to form a border
◆ Appliqué on the insertion lace around the white square, insert the ribbon, and appliqué the square to the pink blanket top

◆ Appliqué the eyelet lace and edging lace to the sides of the pieced square, and insert the ribbon
◆ Cut the backing 23⅝ × 37" (60 × 74 cm), which includes an additional 6" (15 cm) for an extra part at the bottom that will be folded inside the blanket
◆ Put the blanket top and backing together, right sides facing, and stitch the three sides, leaving the bottom side with the extension open to insert the batting. This will let you transform the lightweight blanket into a warmer blanket for the cold seasons
◆ Turn blanket right-side out and finish by hemming the extension that will be folded inside.
◆ Cut batting to fit and insert when needed.

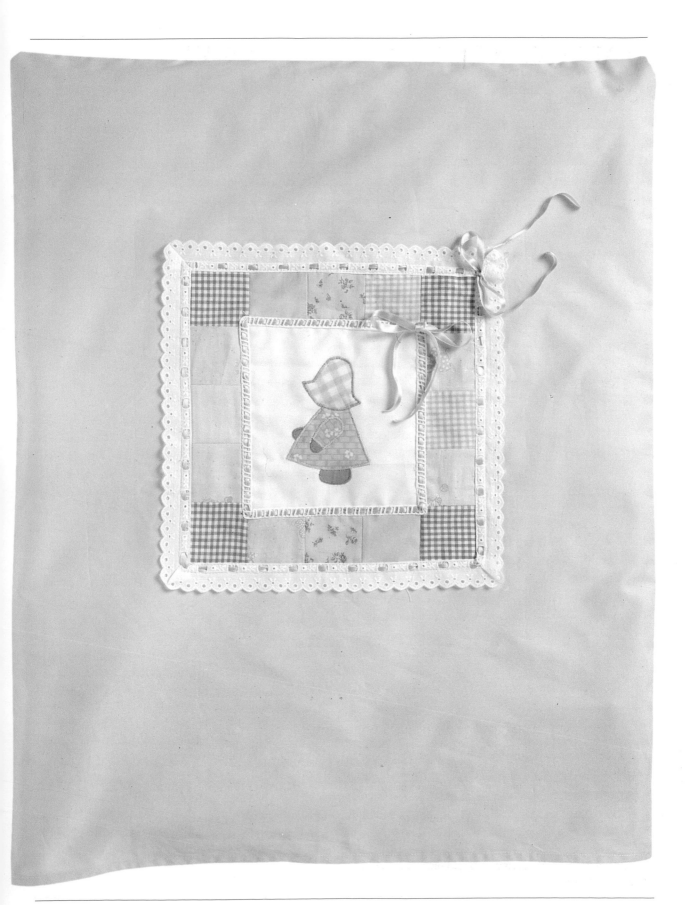

# HEARTS QUILT

**TECHNIQUES**
*Appliqué, American piecing*

**PATTERN**
*Heart*

**SIZE**
*39¼ × 50¼" (100 × 128 cm)*

**MATERIALS**
- *Many colors and patterns for hearts*
- *Pink fabric for the background*
- *Dark pink fabric for border*
- *Checked pink fabric for backing*
- *Batting*

*Opposite: Quilt by G. Berti.*

## DIRECTIONS

◆ Add seam allowances to all cutting dimensions given below
◆ From the pink background fabric cut a rectangle 27½ × 38½" (76 × 98 cm)
◆ See p. 374 for heart pattern; enlarge to fit 5½" (14 cm) square
◆ Prepare the hearts for appliqué (French method) and lay them out on the base fabric that has been ruled into 5½ × 5½" (14 × 14 cm) squares, marked with a water-soluble nonpermanent pencil
◆ Pin, baste, and appliqué the hearts in place
◆ Cut the border 2" (5 cm) wide from the dark pink fabric, and stitch it to the hearts rectangle
◆ Cut the batting about 45¼ × 53" (115 × 135 cm)
◆ Cut the backing 49¼ × 60¼" (125 × 153 cm), which includes extra for the outer border width
◆ Stitch together the three layers (quilt top, batting, and backing). Baste and quilt the squares and around the hearts; trim excess batting
◆ Fold excess backing to the front for 2nd border, hemstitch in place, and quilt the second border if desired.

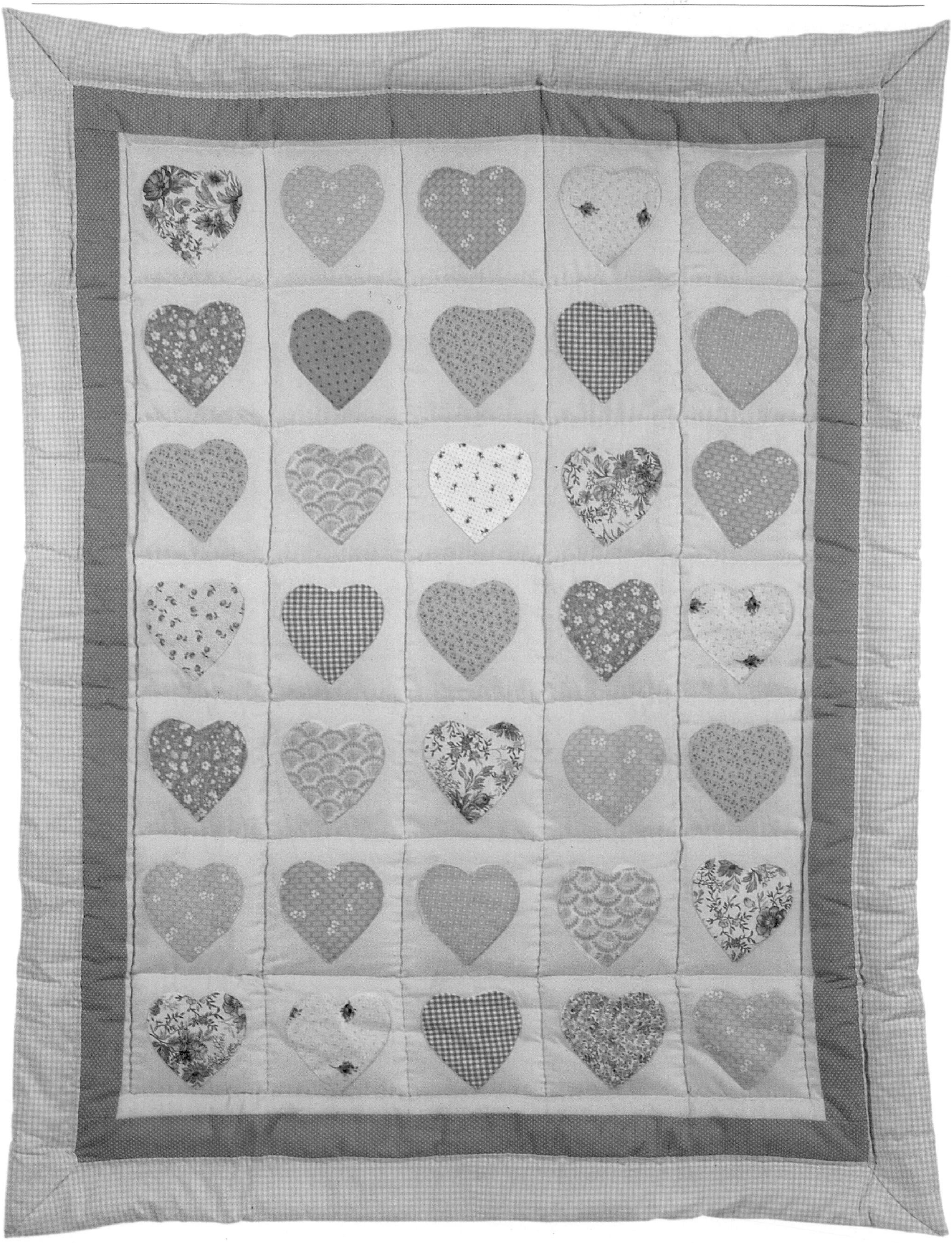

# FOUR-LEAF CLOVER QUILT

**TECHNIQUES**
Appliqué, American piecing

**PATTERN**
Heart

**SIZE**
Block: 6¼ × 6¼" (16 × 16 cm)
Quilt: 54¼ × 65¼" (138 × 166 cm)

**MATERIALS**
• Many colors and patterns of fabric for hearts, lattice strips, and borders
• Ecru fabric for background squares and borders
• Batting
• Backing fabric

*Quilt by
F. Morini.*

## DIRECTIONS

◆ Add seam allowances to all cutting dimensions given
◆ Cut the ecru background squares 6⁵⁄₁₆ × 6⁵⁄₁₆" (16 × 16 cm)
◆ Cut out and make the hearts by the French method; appliqué them to the squares
◆ Cut the lattice strips 1³⁄₁₆" (3 cm) wide
◆ Stitch the appliquéd squares and lattice strips together in rows; see p. 423 for diagram
◆ Stitch the rows together to form the central part of the quilt top
◆ Cut the first ecru borders 4⁵⁄₁₆" (11 cm) wide and stitch to center of quilt on all sides
◆ Cut and piece the first print border 1³⁄₁₆" (3 cm) wide; stitch to quilt all around
◆ Cut two ecru strips 5" (13 cm) wide for ecru top and bottom second borders; appliqué hearts, turned up and down, to borders and stitch to quilt
◆ Cut and piece the second and third print borders 1³⁄₁₆" (3 cm) wide and stitch on
◆ Cut and stitch on the ecru outer border 2⅜" (6 cm) wide, which includes 2" (5 cm) to finish
◆ Cut the batting and backing about 54¼ × 65⅜" (138 × 166 cm)
◆ Assemble the three layers (quilt top, batting, and backing); baste and quilt
◆ Fold excess outer border to back; hemstitch in place.

# BASKET QUILT

## DIRECTIONS

◆ Add seam allowances to all cutting dimensions given below

To make the pieced Basket blocks:
◆ Cut 1³⁄₁₆ × 1³⁄₁₆" (3 × 3 cm) white squares and 1³⁄₁₆ × 1³⁄₁₆ × 1¹¹⁄₁₆" (3 × 3 × 4¼ cm) right triangles out of white and print fabrics
◆ Stitch together the squares and triangles in rows to form the lower part of the basket; see diagrams on p. 426
◆ Cut the large white right triangles 7 × 7 × 10" (18 × 18 × 25.5 cm) and small right triangles 2⅜ × 2⅜ × 3⁵⁄₁₆" (6 × 6 × 8.5 cm)
◆ Cut, prepare, and appliqué the basket handles to the large triangles
◆ Stitch the large triangle (with handle) above the pieced basket and stitch the small triangle below the basket to make a complete Basket block, 7 × 7" (18 × 18 cm)

To make the quilt top:
◆ Cut white squares 7 × 7" (18 × 18 cm), which will go between Basket blocks. Cut half-square triangles 7 × 7 × 10" (18 × 18 × 25.5 cm) and quarter-square triangles 5 × 5 × 7" (12.5 × 12.5 × 17.7 cm)
◆ Stitch together the quarter-square triangles, pieced Basket blocks, and half-triangle squares in angled rows (see p. 427 for diagrams)
◆ Stitch the rows together to form the quilt center
◆ Cut and stitch on a white border 6" (15 cm) wide to the top and bottom of the quilt center

### TECHNIQUES
*Appliqué, American piecing*

### PATTERN
*Basket*

### SIZE
*Square: 7 × 7" (18 × 18 cm)*
*Quilt: 63¾ × 95¼" (162 × 242 cm)*

### MATERIALS
• *White fabric for background and borders*
• *Many colors and patterns of fabric for baskets and borders*
• *Batting*
• *Backing (white or color)*

*Opposite: Basket quilt by Coin.*

◆ Make sawtooth borders by cutting and stitching together 2 × 2 × 2¾" (5 × 5 × 7 cm) white and colored right triangles
◆ Stitch on a sawtoothed border 2" (5 cm) wide, a white border 4" (10 cm) wide, a sawtoothed border 2" (5 cm) wide, and a white border 4" (10 cm) wide all around
◆ Cut the batting about 63¾ × 95¼" (162 × 242 cm) and backing 67 × 90½" (170 × 230 cm)
◆ Assemble the three layers (quilt top, batting, and backing); baste and quilt
◆ Fold excess backing to the front of the piece; hemstitch in place.

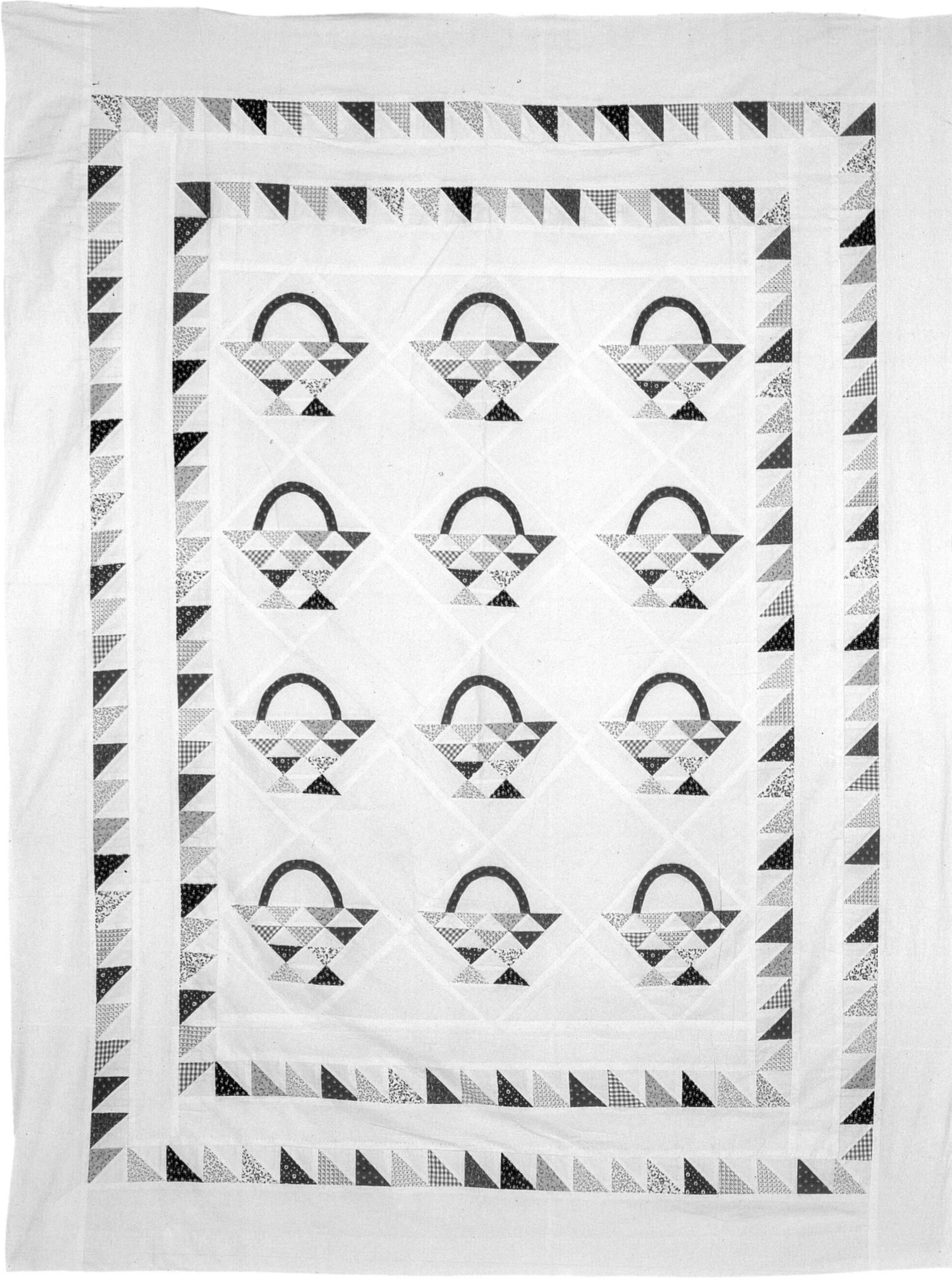

# LOG CABIN INFANT CARRIER

### TECHNIQUES
*American piecing, appliqué*

### PATTERNS
*Log Cabin*
*Heart*

### SIZE
*Block: 7¾ × 7¾" (19.5 × 19.5 cm)*
*Blanket: 35½ × 23⅝" (90 × 60 cm)*

### MATERIALS
• *Many colors and patterns of fabric for Hearts and Log Cabin blocks*
• *Fabric for the background*
• *Checked fabric for backing*
• *Batting*

# DIRECTIONS

This carrier is particularly useful because it can serve several functions: open, as a carriage or cradle blanket; tied closed, as an infant carrier

◆ Add seam allowances to all cutting dimensions given below

◆ Make 3 Log Cabin squares (see p. 182 for details) that are 7¾ × 7¾" (19.5 × 19.5 cm) and make 3 hearts of strip-pieced fabric

◆ Cut the background fabric 35½ × 23⅝" (90 × 60 cm) and appliqué the squares and hearts by machine or hand to the background

◆ Cut the batting 35½ × 23⅝" (90 × 60 cm) and the backing 39½ × 27½" (100 × 70 cm)

◆ Assemble the carrier top, batting, and backing, and quilt together

◆ Pin and stitch the excess backing to the front to form the border; leave an opening so a tie-strip 1³⁄₁₆" (3 cm) wide can be inserted at the bottom. Make the strip and insert.

*Infant carriers by
G. Berti.*

263

# LITTLE DUCKS QUILT

## TECHNIQUES
*Paper piecing method, embroidery*

## PATTERN
*Square-in-a-Square*

## SIZE
*Block: 6⁵⁄₁₆ × 6⁵⁄₁₆" (16 × 16 cm)*
*Quilt: 30¼ × 36½" (77 × 93 cm)*

## MATERIALS
• *Blue-on-white and blue-on-blue prints for squares and borders*
• *Yellow fabric for the sawtooth border*
• *Navy blue fabric for outer border*
• *Aida cloth for embroidery*
• *Embroidery thread in yellow, black, orange, and blue-green*
• *Batting*
• *Backing fabric*

## DIRECTIONS

◆ Add seam allowances to all cutting dimensions given below
◆ Cross-stitch the pattern (p. 428) on Aida cloth and cut the squares 3⅛ × 3⅛" (8 × 8 cm)
◆ Plan, cut out, and assemble the Square-in-a-Square squares 6⁵⁄₁₆ × 6⁵⁄₁₆" (16 × 16 cm), by paper piecing (see p. 92 and 428)
◆ Cut the whole-cloth squares of blue-on-white fabric 6⁵⁄₁₆ × 6⁵⁄₁₆" (16 × 16 cm)
◆ Stitch the pieced squares to the whole-cloth ones to make horizontal rows
◆ Stitch the rows together to make the quilt top, which is 18⅞ × 25³⁄₁₆" (48 × 64 cm)
◆ Press, and tear off the paper from paper piecing
◆ Cut the first border 2⅜" (6 cm) wide and stitch on
◆ Make the sawtooth border by cutting strips 1⅜" (3.5 cm) wide of yellow and blue-on-blue
  ◆ Stitch strips together and cut 2-triangle squares 1⅜ × 1⅜" (3.5 x 3.5 cm) for sawtooth border (see p. 90). Make sawtooth borders, and stitch them to the quilt top
    ◆ Cut 3rd border 1⅜" (3.5 cm) wide and the 4th 2⅝" (6.5 cm) wide from navy blue, which includes 2" (5 cm) to finish. Stitch on borders
      ◆ Cut batting and backing 30¼ × 36½" (77 × 93 cm)
      ◆ Assemble the backing, batting, and quilt top; baste and quilt
      ◆ Trim batting; fold excess of outer border to back and hemstitch in place.

*Label used to personalize a quilt.*

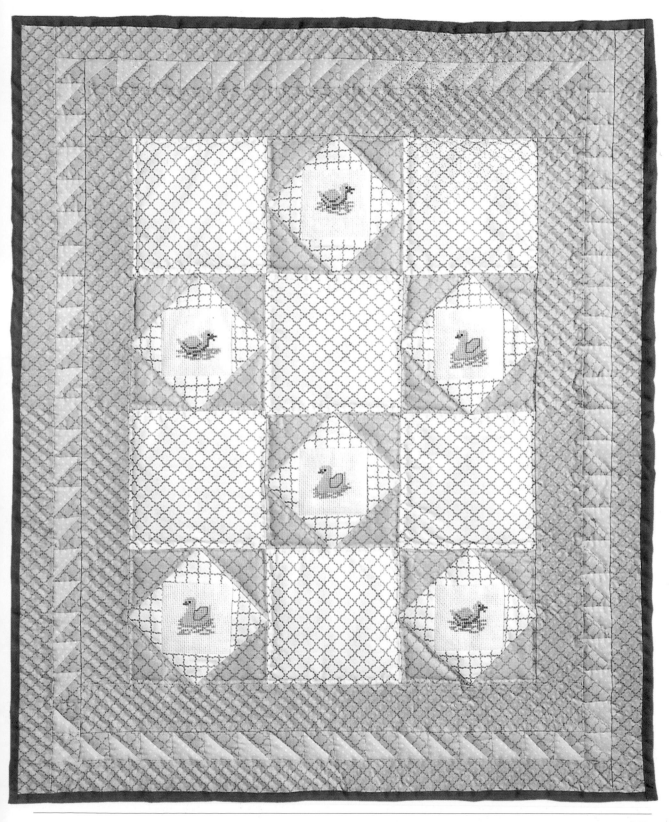

# DRESSES QUILT

*Opposite: By G. Berti from an idea in Quilts for Kids.*

**TECHNIQUES**
*Paper piecing method, quilting*

**PATTERN**
*Dress*

**SIZE**
Block: 6⁵/₁₆ × 6⁵/₁₆" (16 × 16 cm)
Quilt: 37 × 45¾" (94 × 116 cm)

**MATERIALS**
• Many colors and prints for dress squares
• Light pink fabric for background
• Pink fabric for 1st border
• Print fabric with red for 2nd border
• Solid red for 3rd border
• Batting fabric
• Backing fabric
• Buttons, ribbons, lace, for decoration

# DIRECTIONS

◆ Add seam allowances to all cutting dimensions given below
◆ Enlarge patterns, cut, and stitch together the dress blocks in three sections (block size, 6⁵/₁₆ × 6⁵/₁₆" or 16 × 16 cm) using the paper piecing method; see p. 429 for pattern and sections
◆ Press, and tear off the paper
◆ Decorate dress squares with buttons, lace, etc.
◆ From background fabric, cut: 6⁵/₁₆ × 6⁵/₁₆" (16 × 16 cm) squares; 6⁵/₁₆ × 6⁵/₁₆ × 8⁷/₈" (16 × 16 × 22.6 cm) right triangles; and 4⁵/₁₆ × 4⁵/₁₆ × 6⅛" (11 × 11 × 15.5 cm) right triangles (for corners)
◆ Lay out and stitch together pieced and whole-cloth squares and triangles in rows; see p. 429
◆ Stitch the rows together to form the quilt center, 26 × 34⅝" (66 × 88 cm)
◆ Cut the 1st border 1³/₁₆" (3 cm) wide; the 2nd border 4" (10 cm) wide; and 3rd one 2⅜" (6 cm) wide, which includes 2" (5 cm) to finish; stitch on borders
◆ Cut the batting and backing 37 × 45¾" (94 × 116 cm)
◆ Assemble backing, batting, and quilt top; baste and quilt
◆ Trim excess batting; fold extra part of 3rd border to back; hemstitch in place.

*Little toffee-shaped cushion with the Dress pattern (G. Berti).*

# CHRISTMAS TREE PANEL

**TECHNIQUES**
*Paper piecing method, quilting*

**PATTERNS**
*Tree*
*House*

**SIZE**
*Block: 6⁵⁄₁₆ × 6⁵⁄₁₆" (16 × 16 cm)*
*Quilt: 26¾ × 33" (68 × 84 cm)*

**MATERIALS**
• *Many green prints for Tree blocks and 2nd border*
• *Brown fabric for tree trunks*
• *Print fabric for background*
• *Red fabric for the 1st border*
• *Prints for house*
• *Batting*
• *Backing fabric*

## DIRECTIONS

◆ Add seam allowances to all cutting dimensions given below

◆ Trace, cut pieces, and make Tree blocks using the paper piecing method. Make House blocks (see p. 430) in 3 sections. Blocks are 6⁵⁄₁₆ × 6⁵⁄₁₆" (16 × 16 cm). Stitch sections together

◆ Press, and tear off the paper

◆ Stitch blocks together in horizontal rows

◆ Stitch rows together to form the quilt center, 18⅞ × 25³⁄₁₆" (48 × 64 cm)

◆ Cut the 1st border ¾" (2 cm) wide and the 2nd border 5⅛" (13 cm) wide, which includes 2" (5 cm) to finish

◆ Cut batting and backing 26¾ × 33" (68 × 84 cm)

◆ Assemble the backing, batting, and quilt top; baste and quilt

◆ Fold the excess 2nd border to back; hem-stitch in place.

*Pieced block with the same pattern on a Christmas package (G. Berti).*

*Quilt by G. Berti from an idea in Go Wild with Quilts.*

# HOUSES AND GARDENS QUILT

**TECHNIQUES**
*Paper piecing method, strip piecing, quilting*

**PATTERNS**
*House, Tree*

**SIZE**
*Block: 6 × 6" (15 × 15 cm)*
*Quilt: 39¾ × 46" (101 × 117 cm)*

**MATERIALS**
• *Many colors and prints for the pieced blocks and 2nd border*
• *Green fabrics for the horizontal bands and borders*
• *Batting*
• *Backing fabric*

## DIRECTIONS

◆ Add seam allowances to all cutting dimensions given below
◆ Draw, cut, and stitch together the pieced blocks of the House pattern, 3 × 3" (7.5 × 7.5 cm), and the Pine tree pattern, 1.5 × 3" (3.7 × 7.5 cm), using the paper piecing method; see p. 431 for patterns
◆ Stitch the blocks together in rows
◆ Cut green strips 1⁹⁄₁₆" (4 cm) wide and stitch between pieced rows to make the quilt center, 29½ × 35¾" (75 × 91 cm)
◆ Cut the 1st border 1⁹⁄₁₆" (4 cm) wide from green fabric and stitch on
◆ Make the 2nd border of strip-pieced fabric 3⅛" (8 cm) wide and stitch it to the 1st border
◆ Cut the 3rd border 2⅜" (6 cm) wide from green fabric, which includes 2" (5 cm) to finish
◆ Cut the batting and backing about 39¾ × 46" (101 × 117 cm)
◆ Assemble the backing, batting and quilt top; baste and quilt
◆ Fold the excess of the 3rd border to the back and hemstitch in place.

*Bottle carrier of strip-pieced fabric (G. Berti).*

*Quilt by G. Berti, from an idea in Miniature Quilts, September 1995.*

# GREEN EMBROIDERED QUILT

*Opposite: Quilt by G. Berti.*

**TECHNIQUES**
*Paper piecing method, appliqué, embroidery*

**PATTERNS**
*Log Cabin*
*Heart*

**SIZE**
*Block: 9¹³/₁₆ × 9¹³/₁₆" (25 × 25 cm)*
*Quilt: 38½ × 48" (98 × 122 cm)*

**MATERIALS**
• *Print and checked fabrics in various tones of green for squares, hearts, and borders*
• *Aida cloth*
• *Batting*
• *Backing fabric*
• *Green embroidery thread*

## DIRECTIONS

◆ Add seam allowances to all cutting dimensions given
◆ Cross-stitch the letters (see p. 432) on the Aida cloth (BUONA NOTTE, or another message) and cut the Aida squares 4 × 4" (10 × 10 cm)
◆ Draw, cut, and assemble the Log Cabin blocks from strips 1" (2.5 cm) wide, using the paper piecing method; see p. 222 for a similar Log Cabin block
◆ Press, and tear off the paper
◆ Stitch the blocks together to form horizontal rows
◆ Stitch the rows together to form the quilt center 29½ × 39⅜" (75 × 100 cm)
◆ Cut the 1st border ⅝" (1.5 cm) wide; the 2nd one 3⅛" (8 cm) wide; and the 3rd one 2¾" (7 cm) wide, which includes 2" (5 cm) to finish; stitch borders to quilt center
◆ Cut, prepare, and hand-appliqué the hearts
◆ Cut the batting and backing 38½ × 48" (98 × 122 cm)
◆ Assemble backing, batting, and quilt top; baste and quilt
◆ Fold excess border to back; hemstitch in place.

*Squares with Log Cabin pattern and cross-stitched tree (G. Berti).*

# PINK HOUSE QUILT

**TECHNIQUES**
*Paper piecing method, embroidery*

**PATTERN**
*Log Cabin*

**SIZE**
*Block: 6¹¹/₁₆ × 6¹¹/₁₆" (17 × 17 cm)*
*Quilt: 24 × 30¾" (61 × 78 cm)*

**MATERIALS**
• *Fabrics in shades of green and pink for blocks, borders, and backing*
• *Batting*
• *Aida cloth*
• *Pink ribbon*
• *Pink embroidery thread*

## DIRECTIONS

This is a 4-season quilt, usable with or without batting
◆ Add seam allowances to all cutting dimensions given below
◆ Cross-stitch houses on Aida cloth and cut out Aida squares 3⅛ × 3⅛" (8 × 8 cm); see p. 432 for pattern
◆ Make Log Cabin blocks, 6¹¹/₁₆ × 6¹¹/₁₆" (17 × 17 cm) of strips ⅝" (1.5 cm) wide, using paper piecing method
◆ Stitch the blocks together in horizontal rows
◆ Stitch the rows together to make the quilt center, 20 × 26¾" (51 × 68 cm). Press, and tear off the paper
◆ Cut 1st border ⅜" (1 cm) wide and the 2nd border 1⁹/₁₆" (4 cm) wide; stitch borders on
◆ Cut the backing 24 × 37½" (61 × 95 cm), which includes extra fabric to be folded in over the batting
◆ Stitch the quilt top and backing together on top and sides; hem the remaining edges
◆ Stitch ribbons on the lower part. Cut and insert batting

*Pink House quilt by G. Berti.*

# PINWHEELS QUILT

*Opposite:*
*Pinwheels quilt by*
*Coin.*

**TECHNIQUES**
Paper piecing method, quilting

**PATTERN**
Pinwheel

**SIZE**
Block: 5½ × 5½" (14 × 14 cm)
Quilt: 41 × 57½" (104 × 146 cm)

**MATERIALS**
• Many colors and patterns of fabric for Pin-
wheels
• Ecru fabrics for background, border, and
backing
• Batting

## DIRECTIONS

◆ Add seam allowances to all cutting
dimensions given below
◆ Make the Pinwheel blocks 5½ × 5½"
(14 × 14 cm), in two sections (see
p. 433) using the paper piecing method
◆ Press, and tear off the paper
◆ Stitch the blocks together to form horizontal rows
◆ Stitch the rows together to form the
quilt top, 33 × 49¼" (84 × 126 cm)
◆ Cut the border 6" (15 cm) wide, which
includes 2" (5 cm) to finish; stitch on
◆ Draw the quilting patterns on the
border
◆ Cut the batting and backing 41 ×
57½" (104 × 146 cm)

◆ Assemble
the backing, batting, and quilt
top; baste and quilt
◆ Fold the excess border to the
back and hemstitch.

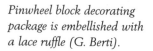

*Pinwheel block decorating*
*package is embellished with*
*a lace ruffle (G. Berti).*

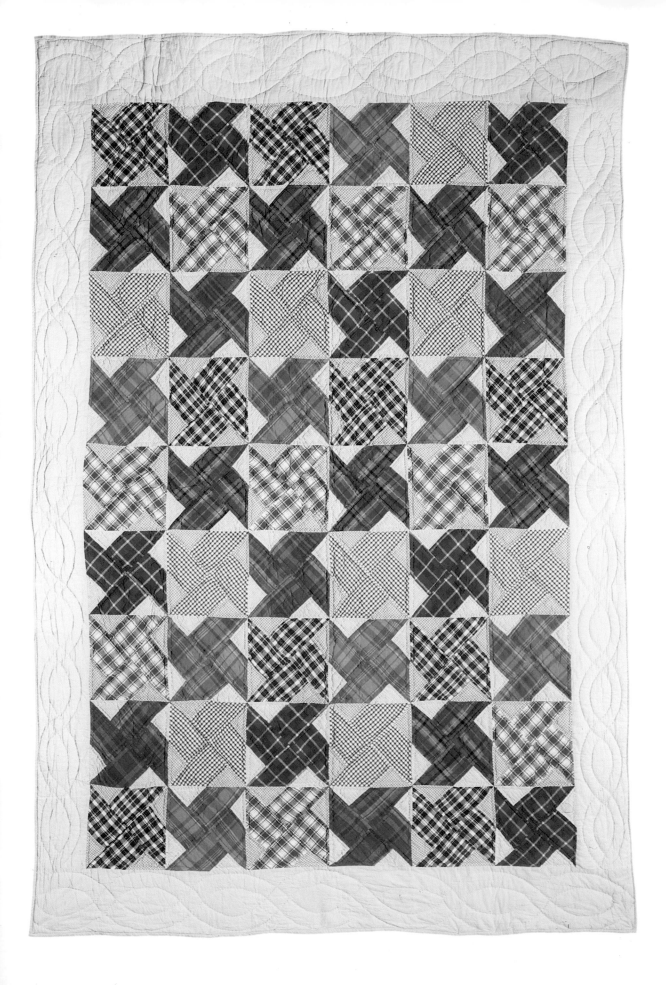

# VIOLETS QUILT

### TECHNIQUES
*Paper piecing method, embroidery*

### PATTERN
*Log Cabin*

### SIZE
*Block: 7 × 7" (18 × 18 cm)*
*Quilt: 36¼ × 29" (92 × 74 cm)*

### MATERIALS
• *Aida cloth*
• *Many shades of green and pink for squares and borders*
• *Batting*
• *Backing fabric*
• *Purple, lavender, yellow, and green embroidery threads*

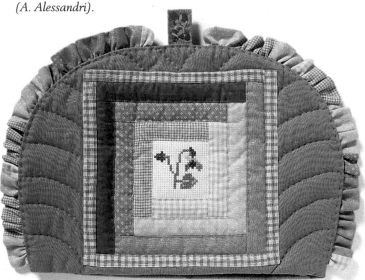

*Tea cozy*
*(A. Alessandri).*

## DIRECTIONS

◆ Add seam allowances to all cutting dimensions given below
◆ Cross-stitch the violets on the Aida cloth (patterns on p. 433) and cut the Aida squares 7 × 7" (18 × 18 cm)
◆ Cut and stitch the Log Cabin blocks from strips ¾" (2 cm) wide
◆ Stitch the blocks together in rows
◆ Stitch the rows together to make the quilt center, 29½ × 21¼" (75 × 54 cm)

◆ Cut 1st border 1" (2.5 cm) wide; 2nd border 2½" (6.3 cm) wide; 3rd one 2⅜" (6 cm) wide, which includes 2" (5 cm) to finish;
◆ Stitch on borders. Cut batting and backing 36¼ × 29" (92 × 74 cm)
◆ Assemble backing, batting, and quilt top; baste and quilt
◆ Fold excess border to back; hem-stitch.

*Violets quilt by the Parma*
*Patchwork Club.*

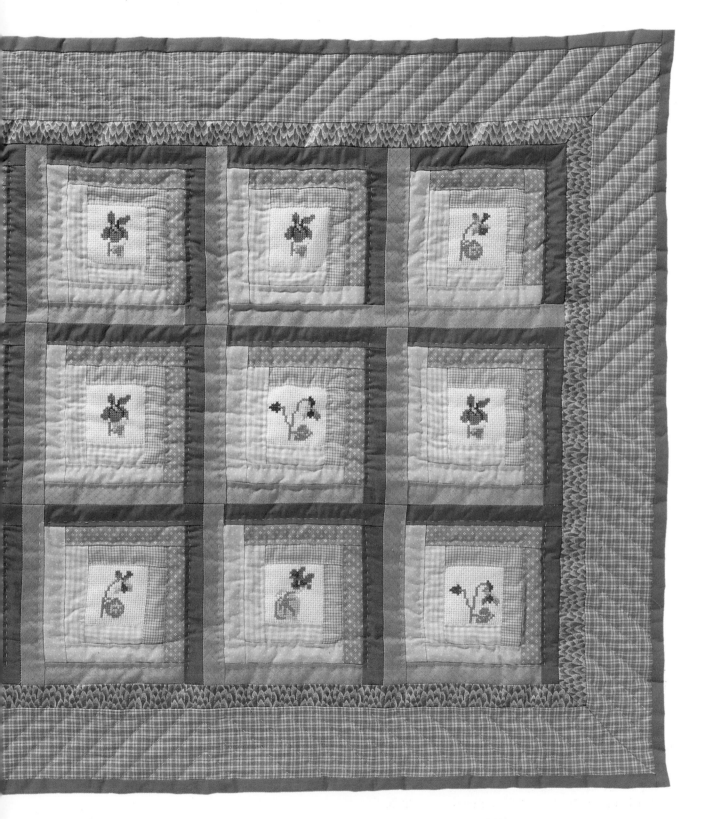

# LITTLE RABBITS QUILT

**TECHNIQUES**
*Hand-appliqué, American piecing, embroidery*

**PATTERNS**
*Rabbit*
*Carrot*

**SIZE**
*45¾ × 54½" (116 × 138 cm)*

**MATERIALS**
- *Ecru fabric for background and borders*
- *Variety of blue prints for the appliqués and borders*
- *Batting*
- *Backing fabric*
- *Blue embroidery thread*

## DIRECTIONS

◆ Add seam allowances to all cutting dimensions given below

◆ Cut the ecru background fabric 33⅞ × 42½" (86 × 108 cm)

◆ Cut, prepare, and appliqué the little rabbits and carrots to the background (patterns on p. 436)

  ◆ Embroider the carrot tops

    ◆ For the sawtooth border, cut ecru and light blue strips 2⅜" (6 cm) wide and stitch together on a long side (see p. 89)

      ◆ From the two strips, cut 2-triangle squares 2⅜ × 2⅜" (6 × 6 cm); see p. 90

        ◆ Stitch the squares together to form sawtooth borders

          ◆ Stitch the sawtooth border to the quilt center. Cut the 2nd border 2⅜" (6 cm) wide from ecru and the 3rd border 2³⁄₁₆" (8 cm) wide from blue, which includes 2" (5 cm) to finish

          ◆ Cut the batting and backing about 45¾ × 54½" (116 × 138 cm)

          ◆ Assemble backing, batting, and quilt top; baste and quilt

          ◆ Fold excess outer border to back; hemstitch in place.

*By the Parma*
*Patchwork Club.*

# SUNBONNET SUE MINI-QUILT

**TECHNIQUES**
Hand appliqué, quilting

**PATTERN**
Sunbonnet Sue and friend

**SIZE**
Quilt: 21⅝ × 29½" (55 × 75 cm)

**MATERIALS**
- White print for the background
- Many fabrics for appliqués and backing
- Batting
- Wool blanket, about 43¼ × 31½" (110 × 80 cm)

*Sunbonnet Sue decorates the gift and the smock above (G. Berti).*

## DIRECTIONS

This quilt is warm and cuddly and is particularly recommended for outings and walks, but also for cradles and carriages in several seasons, since the two parts making it up (quilt and wool blanket) can be separated when warmer weather comes.

◆ Add seam allowances to all cutting dimensions given below

◆ Cut the background fabric 19¾ × 27½" (50 × 70 cm)

◆ Cut, prepare, and hand-appliqué the children by the French method (patterns on p. 434 and 435)

◆ Cut the batting 21⅝ × 29½" (55 × 75 cm) and the backing 25½ × 33½" (65 × 85 cm)

◆ Assemble the backing, batting, and quilt top; baste and quilt

◆ To finish, fold the excess backing to the front of the piece to form the border; hemstitch in place

◆ Hemstitch the mini-quilt to a wool blanket 43¼ × 31½" (110 × 80 cm).

*Sunbonnet Sue mini-quilt
by D. Berti Calderini.*

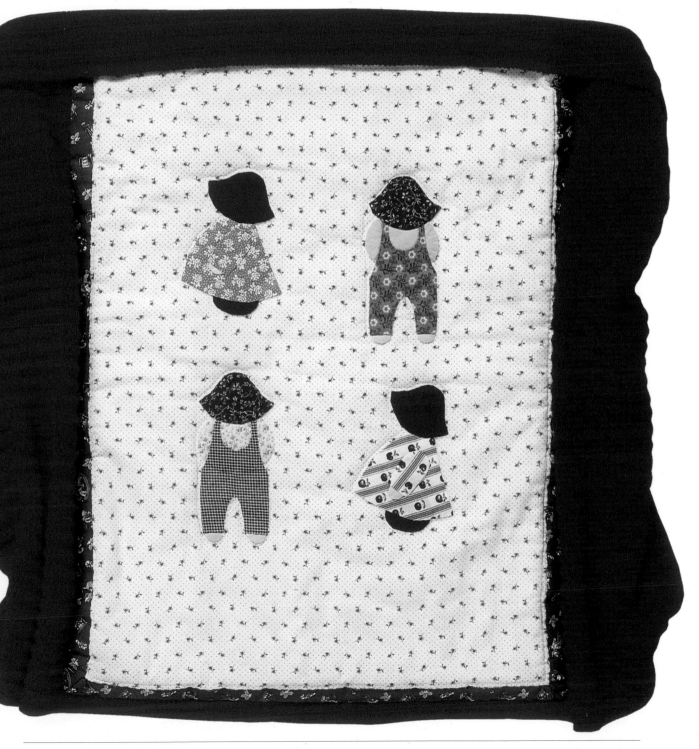

# CUP-AND-SAUCER PANEL

**TECHNIQUES**
*Hand appliqué, piecing, quilting*

**PATTERNS**
*Cup*
*Saucer*

**SIZE**
*Block: 6¼ × 6¼" (16 × 16 cm)*
*Quilt: 38¼ × 30¾" (97 × 78 cm)*

**MATERIALS**
- *White fabric for background*
- *Green and red fabric for the cups, saucers, and borders, including checks and plaids*
- *Dark green fabric for the lattice strips and first border*
- *Batting*
- *Backing fabric*

# DIRECTIONS

◆ Add seam allowances to all cutting dimensions given below

◆ Cut the white background squares 6¼ × 6¼" (16 × 16 cm)

◆ Cut, prepare, and appliqué the cups and saucers to the background (patterns on p. 437)

◆ Cut the green lattice strips and first border 1⅜" (3.5 cm) wide

◆ Stitch the appliqué squares and lattice strips together to form horizontal rows

◆ Stitch the rows together to form the quilt top 31⅞ × 24⅜" (81 × 62 cm)

◆ Stitch on the first (green) border

◆ Cut the white checked border 2" (5 cm) wide and stitch on

◆ To make the triangles border, cut strips 2⅜" (6 cm), fold them in half lengthwise, press, and cut them in sections 2⅜" (6 cm), thus obtaining 2⅜ × 1³⁄₁₆" (6 × 3 cm) rectangles

◆ Make triangles 1³⁄₁₆" (3 cm) tall

◆ Cut and sew the triangles to the back near the edge to form the outer border

◆ Cut the batting 38¼ × 30¾" (97 × 78 cm) and backing 39 × 31½" (99 × 80 cm)

◆ Assemble the backing, batting, and quilt top; baste and quilt

◆ Fold the excess backing under and hemstitch in place on the back to finish.

*Cup-and-Saucer panel by R. Ranieri.*

# LITTLE BEARS QUILT

**TECHNIQUES**
*Appliqué, quilting*

**PATTERNS**
*Bears*
*Basket*

**SIZE**
*37½ × 49¼" (95 × 125 cm)*

**MATERIALS**
• *Several pink and green prints for bears*
• *Pink fabric for the background*
• *Batting*
• *Backing fabric*

*Bears quilt by*
*G. Berti.*

## DIRECTIONS

◆ Add seam allowances to all cutting dimensions given below

◆ Cut the background fabric 30¾ × 42½" (78 × 108 cm). Rule diamonds on quilt background with nonpermanent pencil

◆ Trace the patterns from p. 437. Cut out the little Bears and basket handle from fabric and appliqué them by machine or by hand to background

◆ Cut front and back of large Bear, and sew together with right sides facing, leaving an opening for stuffing.

Turn right-side out, stuff with batting, and close the seam

◆ Cut the basket, line it, and appliqué it on, leaving the upper part detached from the background to hold the stuffed bear

◆ Cut the 1st border ⅝" (1.5 cm) wide and the 2nd one 4¾" (12 cm) wide, which includes 2" (5 cm) to finish

◆ Cut the batting and backing 37½ × 49¼" (95 × 125 cm)

◆ Assemble the backing, batting and quilt top; baste and quilt

◆ Fold the excess border to back; hemstitch in place.

# BABY CARRIAGES MINI-QUILT

**TECHNIQUES**
*Appliqué, quilting*

**PATTERN**
*Carriage*

**SIZE**
*23½ × 29½" (60 × 75 cm)*

**MATERIALS**
- *Pink checked background fabric*
- *Various print fabrics for the carriages*
- *Flowered fabric for first border*
- *Batting*
- *Rose pink backing fabric*
- *Pink ribbon*

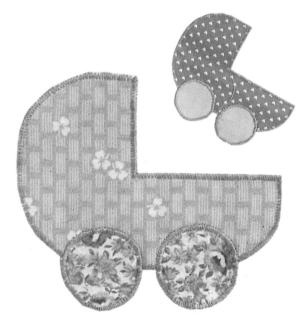

# DIRECTIONS

◆ Add seam allowances to all cutting dimensions given below
◆ Cut the background fabric and draw the quilting lines with a non-permanent pencil to make diamonds 6⁵⁄₁₆ × 6⁵⁄₁₆" (16 × 16 cm)
◆ Prepare and appliqué the carriages to the background (pattern on p. 438)
◆ Cut the flowered border 2⅜" (6 cm) wide and stitch on

◆ Stitch on the ribbons
◆ Cut the batting 23½ × 29½" (60 × 75 cm) and backing 26¾ × 32¾" (68 × 83 cm)
◆ Assemble the backing, batting, and quilt top; baste and quilt
◆ Fold the excess backing to the front of the piece to form a border; hemstitch in place.

# PEACEFUL CRADLE COVERLET

**TECHNIQUES**
*Appliqué, American piecing*

**PATTERNS**
*Bird*
*Clouds*
*Cradle*
*Leaf*

**SIZE**
*Appliqué block and frame:*
*14½ × 13" (37 × 33 cm)*
*Cover: 23⅝ × 28¼" (60 × 73 cm)*

**MATERIALS**
• *Pink fabric for the blanket front and back*
• *White fabric for appliqué background*
• *Various colors and patterns for the appliqués and border*
• *Edging lace, ribbon, and insertion lace*
• *Batting*

## DIRECTIONS

◆ Add seam allowances to all cutting dimensions given below
◆ Sew the various appliqués (see p. 438), as well as the cradle lace, on a white background square 9¾ × 8¼" (25 × 21 cm)
◆ Make strips of multicolored pieces and stitch them to the white square to form a border 2⅜" (6 cm) wide
◆ Cut the pink top of the cover 23½ × 28¼" (60 × 73 cm), and appliqué the pieced center rectangle to it
◆ Outline the rectangle with insertion lace and edging lace
◆ Cut the back of the cover 23½ × 35½" (60 × 90 cm), which includes an extra hem to be folded in
◆ Assemble the blanket top and back with right sides together, and stitch closed on three sides; leave the fourth side open but hem it
◆ Sew pink ribbons on the lower part for decoration.
◆ Cut batting and insert as needed.

*Opposite: This 4-season coverlet can be used in the cold weather if you insert batting in the coverlet. By G. Berti.*

# CHRISTMAS TREE SKIRT

*Tree skirt and holiday decorations (opposite) by G. Berti.*

**TECHNIQUES**
*Appliqué, piecing*

**PATTERNS**
*Tree*
*Bell*
*People*

**SIZE**
*39¾" (100 cm) in diameter*

**MATERIALS**
• *Red fabric with stars for background and ruffle*
• *Colorful prints for the appliqués*
• *Red ribbons*

## DIRECTIONS

◆ Add seam allowances to all cutting dimensions given below
◆ From the red fabric, cut a circle for the base of radius 19¾" (50 cm) and a ruffle 2" (5 cm) wide

◆ Cut out the children, pine trees and bells, and appliqué them to the circle (patterns on p. 439)
◆ Hem the opening of the circle
◆ Prepare and stitch on the ruffle and ribbons for closing.

# SHELLS COVERLET

*Below: wreaths to announce a birth. Opposite: Shells coverlet by G. Berti.*

**TECHNIQUES**
*Appliqué, quilting*

**PATTERN**
*Shell*

**SIZE**
*26¼ × 30¼" (67 × 77 cm)*

**MATERIALS**
- *Pink prints for the appliqués*
- *White and pink solid fabric for appliqués*
- *Checked fabric for the base (will not show)*
- *Batting*
- *Pink fabric for backing*

## DIRECTIONS

◆ Add seam allowances to all cutting dimensions given below
◆ Cut the base fabric 26⅜ × 30⁵⁄₁₆" (67 × 77 cm), preferably

from checked cloth, since it can serve as a guide for laying out shells; it will not show in the final work

◆ Cut seven 3 × 3" (7.5 × 7.5 cm) squares out of the many patterns of fabric and stitch them together in a horizontal row (see p. 439)

◆ Pin the pieced row to the top of the base fabric

◆ Prepare the fabric shells using the French method of appliqué (pattern on p. 439)

◆ Starting at the top, put the first line of shells on the checked row; pin, baste, and hemstitch them in place (see p. 439). The sides of some shells will stick out over the base

◆ Place a second line of shells

partially overlapping the first row; pin, baste, and hemstitch in place

◆ Proceed with more rows until the entire base fabric is covered

◆ Trim off the parts of the shells that extend beyond the base

◆ Cut the batting 26¼ × 30¼" (67 × 77 cm) and backing 31½ × 35½" (80 × 90 cm)

◆ Assemble the backing, batting, and quilt top; baste and quilt

◆ Fold the excess backing to the front of the piece to form a border 2" (5 cm) wide; hemstitch in place.

# SUNBONNET SUE PILLOW

## TECHNIQUES
*Appliqué, quilting*

## PATTERN
*Sunbonnet Sue*

## SIZE
*11¾ × 11¾" (30 × 30 cm)*

## MATERIALS
• *Ecru fabric for appliqués and background squares*
• *Pink-and-white and black-and-white checked fabrics for the appliqués, border, and backing*
• *Fabric for lining*
• *Batting*
• *Stuffing*

## DIRECTIONS

◆ Add seam allowances to all cutting dimensions given below
◆ Cut the appliqué background square 9 × 9" (23 × 23 cm) from the ecru fabric
◆ Prepare the appliqués and hemstitch them to the ecru square (Sunbonnet Sue pattern is on p. 440)
◆ Cut the pink checked border 1⅜" (3.5 cm) wide; stitch the pink border on the ecru square
◆ Make sawtooth border from 2-triangle squares of red-checked and black-checked fabric

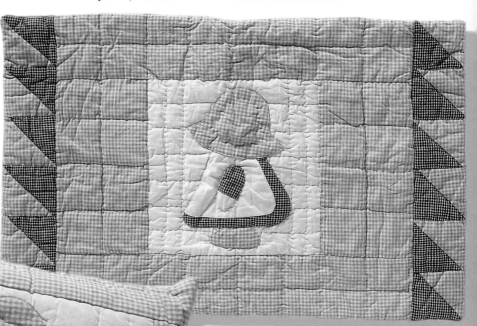

*Bedside throw rug.*

*Pillow.*

◆ Cut a layer of batting and lining fabric 11¾ × 11¾" (30 × 30 cm)
◆ Assemble the quilt top, batting, and lining; baste and quilt
◆ Cut the pillow back 11¾ × 11¾" (30 × 30 cm)
◆ Assemble the pillow front and back (right sides facing); stitch together on 3½ sides, leaving a 6" (15 cm) opening; turn right-side out
◆ Stuff pillow and stitch the opening closed.

*Sunbonnet Sue is featured on this mini-quilt,
accented by a sawtooth border (Coin).*

# HEARTS INFANT CARRIER

**TECHNIQUES**
*Appliqué, strip piecing, quilting*

**PATTERN**
*Heart*

**SIZE**
*33½ × 21" (85 × 53 cm)*

**MATERIALS**
• *Checked fabric for background and tie*
• *Several patterns for the appliqués*
• *Backing fabric*
• *Batting*

## DIRECTIONS

◆ Add seam allowances to all cutting dimensions given below

◆ Cut background fabric 33½ × 21" (85 × 53 cm)

◆ Cut out and appliqué the hearts (made with strip-pieced fabric) to the background fabric

◆ Cut the batting 33½ × 21" (85 × 53 cm) and backing 37½ × 24¾" (95 × 63 cm)

◆ Assemble the backing, batting, and quilt top; baste and quilt

◆ Fold the backing to the front of the piece to make a border 1" (2.5 cm) wide; stitch in place but leave openings on bottom for tie

◆ Cut the tie ¾" (2 cm) wide, fold, and stitch it closed. Insert it in the lower border to tie the carrier closed.

*Infant carrier opened (opposite) and closed (above); by G. Berti.*

299

# HEARTS QUILT

**TECHNIQUES**
*American piecing, appliqué, quilting*

**PATTERN**
*Heart*

**SIZE**
*Block: 7 × 7" (18 × 18 cm)*
*Quilt: 42 × 51¼" (107 × 130 cm)*

**MATERIALS**
• *Ecru fabric for background squares and backing*
• *Several colors and patterns for Hearts*
• *Green checked fabric for 2nd border*
• *Floral pattern for lattice strips and 1st border*
• *Batting*

## DIRECTIONS

◆ Add seam allowances to all cutting dimensions given below
◆ Cut the ecru squares 7 × 7" (18 × 18 cm)
◆ Cut, prepare, and appliqué the hearts to the squares (pattern on p. 440)
◆ From the floral fabric cut 2" (5 cm) wide lattice strips and 2 × 2" (5 × 5 cm) lattice squares
◆ Stitch together the Heart blocks and lattice strips to form horizontal rows
◆ Stitch 4 lattice strips and 3 lattice squares together to form horizontal bands for between the Heart block rows
◆ Stitch the bands and Heart block rows together to form the quilt top, 34¼ × 43¼" (87 × 110 cm)
◆ Cut the 1st border 2" (5 cm) wide of floral fabric and the 2nd of green checked fabric 1½" (4 cm) wide; stitch on
◆ Cut the batting 42 × 51¼" (107 × 130 cm) and backing 43¼ × 52¼" (110 × 133 cm)
◆ Assemble the backing, batting, and quilt top; baste and quilt
◆ Fold the excess backing to the front of the piece for an outer border; hemstitch in place.

*Wreath by G. Berti. Opposite: Hearts quilt by S. Ognibene.*

# CHILDREN AT THE WINDOW QUILT

## TECHNIQUES
*American piecing, appliqué, quilting*

## PATTERN
*Children*

## SIZE
*Checkerboard block: 9¾ × 9¾" (25 × 25 cm)*
*Quilt: 43 × 48¾" (109 × 124 cm)*

## MATERIALS
- *Ecru fabric for background and second border*
- *Gray fabric for the windowsill*
- *Several colors and patterns for the checker-board squares*
- *Dark gray fabric for the first border, appliqués, and backing*
- *White, pink, and brown fabric for appliques*
- *Batting*
- *Embroidery thread for faces*

## DIRECTIONS

◆ Add seam allowances to all cutting dimensions given below
◆ From the ecru fabric cut rectangles for the background 9¾ × 6" (25 × 15 cm)
◆ From the gray fabric cut strips for the windowsills, 9¾ × 2" (25 × 5 cm)
◆ From many colors of fabric, cut 2 × 2" (5 × 5 cm) squares and stitch them in rows of 5 to form the checkerboard blocks 9¾ × 9¾" (25 × 25 cm)
◆ Stitch the background rectangles, windowsill strips, and checkerboard blocks in 3 columns (see diagram on p. 441)
◆ Stitch the columns together to form the quilt center, 29½ × 35½" (75 × 90 cm)
◆ Cut the dark gray 1st border 1⁹⁄₁₆" (4 cm) wide and the ecru 2nd border 4" (10 cm) wide; stitch to the quilt center
◆ Cut, prepare, and appliqué the children to the quilt (see photo)
◆ Cut the batting 43 × 48¾" (109 × 124 cm) and backing 45¼ × 51¼" (115 × 130 cm). Assemble the backing, batting, and quilt top; baste and quilt
◆ Fold excess backing to the front of quilt for outer border; hemstitch in place.

# WALL HANGING WITH SQUARES

*Quilt by Coin.*

**TECHNIQUES**
*American piecing, quilting*

**PATTERN**
*Squares*

**SIZE**
*52½ × 22" (133 × 56 cm)*

**MATERIALS**
- *Many colors and patterns of blue-gray fabric*
- *Small blue-on-white print for border, loops, and backing*
- *Batting*

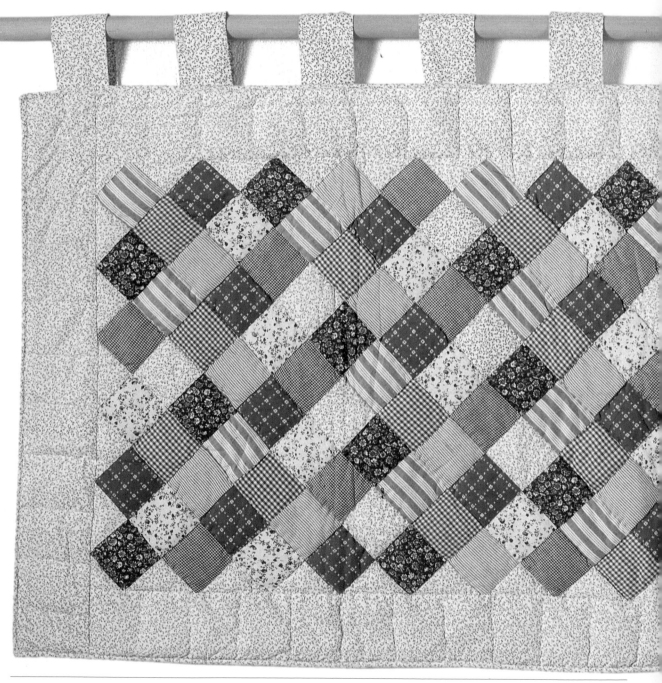

# DIRECTIONS

◆ Add seam allowances to all cutting dimensions
◆ Cut 2 × 2" (5 × 5 cm) squares from the blue-gray and blue-on-white print fabrics; cut 2 × 2 × 2¾" (5 × 5 × 7 cm) and 1⅜ × 1⅜ × 2" (3.5 × 3.5 × 5 cm) right triangles (for corners) from blue-on-white fabric
◆ Stitch the squares and triangles together to form strips (see p. 442)
◆ Stitch the strips at an angle to form the quilt top center, 47 × 16½" (119 × 42 cm)

◆ Cut the blue-on-white print border 2¾" (7 cm) wide
◆ Cut blue-on-white strips 4" (10 cm) wide. Cut them into sections 7" (18 cm) long and make the loops for the rod
◆ Pin and baste loops to upper part of wall hanging
◆ Cut the batting and backing 52½ × 22" (133 × 56 cm)
◆ Assemble the backing, batting, and quilt top; quilt the layers
◆ Fold and pin the quilt top and backing edges in so they meet perfectly; machine-stitch edges closed.

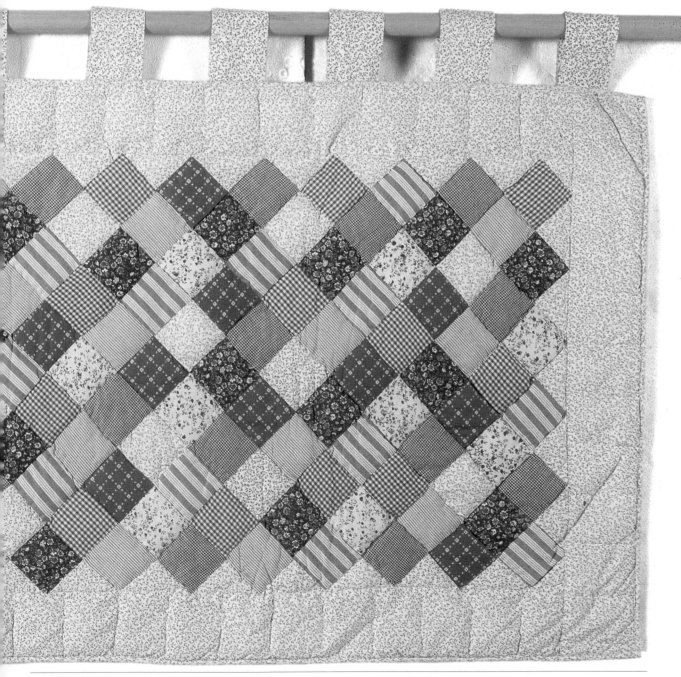

# RAIL FENCE QUILT

## TECHNIQUES
*Strip piecing, quilting*

## PATTERN
*Interlocked Squares
(Rail Fence)*

## SIZE
*Block: 4¾ × 4¾" (12 × 12 cm)
Quilt: 38½ × 57½" (98 × 146 cm)*

## MATERIALS
• *Print fabric in three shades of
green for the blocks*
• *Green fabric for the 2nd
border*
• *Red print fabric for the 1st and
3rd borders*
• *Batting*
• *Backing fabric*

## DIRECTIONS

◆ The patchwork pattern is a lattice
design that can be done in several
ways. The quilt shown was made with
strip-pieced fabric.
◆ Add seam allowances to all cutting
dimensions given below
◆ From the three green print fabrics, cut
strips 1⁹⁄₁₆" (4 cm) wide and stitch
together to create three-strip fabric 4¾"
(12 cm) wide; see p. 443 for diagrams
◆ From the pieced fabric, cut 4¾ × 4¾"
(12 × 12 cm) squares
◆ Lay out the squares with the strips
alternately horizontal and vertical (see
photo), to form horizontal rows that

make the pattern; stitch the squares
together in rows
◆ Stitch the rows together to form the
quilt center, 33 × 52" (84 × 132 cm)
◆ Cut the 1st border ¾" (2 cm) wide;
the 2nd border 4" (10 cm) wide; and
the 3rd one 2¾" (7 cm) wide, which
includes 2" (5 cm) to finish
◆ Cut the batting and backing 38½ ×
57½" (98 × 146 cm)
◆ Assemble the backing, batting, and
quilt top; baste and quilt
◆ Fold the outer border to the back of
the piece; hemstitch in place.

*Print and solid-colored fabric swatches
are helpful in planning a quilt.
Opposite: Rail Fence quilt by G. Berti.*

# MINI-QUILT WITH MILLS

## TECHNIQUES
*English method or paper piecing method, quilting*

## PATTERN
*Mill*

## SIZE
*Block: 5½ × 4¾" (14 × 12 cm)*
*Quilt: 31½ × 39¼" (80 × 100 cm)*

## MATERIALS
- *White and brown print fabrics for the Mills*
- *Light blue and medium blue fabric for the sky, water, and borders*
- *Pink checked fabric for the background, borders, lattice strips, and backing*
- *Batting*

## DIRECTIONS

◆ Add seam allowances to all cutting dimensions given below

◆ Cut and stitch together the Mill blocks 5½ × 4¾" (14 × 12 cm), using the English method or the paper-piecing method. See p. 92 for general paper piecing and p. 444 for pattern

◆ From the pink checked fabric, cut lattice strips 2" (5 cm) wide and 2⅜" (6 cm) wide

◆ Stitch the Mill blocks and 2" (5 cm) wide lattice strips together to form 3 vertical columns

◆ Stitch the columns together with the 2⅜" (6 cm) lattice strips in between to form the quilt center

◆ From the pink checked fabric, cut a top and bottom border 4¼" (11 cm) wide; stitch to quilt center

◆ Cut and stitch on the light blue border ¾" (2 cm) wide, the blue border ¾" (2 cm) wide, and the pink border ¾" (2 cm) wide

◆ Cut the batting 31½ × 39¼" (80 × 100 cm) and backing 35½ × 43¼" (90 × 110 cm)

◆ Assemble the backing, batting, and quilt top; baste and quilt

◆ Fold the excess backing to the front of the piece to make the outermost pink border; hemstitch in place.

*Pajama holders have zippers on the back as well as straps for hanging (E. Santini).*

*Opposite: Mills quilt by G. Berti.*

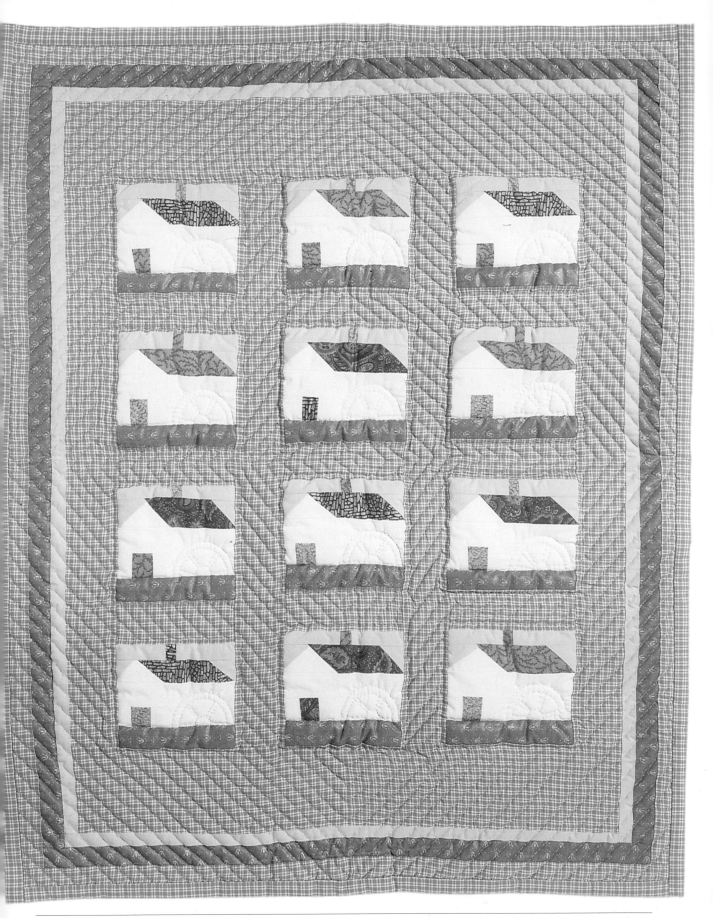

# HERRINGBONE QUILT

## TECHNIQUES
*Speed cutting, English piecing, quilting*

## PATTERN
*Herringbone*

## SIZE
*31½ × 35½" (80 × 90 cm)*

## MATERIALS
• *Many colors and patterns for the Herringbone pattern*
• *Floral red-on-white fabric for triangles*
• *Red-checked fabric for square*
• *Colorful fabric for the first border*
• *Ecru fabric for the second border and backing*
• *Batting*

## DIRECTIONS

◆ Add seam allowances to all cutting dimensions given below
◆ To prepare the Herringbone pattern pieces by the speed method, cut 1⁹⁄₁₆" (4 cm) wide strips of fabric and from these, cut trapezoids whose parallel sides are 3" and 4⁵⁄₁₆" (7.5 and 11 cm); patterns on p. 445
◆ Cut right triangles 4⁵⁄₁₆" × 4⁵⁄₁₆" × 6⅛" (11 × 11 × 15.5 cm) and 3⅛" × 3⅛" × 4⁷⁄₁₆" (8 × 8 × 11.3 cm) from floral fabric
◆ Cut little squares from red checked fabric 1⁹⁄₁₆" × 1⁹⁄₁₆" (4 × 4 cm)
◆ Using the English method, make templates, cut out and press pieces, and stitch them together as shown on p. 445
◆ Whipstitch the sections together to form the quilt center, 18⅞" × 22¹³⁄₁₆" (48 × 58 cm); then stitch on the floral triangles
◆ Cut the 1st border 2" (5 cm) wide and the 2nd one 6" (15 cm) wide, which includes 2" (5 cm) to finish edges; stitch on borders
◆ Cut batting and backing about 31½" × 35½" (80 × 90 cm)
◆ Assemble the backing, batting, and quilt top; baste and quilt
  ◆ Fold back the excess outer border to the back of the piece; hemstitch in place.

*Child's backpack in pastel calico has embroidered cat faces and pieced star.*

*Herringbone quilt by V. Grassi.*

# LATTICE OF CATS QUILT

**TECHNIQUES**
*Paper piecing method, quilting*

**PATTERN**
*Tall Cat*

**SIZE**
*Square: 3⅛ × 3⅛" (8 × 8 cm)*
*Cat block: 3⅛ × 9⅜" (8 × 24 cm)*
*Quilt: 55⅛ × 99¼" (140 × 252 cm)*

**MATERIALS**
• *Many colors and patterns for the Cat blocks and 1st border*
• *Ecru fabric for the background and 2nd border*
• *Batting*
• *Plaid for backing fabric*

**NOTE:** Instructions for the All Ears Cat Quilt shown on this page are on p. 242. Add seam allowances to all cutting dimensions given below

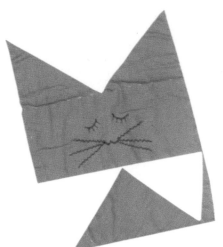

# DIRECTIONS

◆ Cut and make 3⅛ × 3⅛" (8 × 8 cm) squares and make the Cat Blocks, 3⅛ × 9⅜" (8 × 24 cm) by paper-piecing from colored and ecru fabrics (patterns on p. 446)
◆ Lay out and stitch together the ecru squares and rectangles and the patchwork blocks to form horizontal rows
◆ Stitch the rows together to form the quilt top, 47¼ × 95¼" (120 × 232 cm)
◆ Cut 1st border ³⁄₁₆" (.5 cm) wide and 2nd (ecru) border 2" (5 cm) wide; stitch on
◆ Cut the batting 55 × 99¼"(140 × 252 cm) and backing 60 × 104" (152 × 264 cm)
◆ Assemble the backing, batting, and quilt top; baste and quilt
◆ Fold excess backing to the front for the outer border; hemstitch in place.

# ROCKING HORSE BAG

*Little bag, bib, napkin, and placemat in coordinated fabrics (E. Santini).*

**TECHNIQUES**
*Appliqué*

**PATTERN**
*Rocking Horse*

**SIZE**
*11¾ × 13¾" (30 × 35 cm)*

**MATERIALS**
- Ecru and dark red striped and checked fabric
- Dark red fabric
- Cord for tie
- Dark red pearl cotton embroidery thread

## DIRECTIONS

◆ Add seam allowances to all cutting dimensions given below
◆ Cut striped fabric for the bag 23½ × 13¾" (60 × 35 cm)
◆ Cut, prepare, and appliqué the rocking horse to bag (patterns on p. 446)
◆ Prepare an embroidery-thread tassel and stitch it on for a tail
◆ Fold the striped fabric in half, right sides in, and sew closed on two sides to form the bag
◆ Make a casing for tie on the upper part of the bag and insert the little cord to close it.

# GIFTS FOR LITTLE PEOPLE

# QUILT WITH LITTLE PIG

*Opposite: Mini-quilt by Coin.*

# COVERLET WITH HOUSES

*The little House blocks alternate with blocks of various designs (Coin).*

# AT THE CIRCUS

*Characters from the circus enliven this child's quilt (G. Musiari, from Tender Loving Covers).*

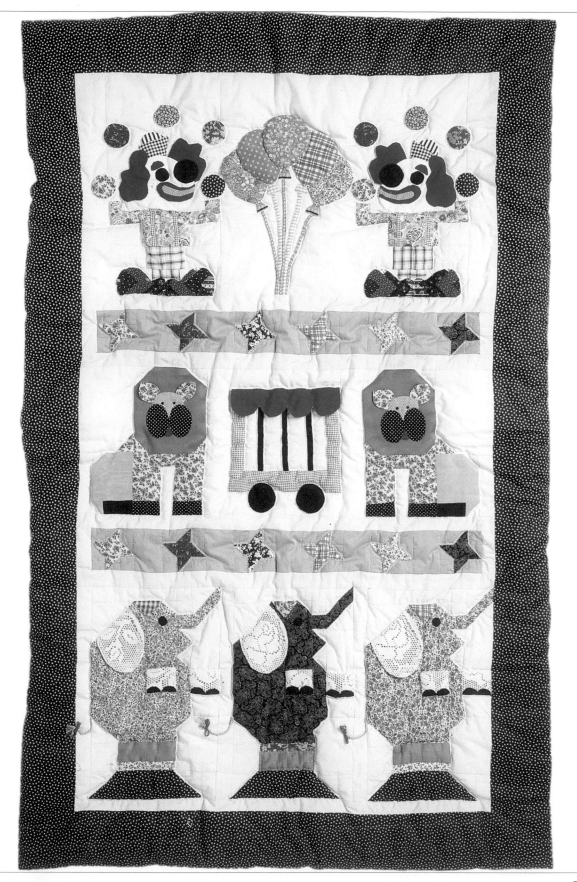

# SCARECROWS

*Mini-quilt in bright colors.*

# HOLIDAY BIBS

*Several shapes of bib with Christmas appliqués (G. Berti).*

# PINK-AND-GREEN LOG CABIN

*Log Cabin squares frame country-style patterns and a baby's photograph, photocopied onto fabric (G. Berti).*

# LITTLE GIRL'S CLOTHING

*Log Cabin in pink for a photo album and multicolored apron (G. Berti).*

*Toy train appliqué decorates a checked apron (P. Visioli).*

*Slippers and purse with appliqués of pink hearts (E. Santini).*

# MINI-QUILT AND BAG

*Opposite: Mini-quilt made up of blocks of different shapes and sizes, decorated with favorite appliqués (Coin).*

*Little bags made of plaid fabrics, in Early American style.*

*Little stuffed and appliquéd
bears and cats liven up
mealtime (E. Santini).*

# QUILT GALLERY

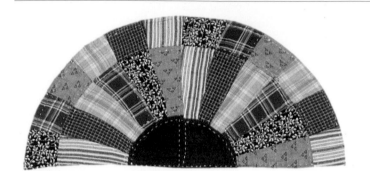

On p. 334 and 335: Quilt by C. Parriaud.

*Below: The interesting arrangement of Fan blocks stands out well against the light background (Bassetti).*

*Opposite: Traditional Wedding Ring quilt, done in many fabrics on a white background (Bassetti).*

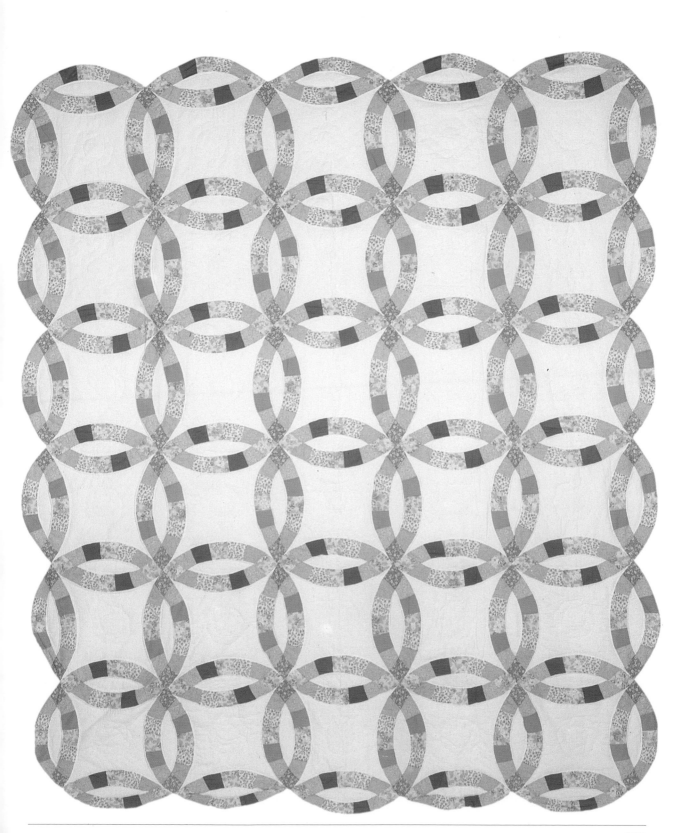

*Trip Around the World pattern
has square pieces that form
concentric squares.*

*Patchwork lilies have appliquéd stems (G. Truffa).*

Below: Dark lattice strips highlight the
geometric blocks in this Album quilt (J. Platt).

Opposite: Folk-style flowers, stars, and hearts are
framed by sawtooth and straight borders (Coin).

*In this quilt, the blocks have traditional*
*appliquéd wreaths (R. Carbone).*

Opposite: *Pleasing earth tones enliven*
*this Log Cabin quilt (M. Todeschi).*

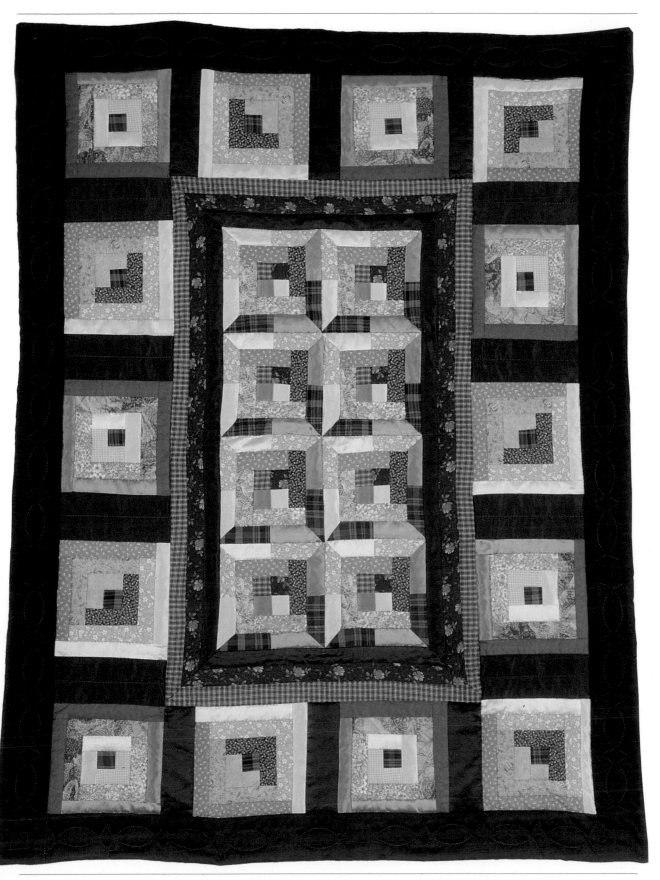

*Lively Cats stand out against the light-colored background, whose negative shapes repeat the Cat pattern (F. Morini).*

*Amusing quilt of stylized, multicolored cats (F. Morini).*

*Simple geometric forms in the corners and large appliqués on the*
*plaid fabric decorate this quilt for a child who loves cars (Coin).*

*Opposite: Mini-quilt with dolls in country-style fabrics and patterns (Coin).*

*Quilt of identical blocks looks contemporary although it uses an early American design (Coin).*

*Stars made of tiny diamonds in pastel colors stand out against the white background and dark lattice strips and border (Coin).*

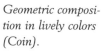

*Geometric composi-*
*tion in lively colors*
*(Coin).*

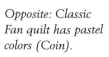

*Opposite: Classic*
*Fan quilt has pastel*
*colors (Coin).*

351

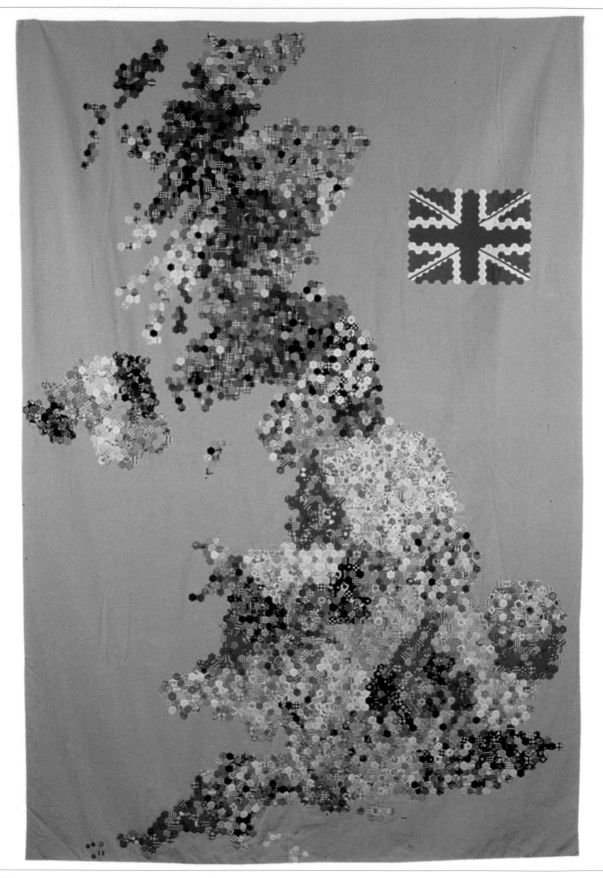

Opposite: Tiny hexagons make a map and flag of Great Britain (P. Hay, National Patchwork Championship).

President Roosevelt's little dog Fola was the inspiration for this clever pattern, which has now become a classic. Here the pattern is highlighted by checkerboard blocks (K. Berenson).

Geometric king-size quilt has Flying
Geese and Square-in-a-Square blocks
(M. Corman).

Opposite: Composition of irregularly sized blocks
in modern fabrics of warm and cool colors
(C. Lavieri Forman).

*In this king size quilt, the simplest geometric shape, the square, is the basis for the design (Bassetti).*

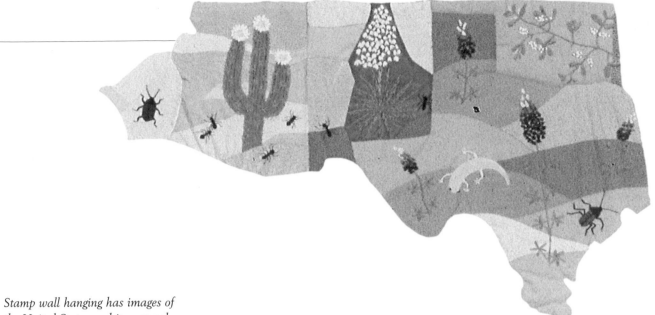

*Stamp wall hanging has images of the United States and its natural beauty (I. Wieland).*

*Below: On this Christmas tree skirt, it is possible to see a mistake inserted on purpose by a superstitious quilter, in accordance with an old pioneer tradition (Coin).*

*Opposite: The careful coordination of colors creates a pleasing three-dimensional effect (S. Ognibene).*

*Regatta is the title of this square quilt,*
*which uses many half-square and quarter-*
*square triangles (R. Ferré).*

*This well-designed king size quilt has a unique version of the classic Tree of Life pattern (R. Ferré).*

*The simplicity of this composition is combined with extraordinarily effective work with colors (I. Hueber).*

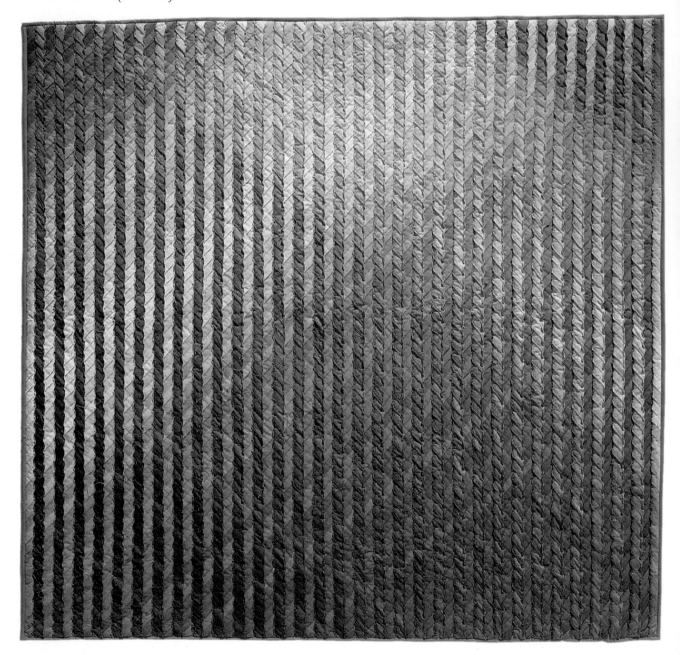

*Opposite: This modern patchwork features simple but effective color modulation and quilting (A. M. Stewart).*

*Appliqué quilt in various blue tones (I. Wieland).*

*This figurative quilt is rich in color and is embellished with appliqué and heavy quilting (H. Thrupp, National Patchwork Championships).*

An Album Quilt of many different block designs, done in appliqué.
The dark lattice strips set off the light-colored background squares
(R. Carbone).

Circular quilt has a central star
made of diamonds in graduated
colors and a broad strip-pieced
border (Flynn Quilt Frame Co.).

Opposite: A simple geometric
composition of intense colors
(J. Chausson).

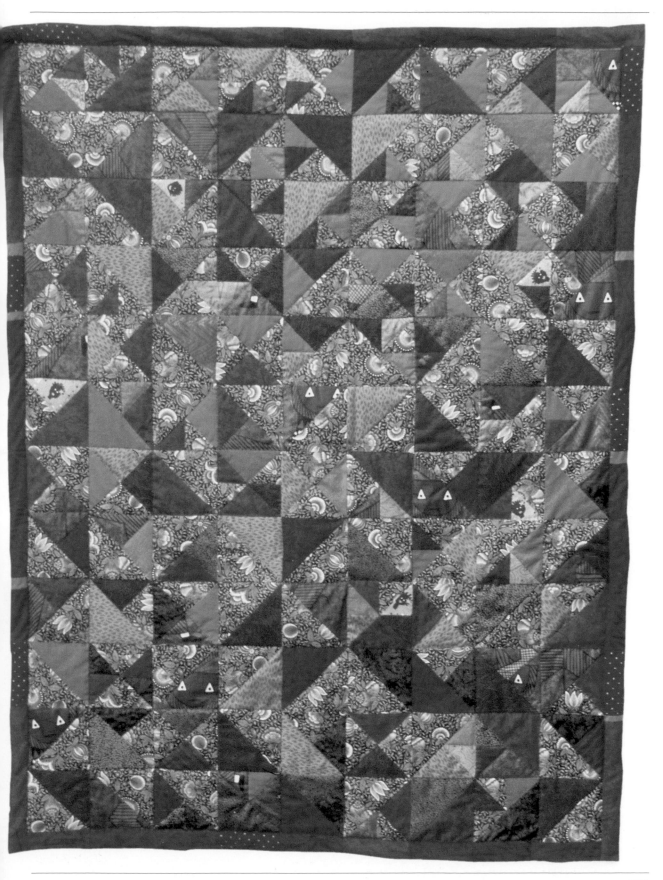

# PATTERNS
# FOR
# PROJECTS

*For all patterns: Adjust pattern sizes if necessary. Add seam allowances to all patterns before cutting.*

# CUP-AND-SAUCER POTHOLDERS (p. 154)
# CUP-AND-SAUCER PANEL (p. 155)

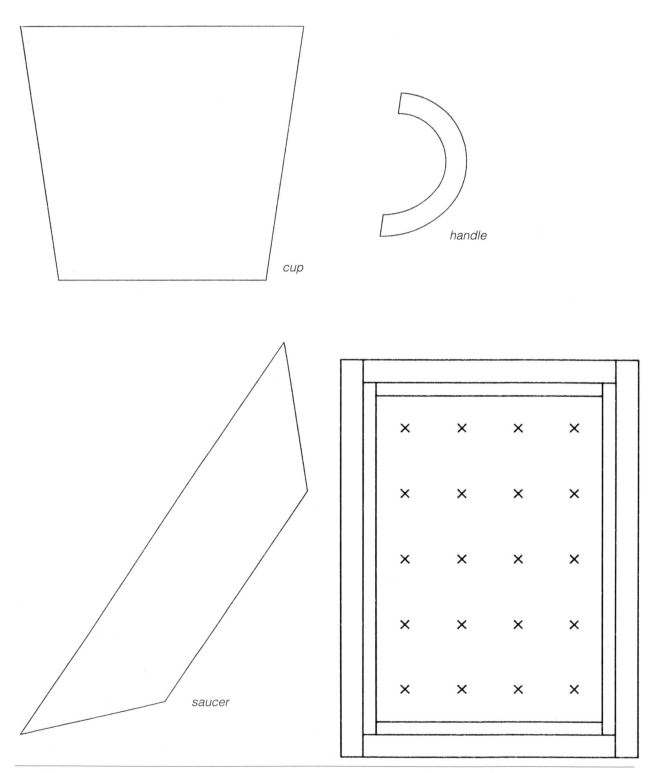

cup

handle

saucer

# HEARTS WALL HANGING

(p. 156)

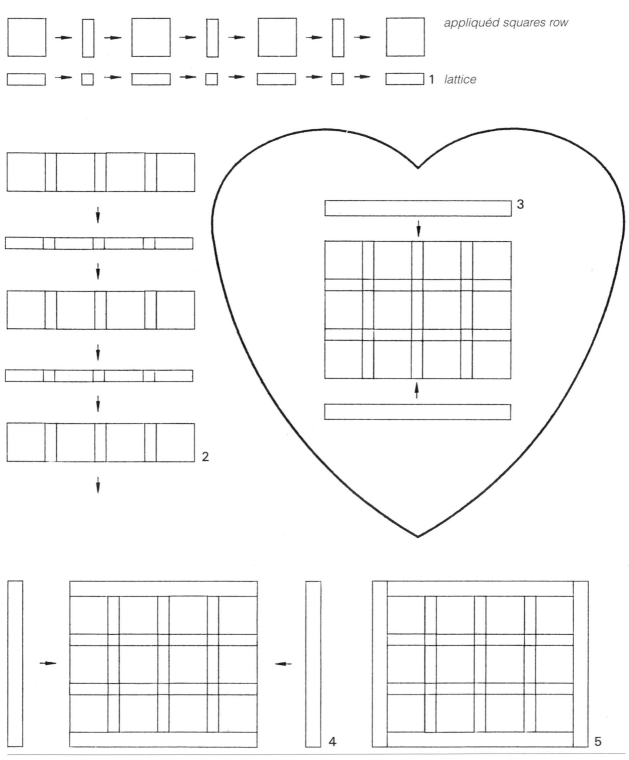

*appliquéd squares row*

**1** *lattice*

**2**

**3**

**4**

**5**

# QUILT WITH HEART WREATHS

(p. 158)

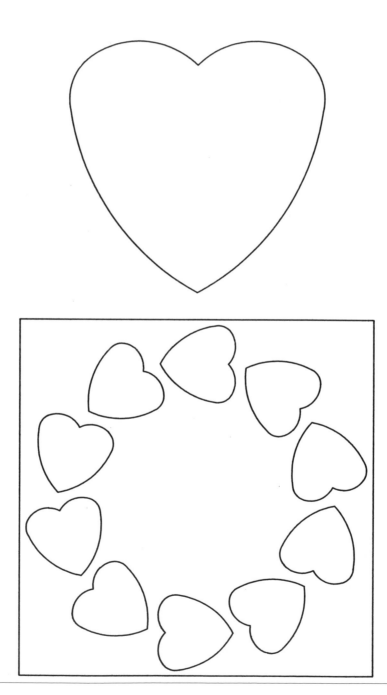

# LITTLE BEAR APPLIQUÉ

(p. 159)

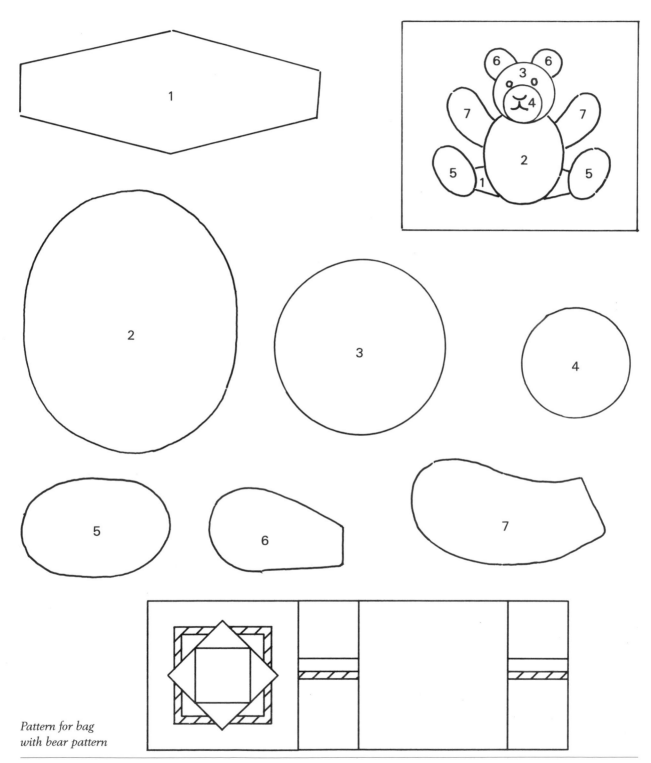

*Pattern for bag with bear pattern*

# LITTLE QUILT WITH SQUARES

(p. 160)

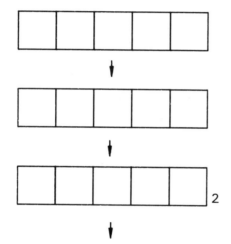

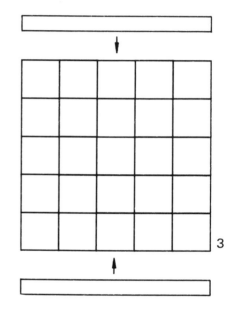

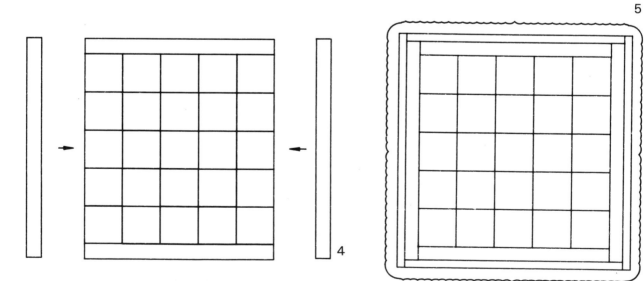

# SHELLS SQUARE

(p. 162)

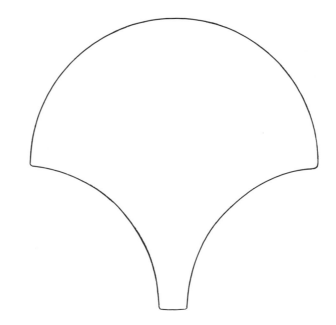

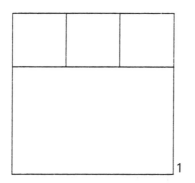

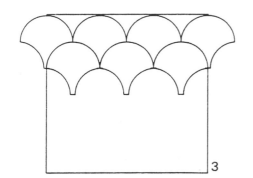

# SUNBONNET SUE QUILT

(p. 164)

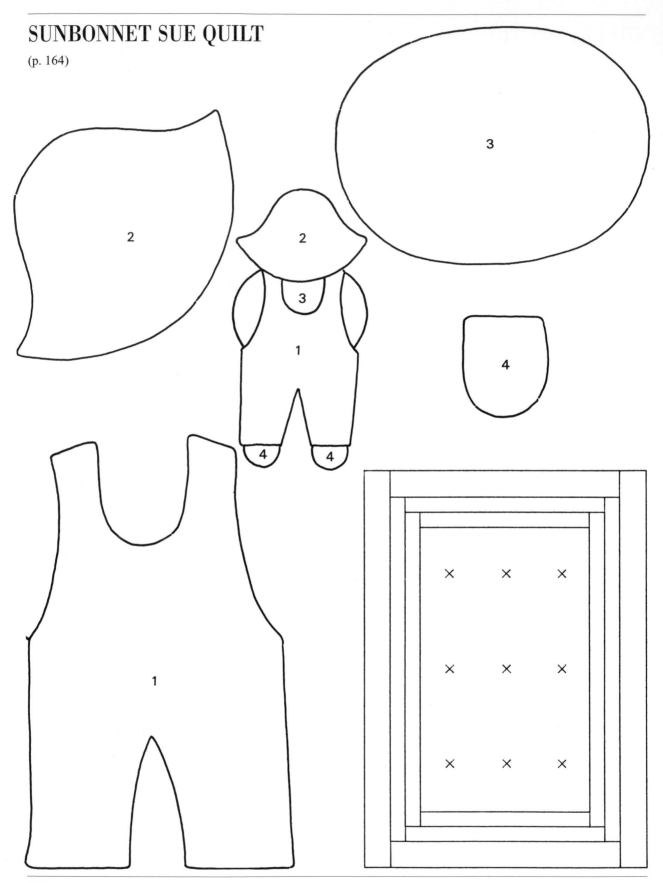

# AFRICAN GIRLS PANEL

(p. 165)

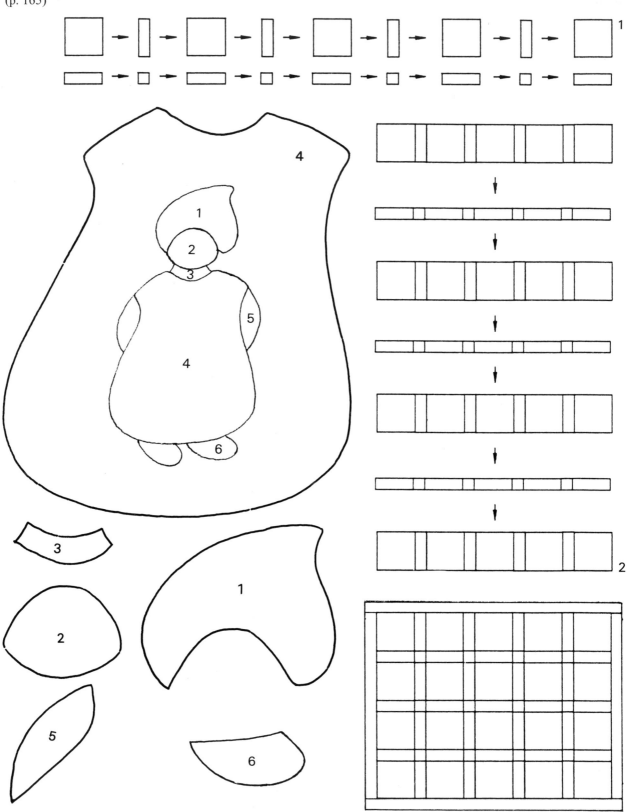

# CHECKERBOARD

(p. 166)

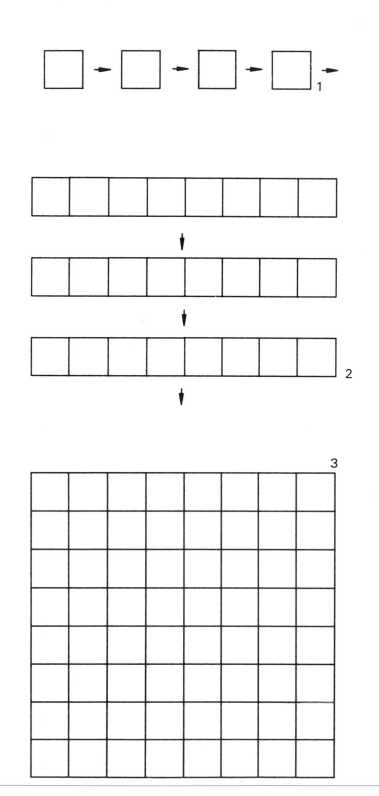

# IRISH CHAIN QUILT

(p. 167)

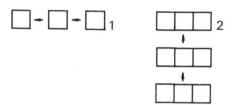

1

2

3

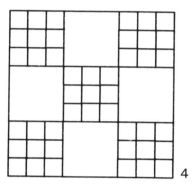

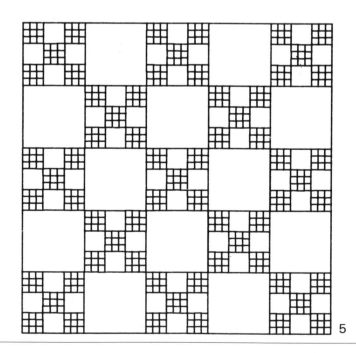

4

5

# 9-PATCH CHECKERBOARD QUILT

(p. 168)

 1

 2

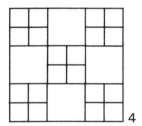 3

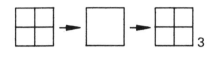 4

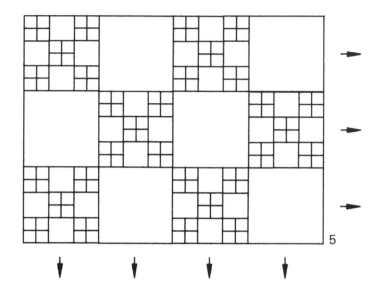

# 16-PATCH QUILT

(p. 169)

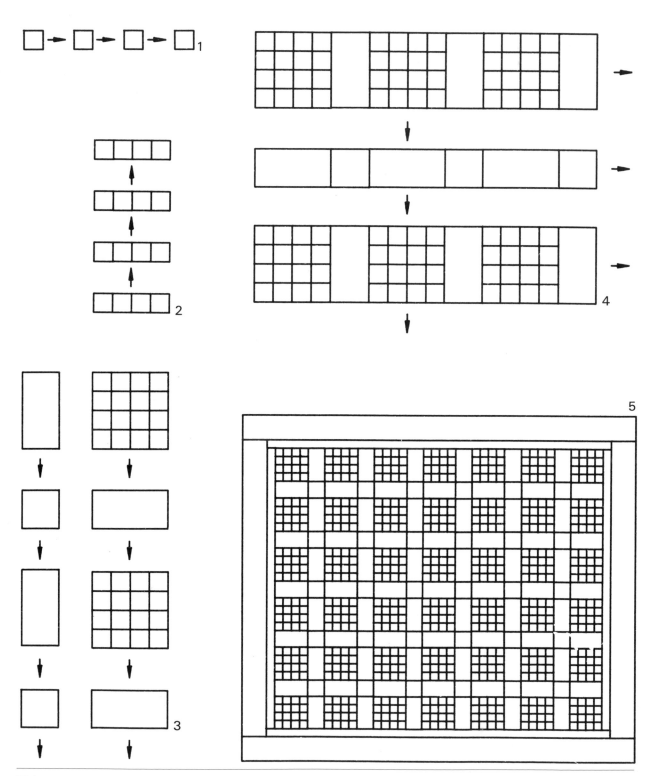

# LITTLE BAG WITH DIAMONDS

(p. 170)

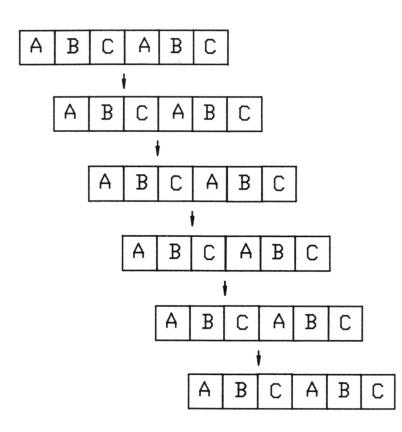

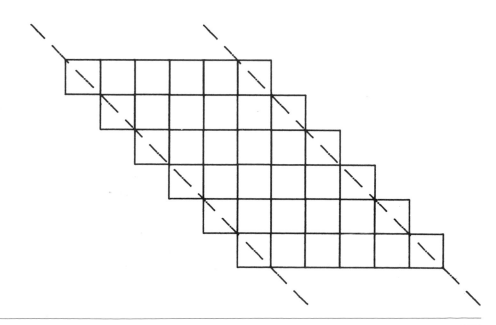

# FAN QUILT

(p. 171)

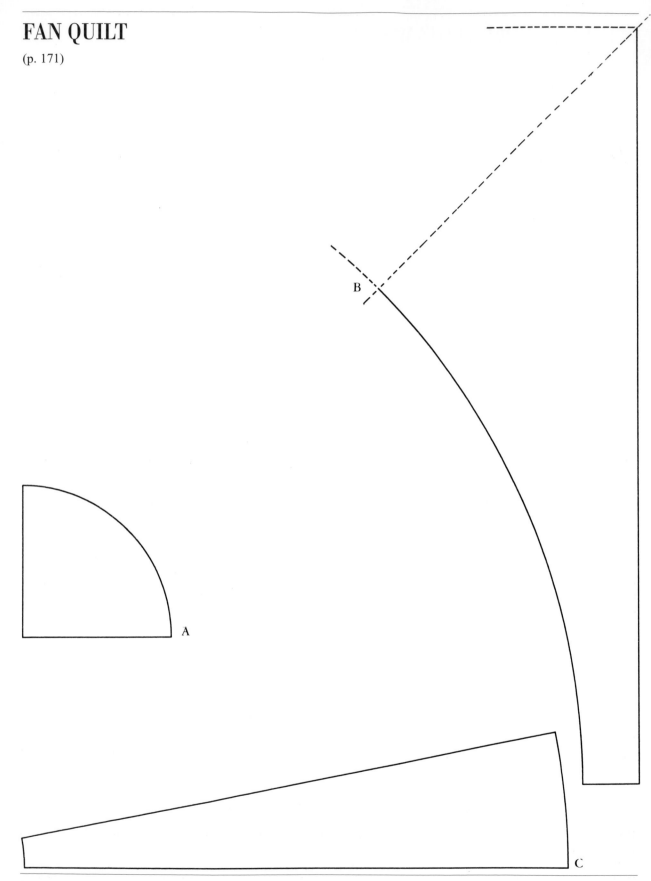

A

B

C

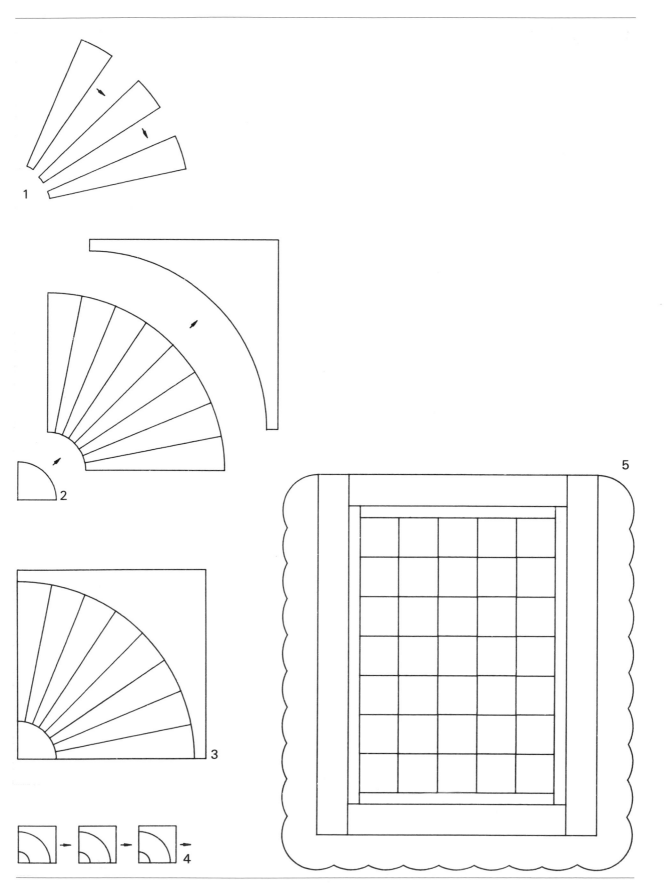

1

2

3

4

5

# BIRDS IN THE AIR PANEL

(p. 172)

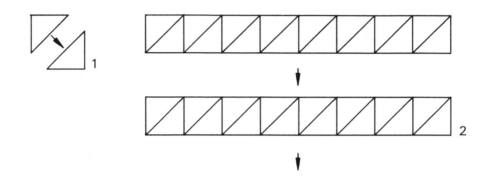

1

2

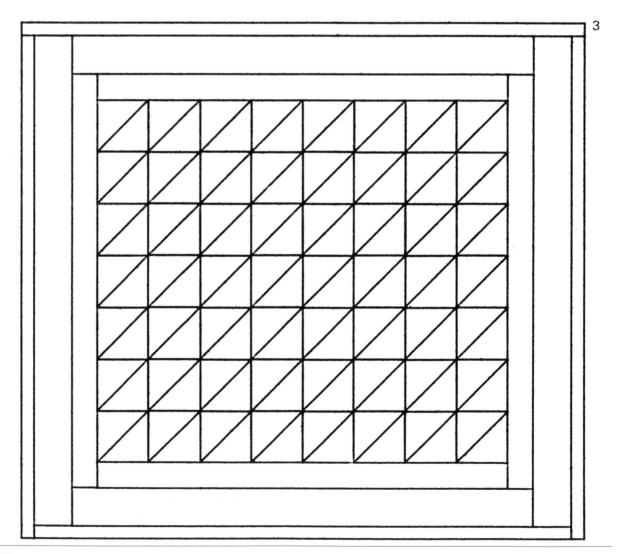

3

# BIRDS IN THE AIR QUILT

(p. 173)

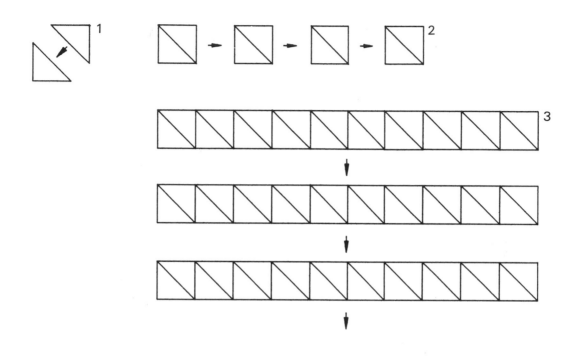

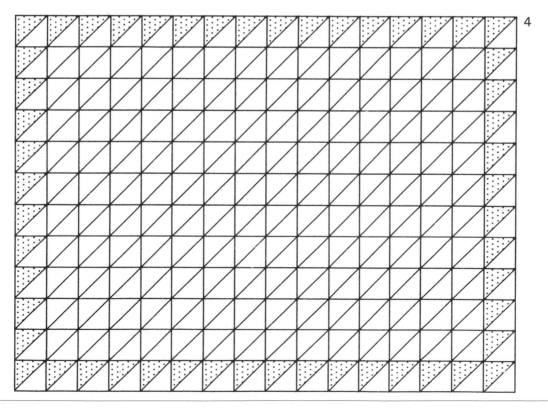

# VELVET STRIP-PIECED PANEL

(p. 174)

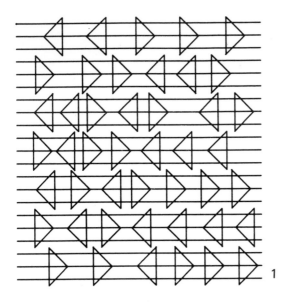

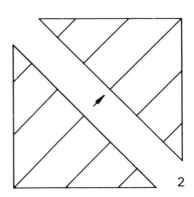

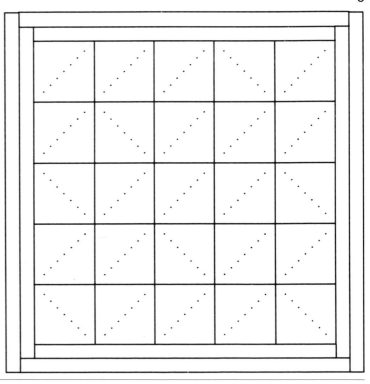

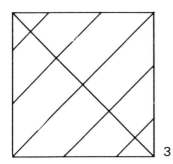

# STRIP-PIECED TEA COZY (p. 175)
# STRIP-PIECED TULIPS (p. 176)

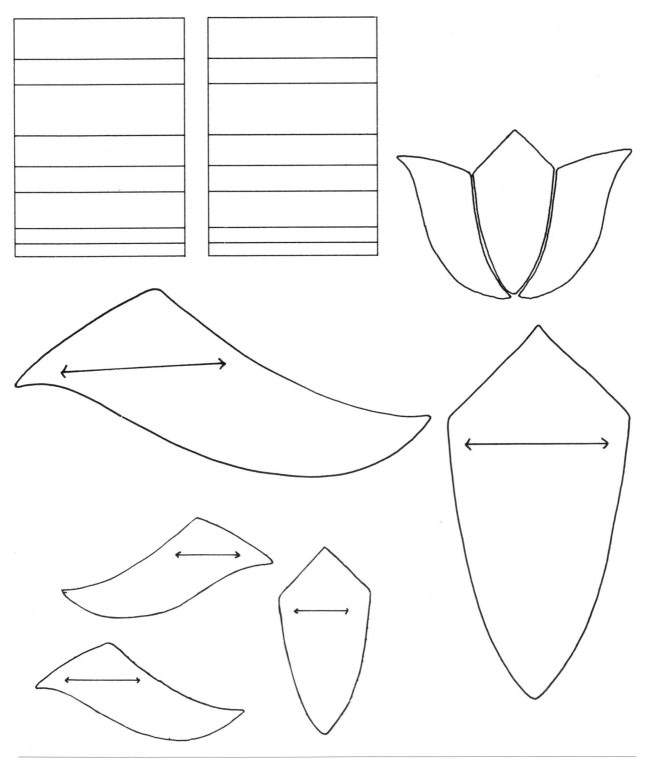

# DOUBLE IRISH CHAIN QUILT (STRIP-PIECED)

(p. 177)

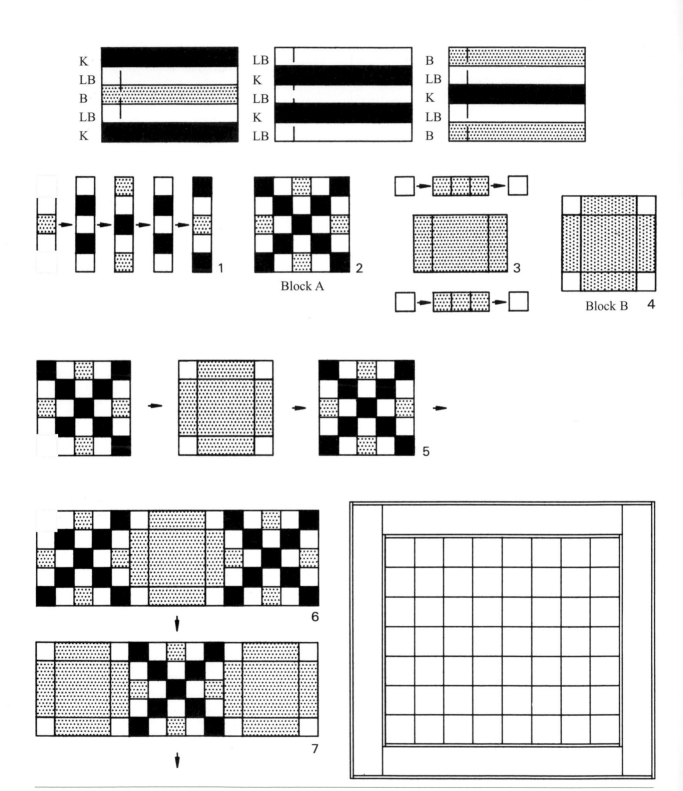

Block A

Block B

# LOG CABIN POTHOLDERS (p. 178)
# LOG CABIN T-SHIRT WITH RECTANGULAR LOG CABIN (p. 180)
# LOG CABIN PLACEMAT (p. 181)

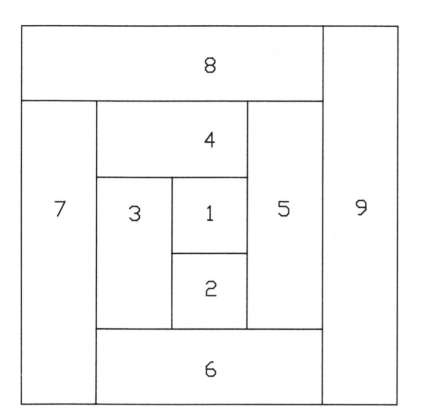

Diagram for Log Cabin block on potholder.

Diagram for Log Cabin block on placemat.

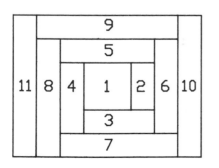

Diagram for Log Cabin block on T-shirt.

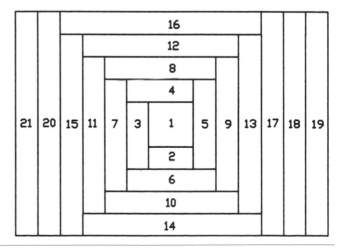

# LOG CABIN INFANT CARRIER

(p. 182)

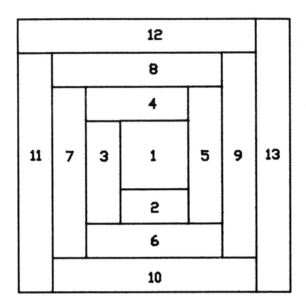

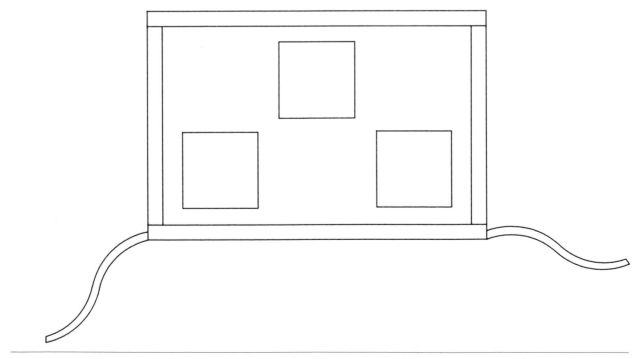

# LOG CABIN QUILT

(p. 184)

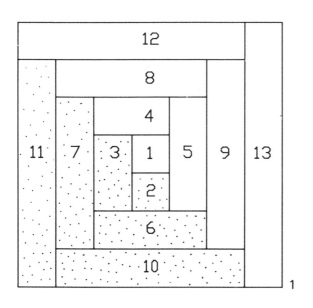

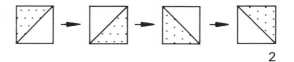

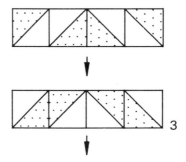

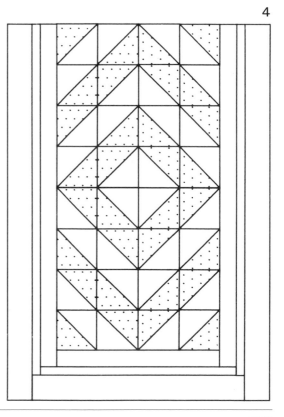

# PLACEMAT WITH HEXAGONS

(p. 186)

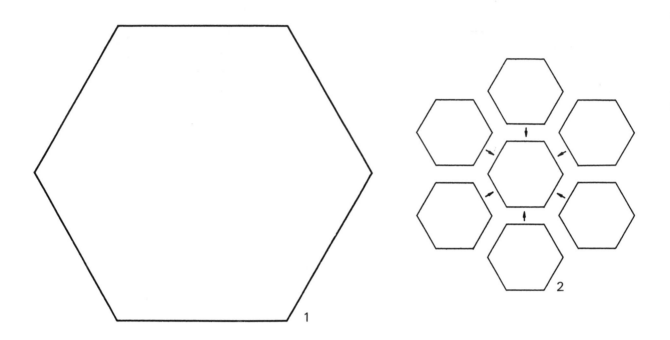

1

2

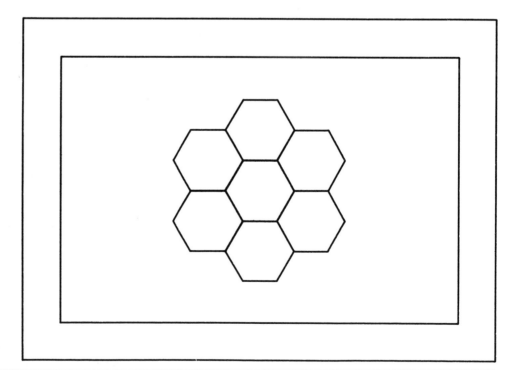

# HEXAGONS QUILT

(p. 187)

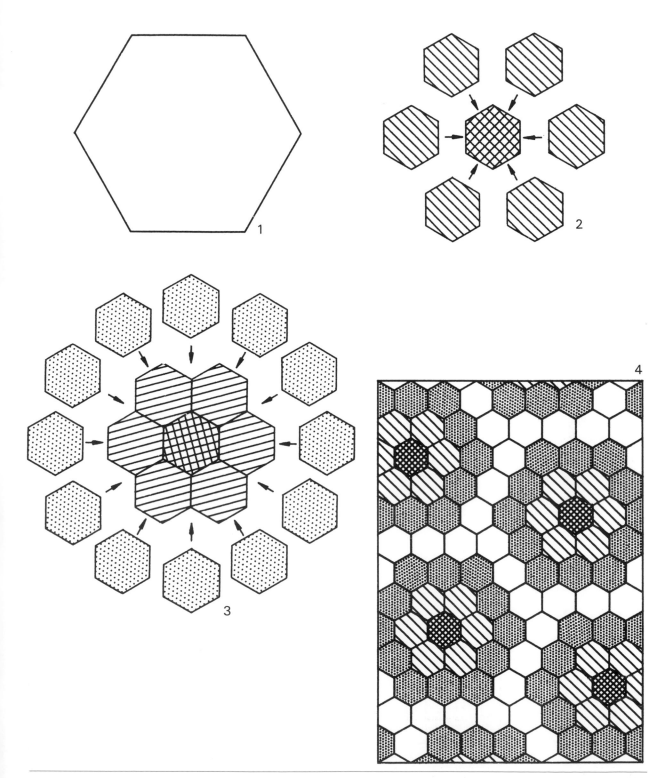

1

2

3

4

# BOW TIE POTHOLDERS (p. 188)
# BOW TIE PILLOW (p. 189)

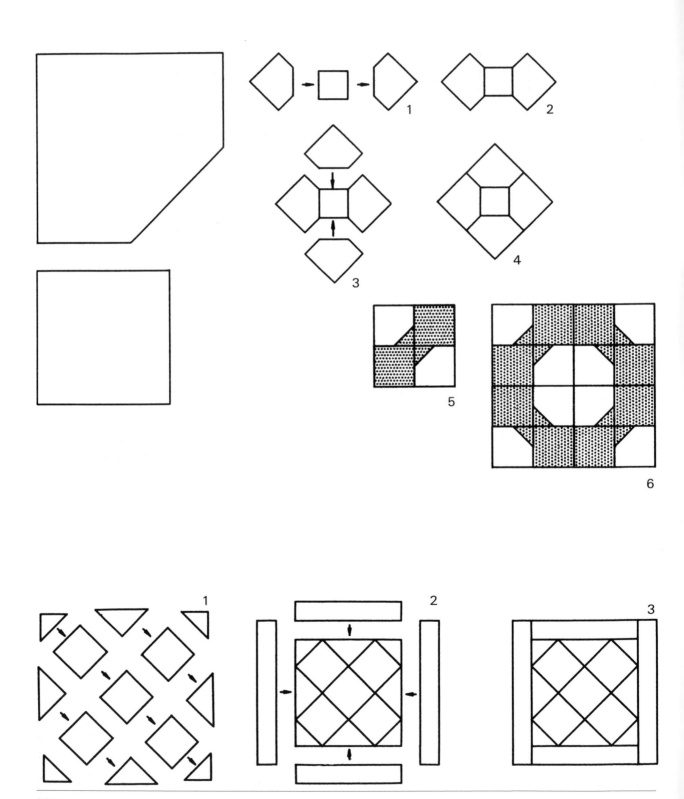

# BOW TIE QUILT

(p. 190)

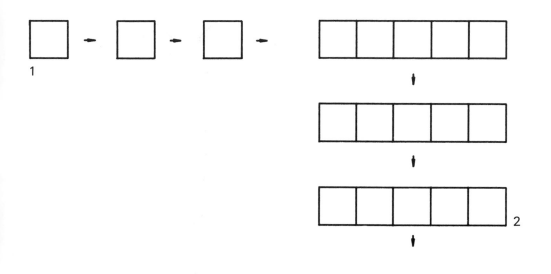

1

2

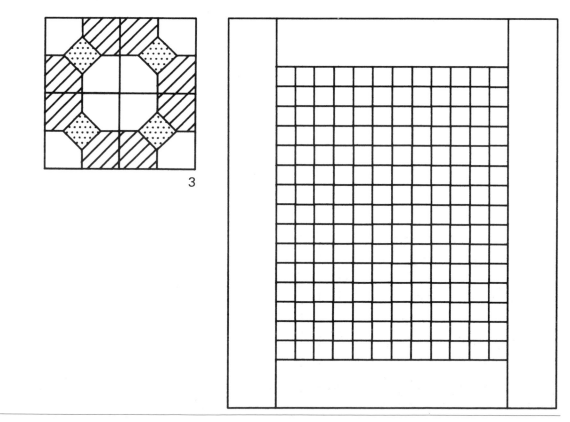

3

# LITTLE SPOOLS BAG

(p. 192)

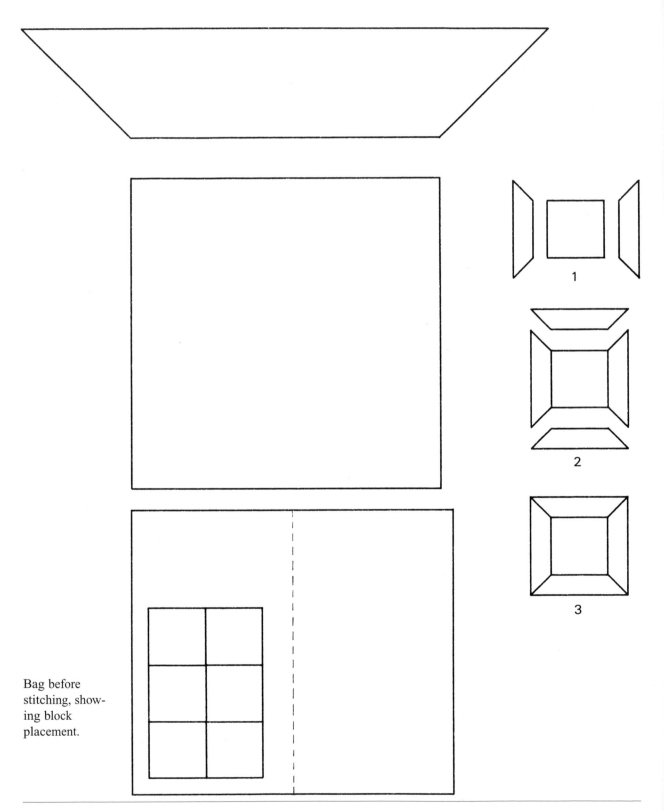

1

2

3

Bag before
stitching, show-
ing block
placement.

# HOUSES WALL HANGING (p. 194)

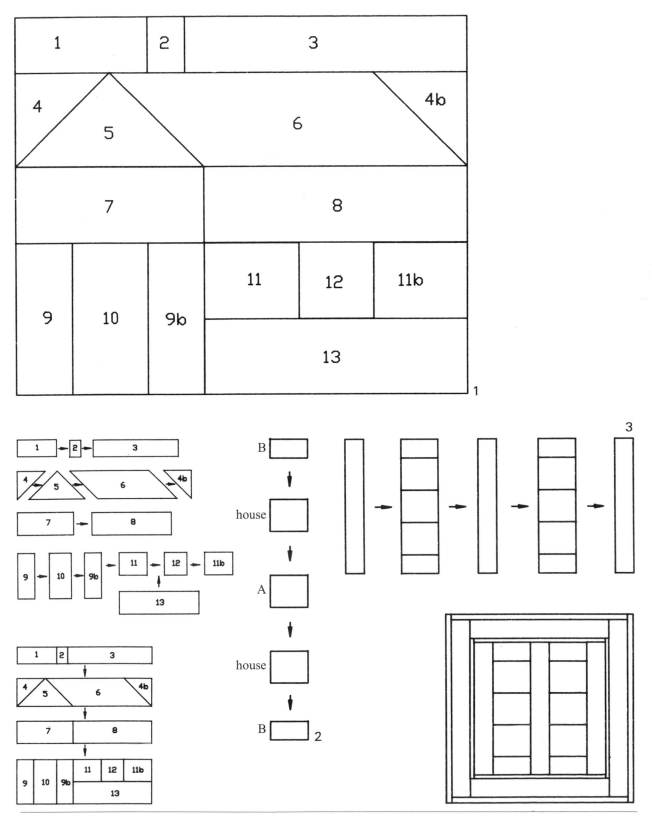

# OHIO STAR TRAY LINER (p. 196)
# OHIO STAR PILLOW (p. 197)

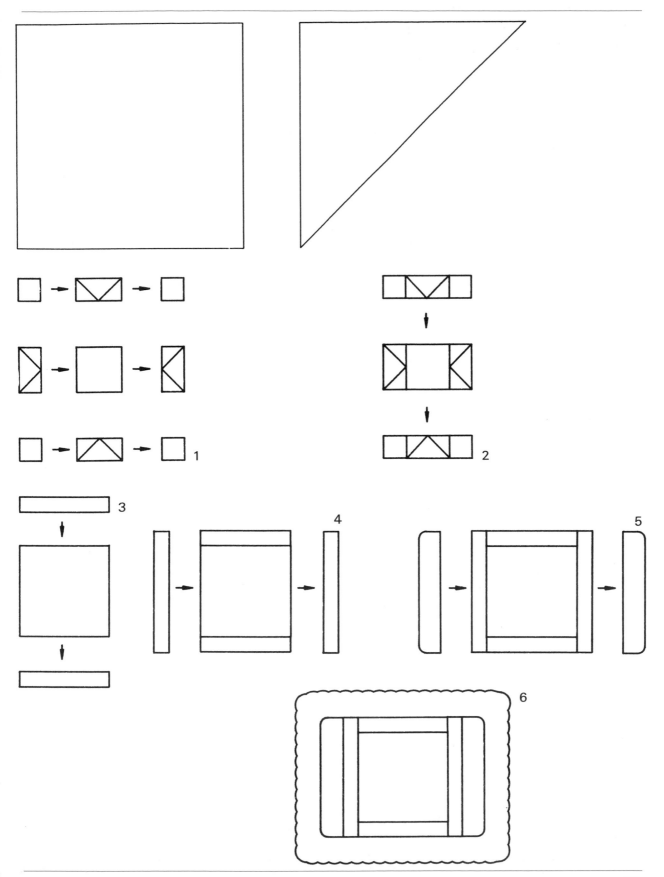

# VIRGINIA STAR QUILT

(p. 198)

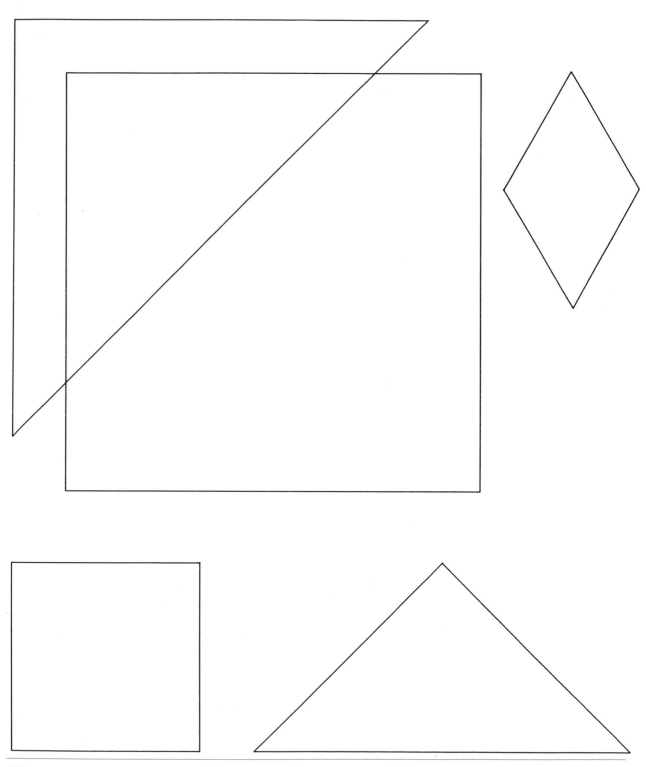

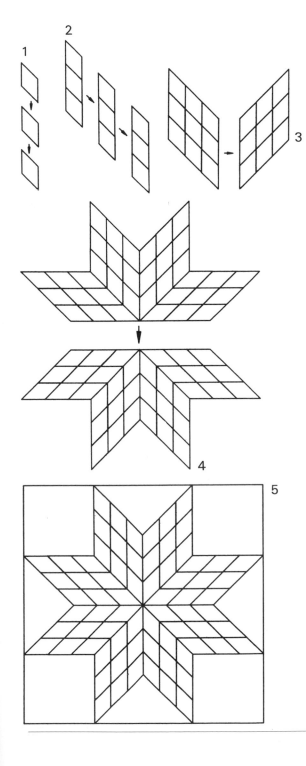

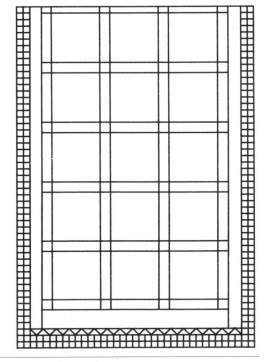

# VIRGINIA STAR PILLOW

(p. 200)

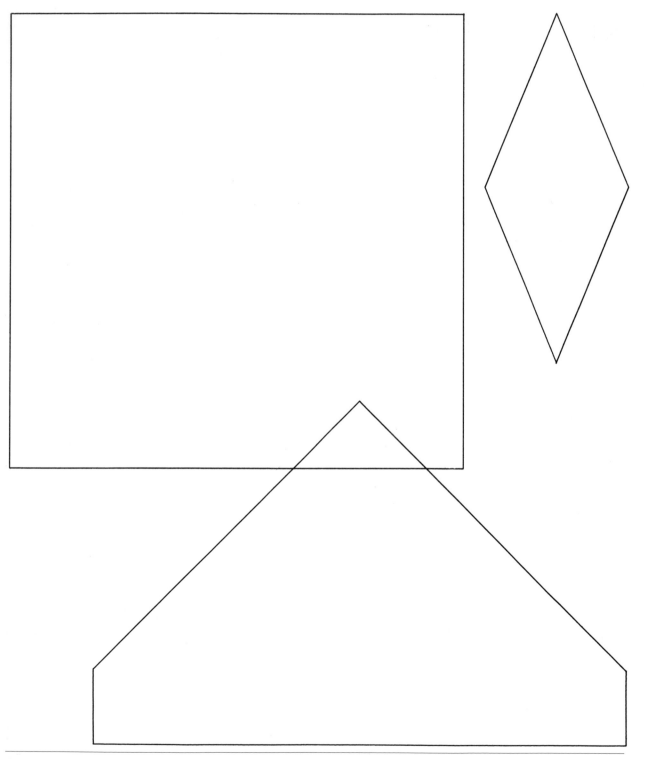

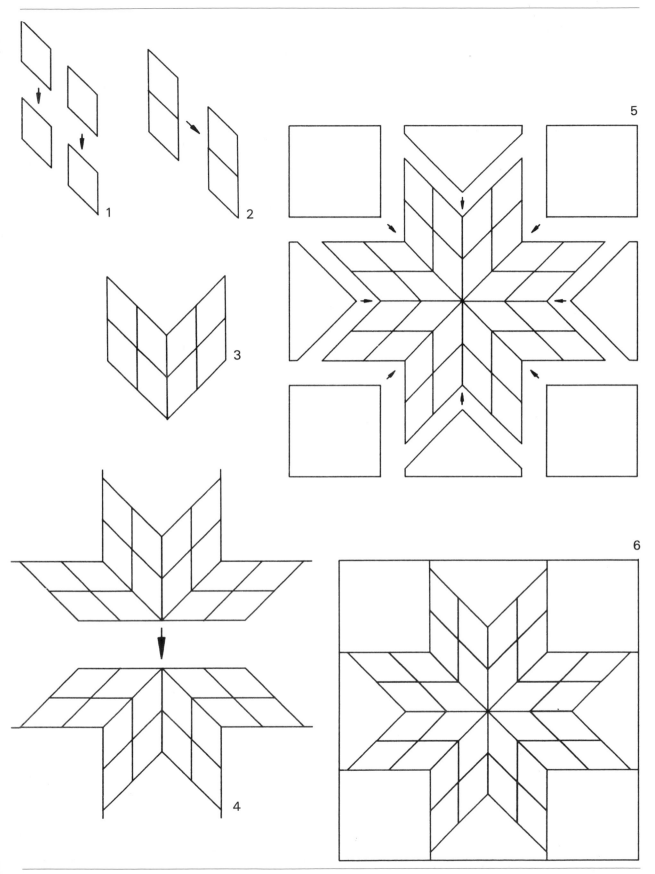

# TRAPEZOIDS WALL HANGING

(p. 201)

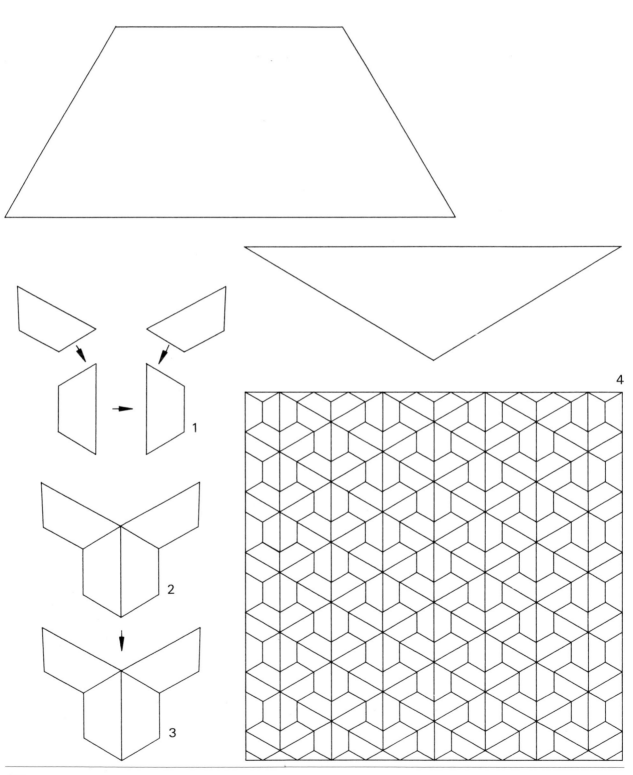

# BABY BLOCKS WALL HANGING

(p. 202)

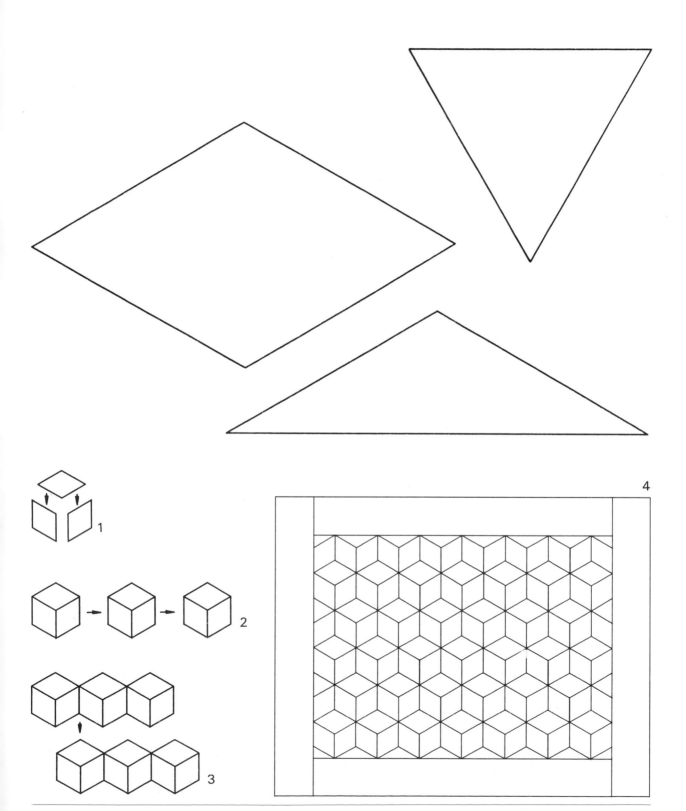

1

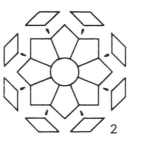

2

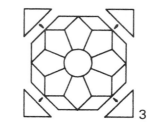

5

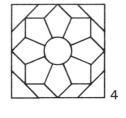

6

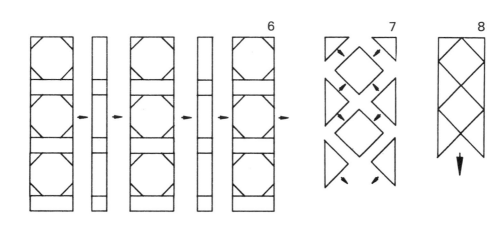

3

4

7

8

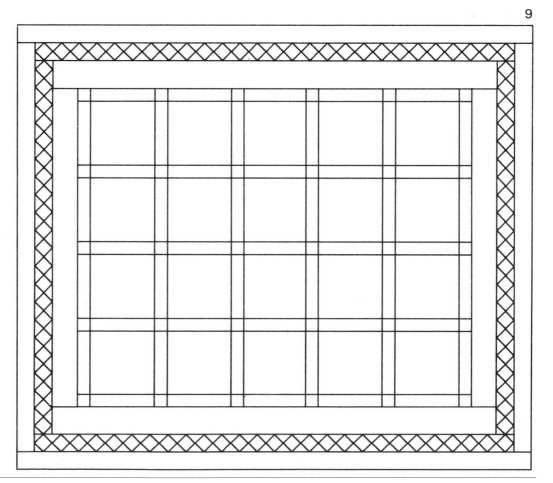

9

# ONE-PATCH QUILT

(p. 232)

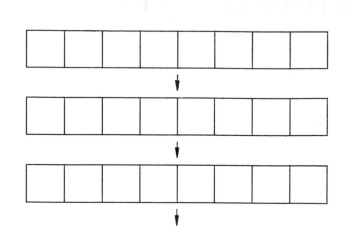

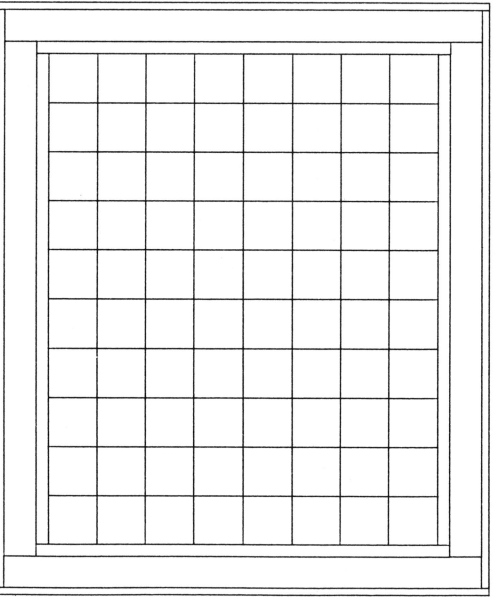

# INDIAN PRINT QUILT

(p. 236)

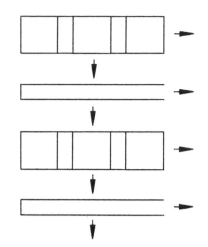

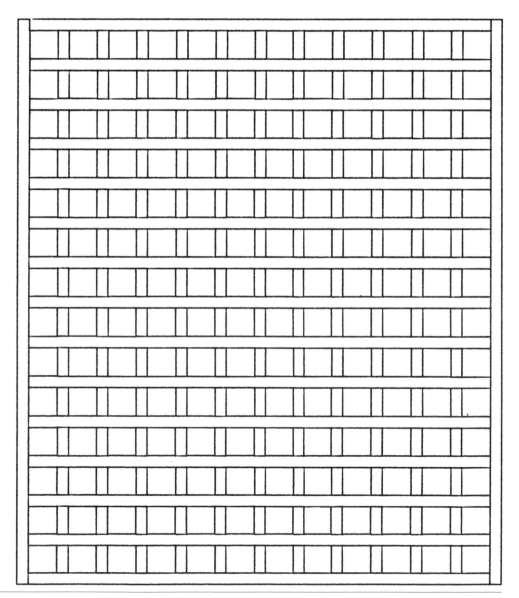

# HOUSES QUILT

(p. 234)

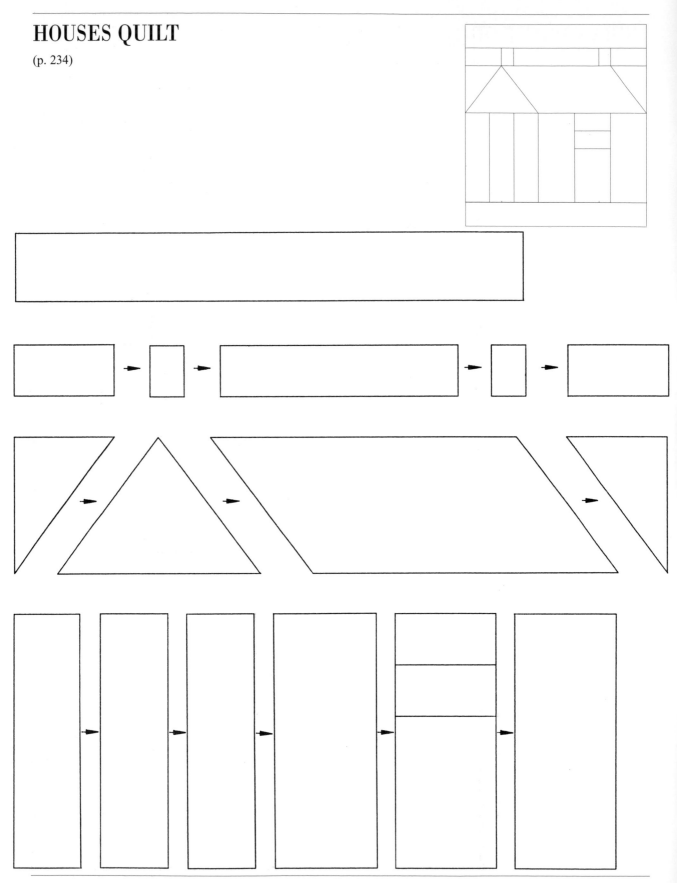

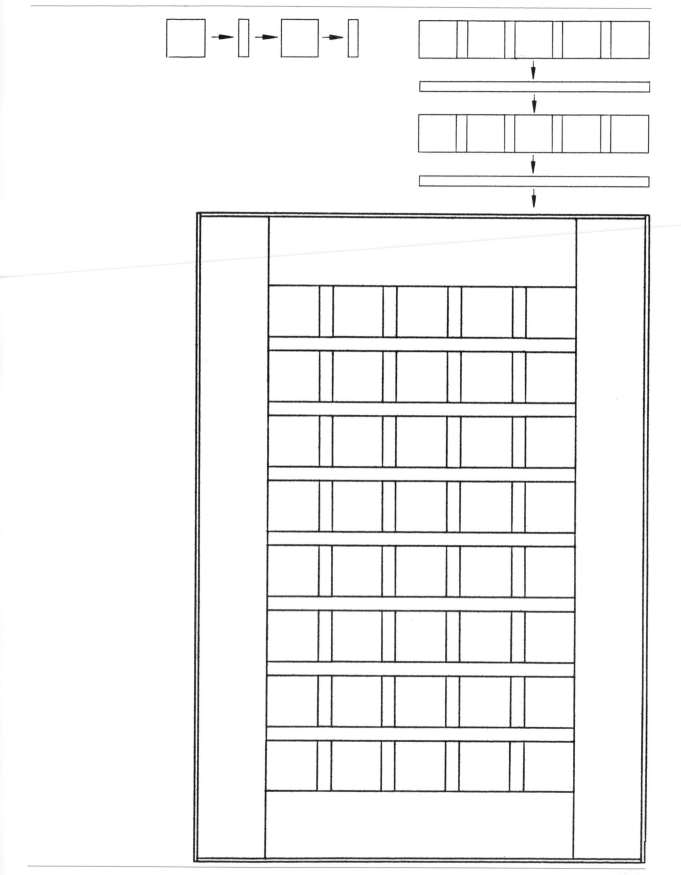

# SCRAP QUILT

(p. 238)

# 9-PATCH QUILT

(p. 240)

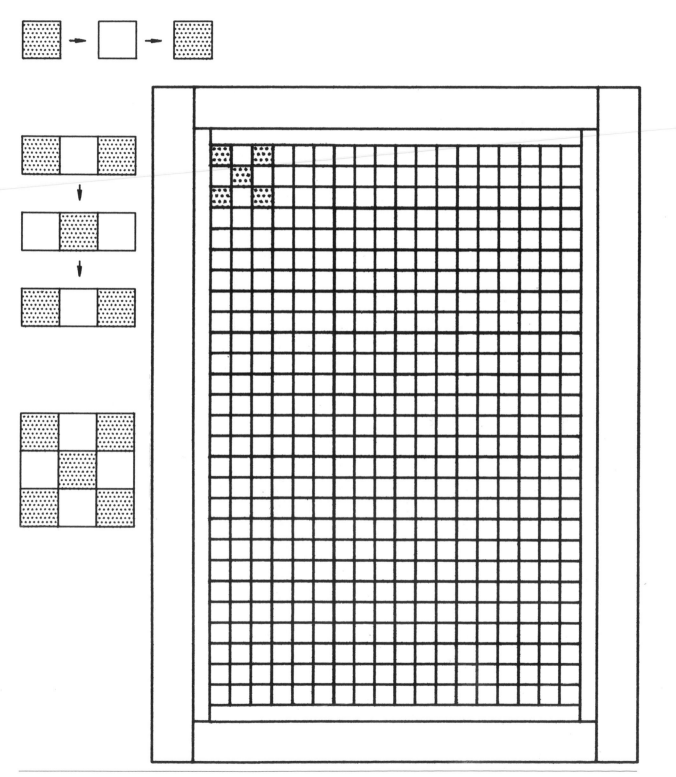

# ALL EARS CAT QUILT

(p. 242)

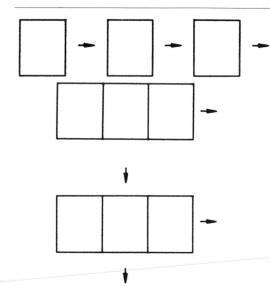

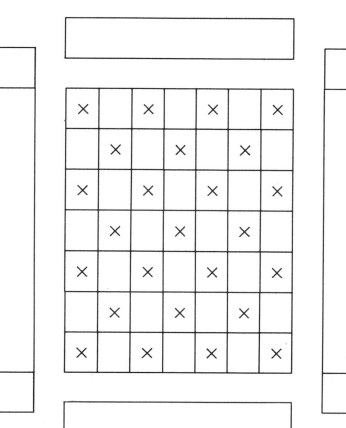

x = pieced block

# TRIANGLES PILLOW SHAM

(p. 244)

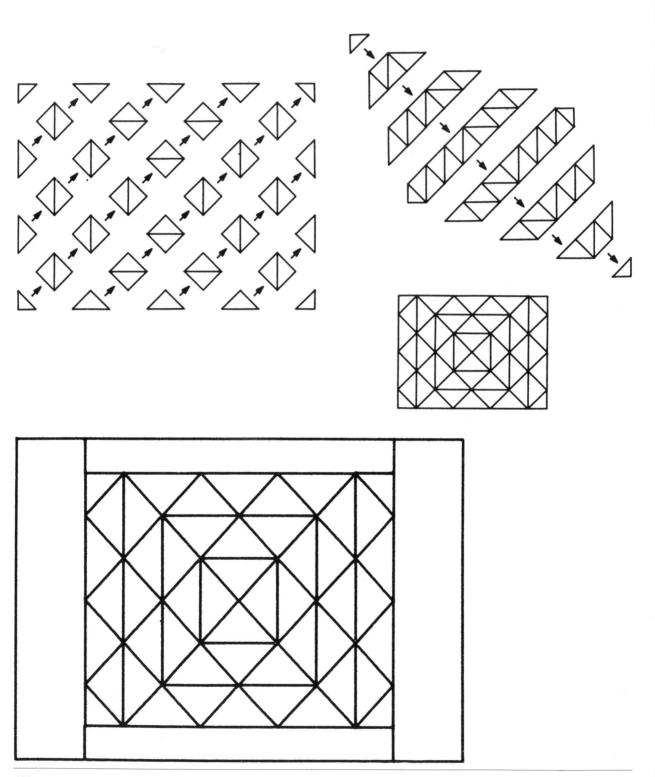

# FLYING GEESE PILLOW SHAM

(p. 246)

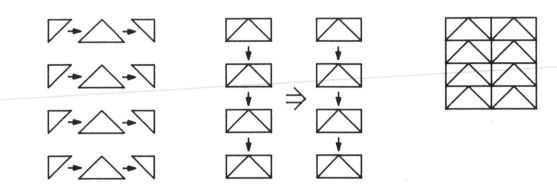

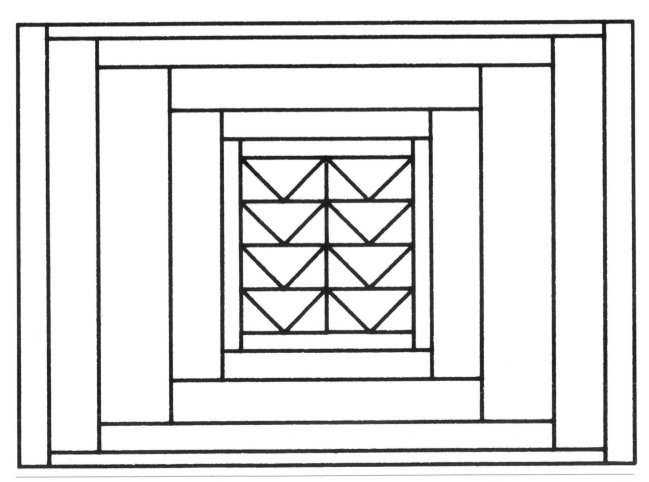

# STRIP-PIECED TABLECLOTH

(p. 252)

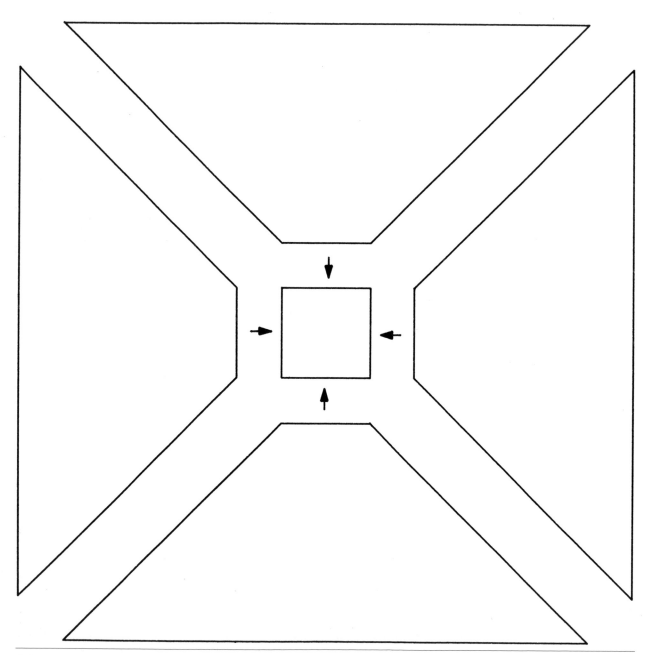

# FOUR-LEAF CLOVER QUILT

(p. 258)

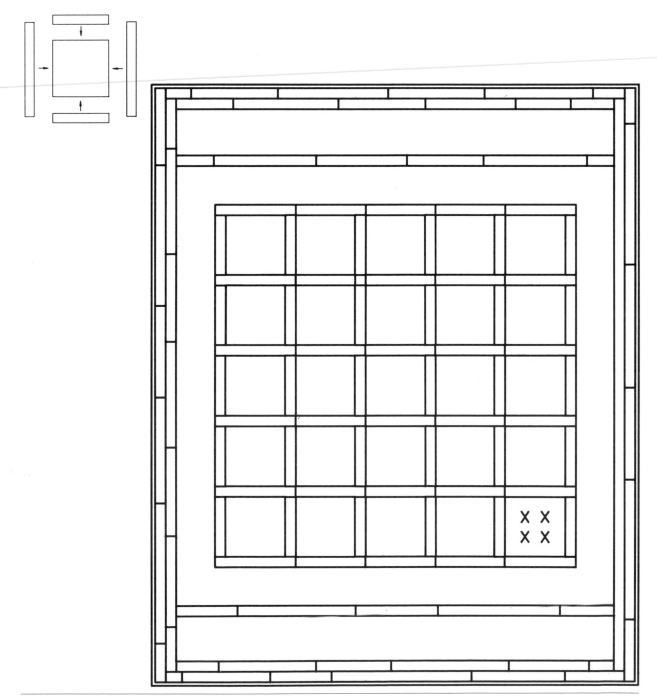

# FOUR SEASONS BABY BLANKET

(p. 254)

# BASKET QUILT

(p. 260)

To assemble a basket:

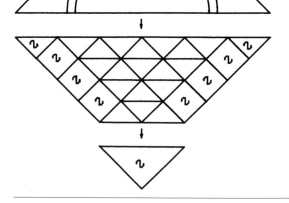

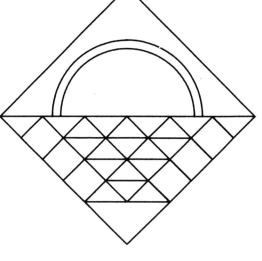

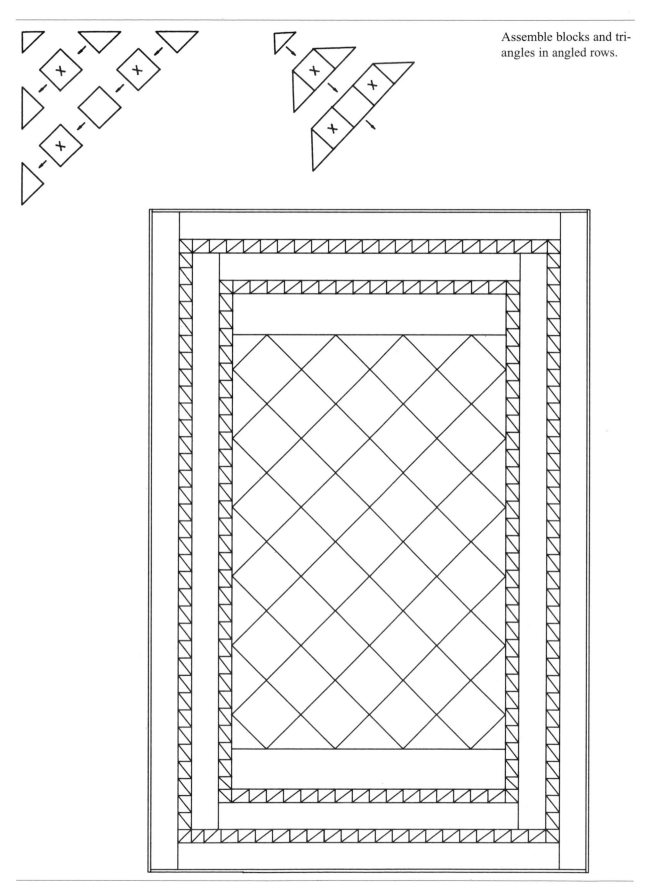

Assemble blocks and triangles in angled rows.

# LITTLE DUCKS QUILT

(p. 264)

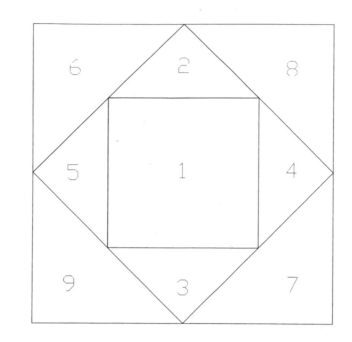

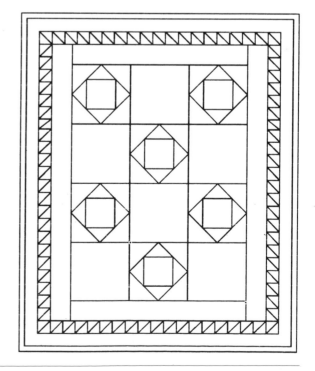

# DRESSES QUILT (p. 266)

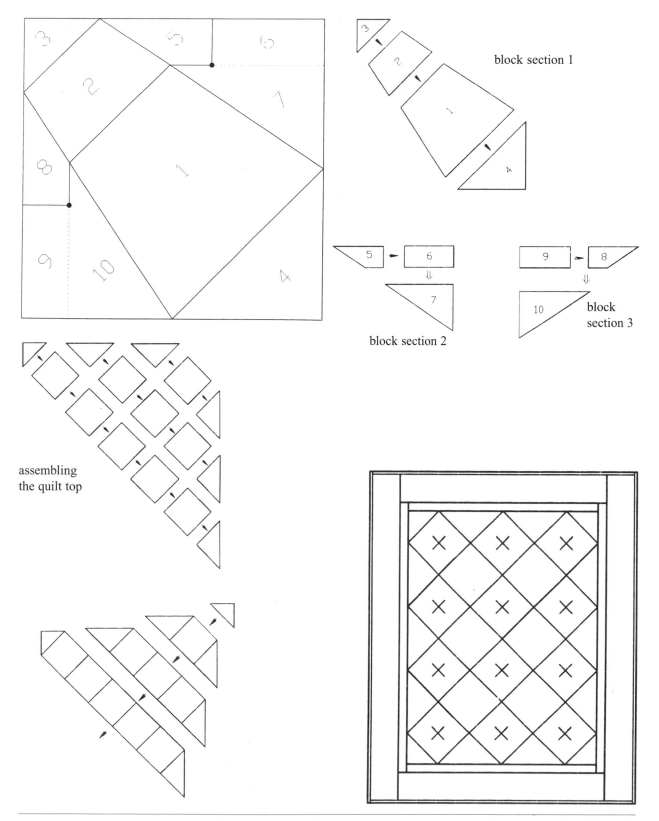

block section 1

block section 2

block section 3

assembling
the quilt top

# CHRISTMAS TREE PANEL (p. 268)

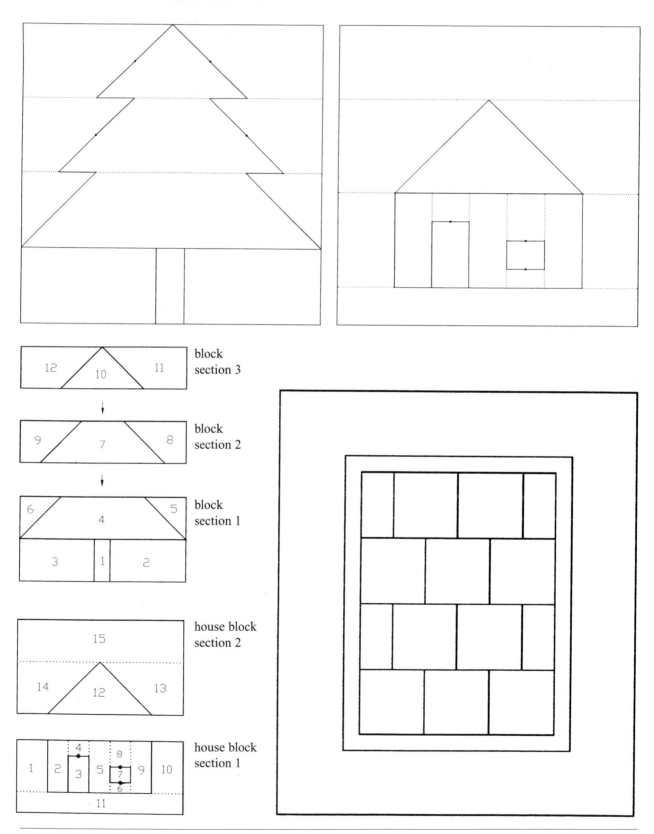

block
section 3

block
section 2

block
section 1

house block
section 2

house block
section 1

# HOUSES AND GARDENS QUILT (p. 270)

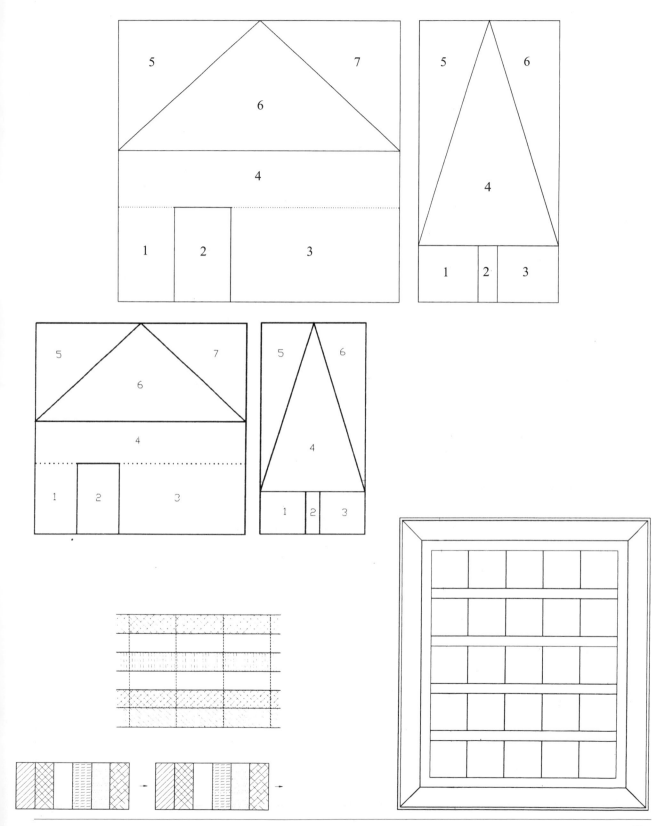

# GREEN EMBROIDERED QUILT (p. 272)

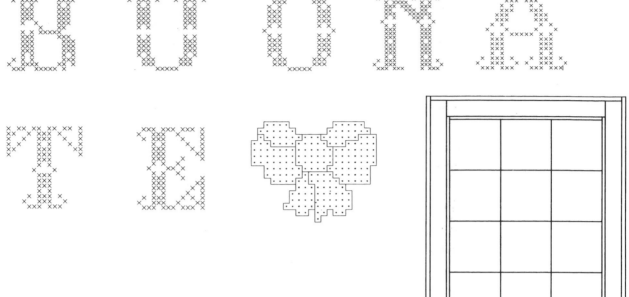

# PINK HOUSE QUILT  (p. 274)

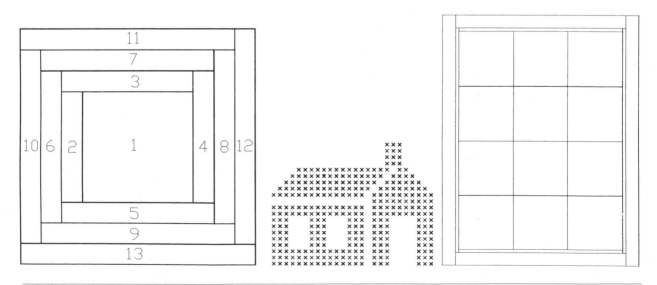

# PINWHEELS QUILT (p. 276)

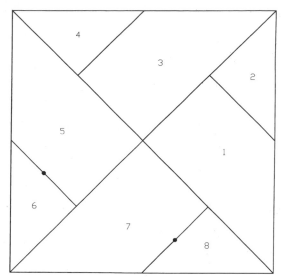

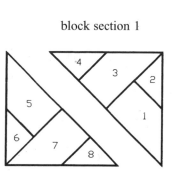

block section 1

block section 2

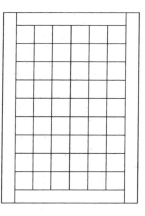

# VIOLETS QUILT (p. 278)

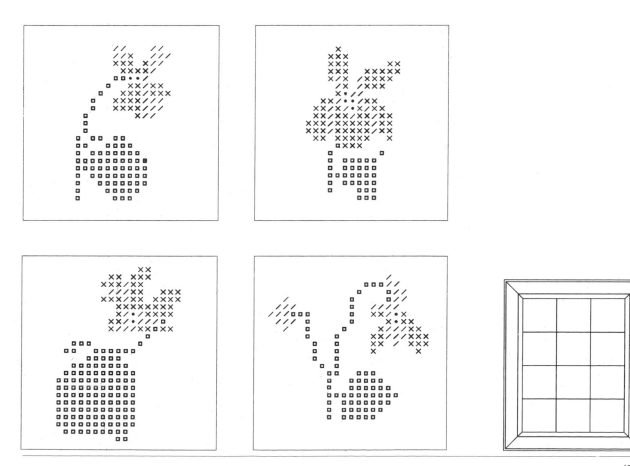

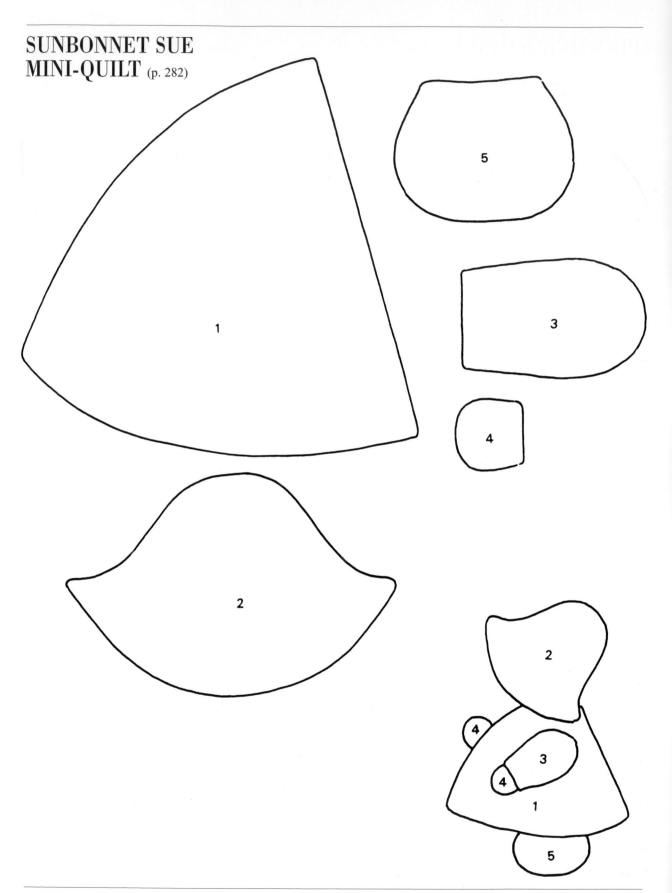

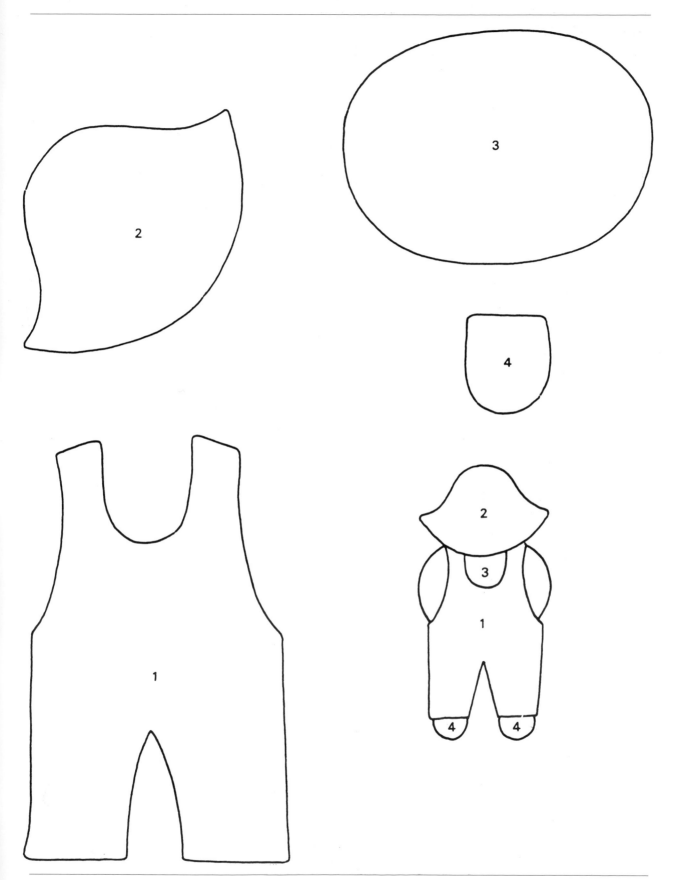

# LITTLE
# RABBITS QUILT
(p. 280)

# CUP-AND-SACUER PANEL (p. 284)

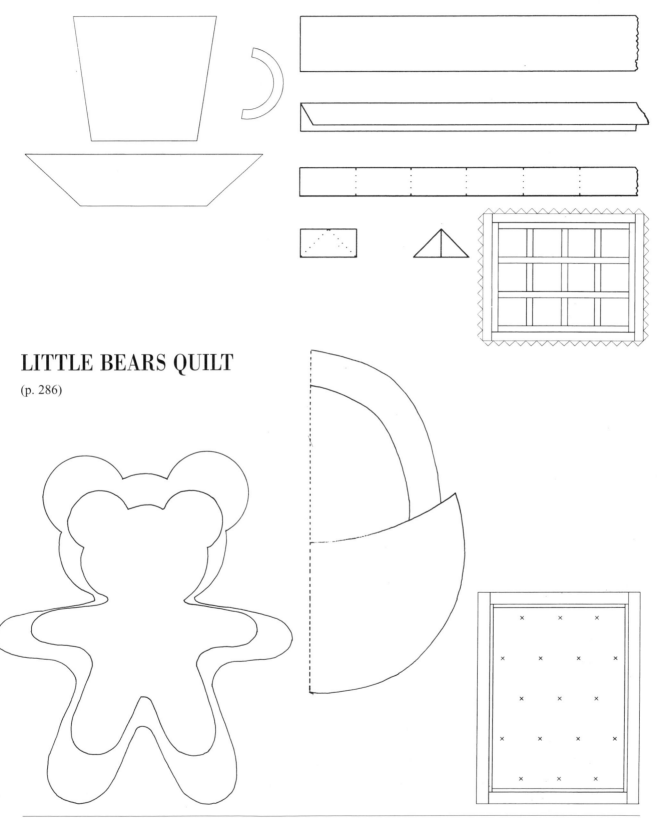

# LITTLE BEARS QUILT

(p. 286)

# BABY CARRIAGES MINI-QUILT (p. 288)

## PEACEFUL CRADLE COVERLET

(p. 290)

# CHRISTMAS TREE
# SKIRT (p. 292)

## SHELLS COVERLET (p. 294)

# SUNBONNET SUE PILLOW

(p. 296)

# HEARTS QUILT (p. 300)

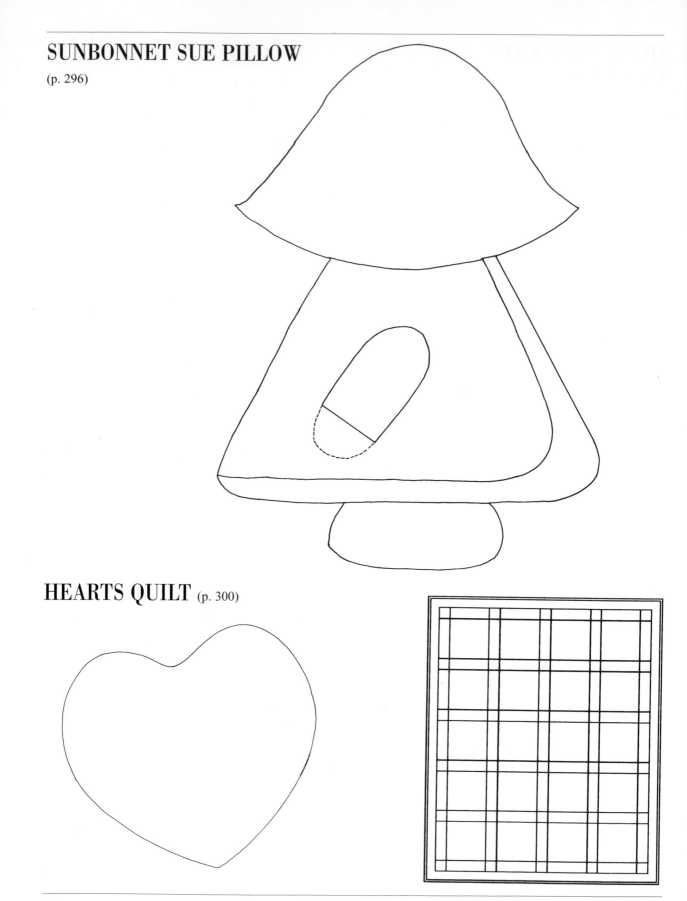

# HEARTS INFANT CARRIER

(p. 298)

# CHILDREN AT THE WINDOW QUILT (p. 302)

# WALL HANGING WITH SQUARES (p. 304)

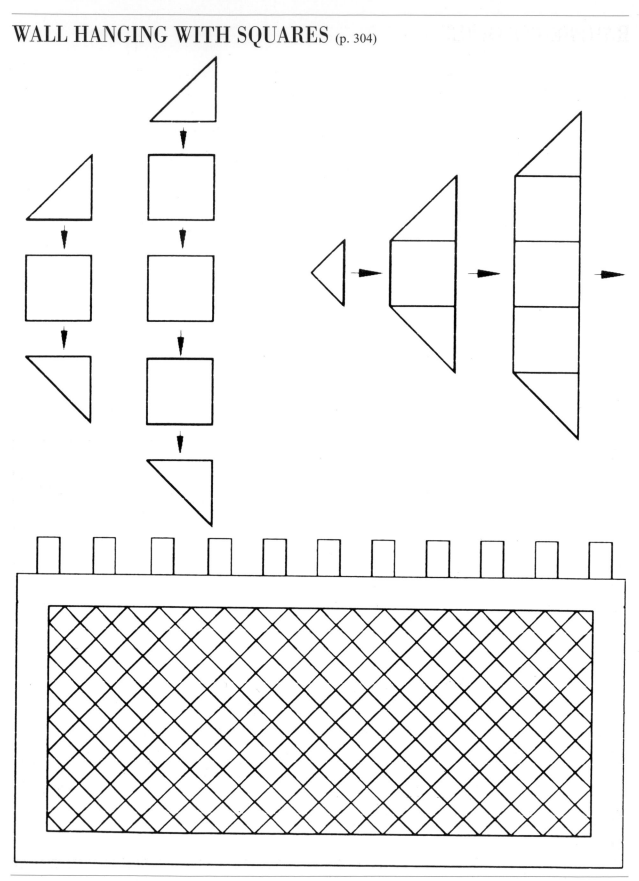

# RAIL FENCE QUILT (p. 306)

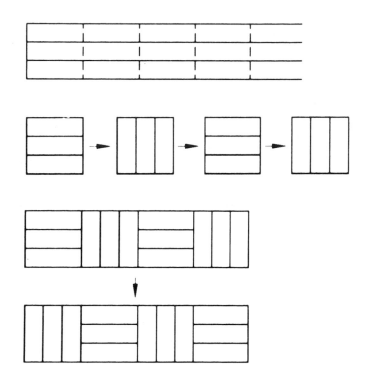

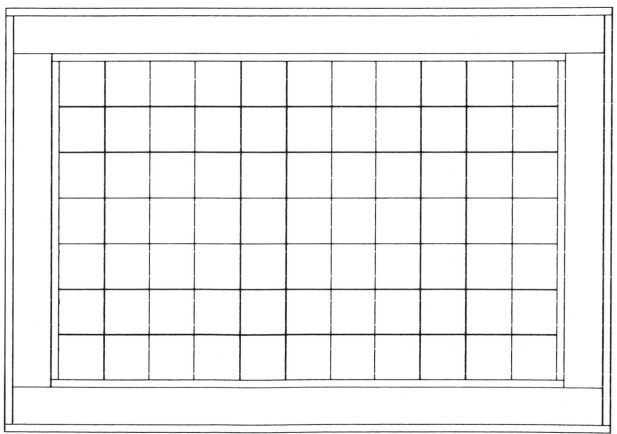

# MINI-QUILT WITH MILLS (p. 308)

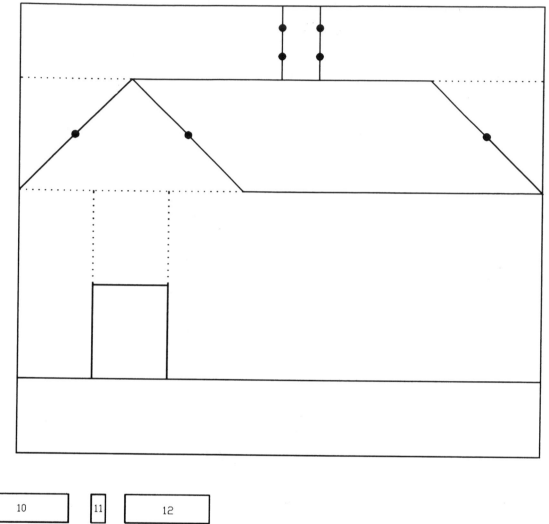

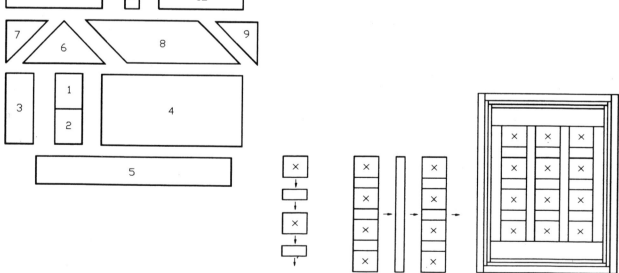

# HERRINGBONE QUILT (p. 310)

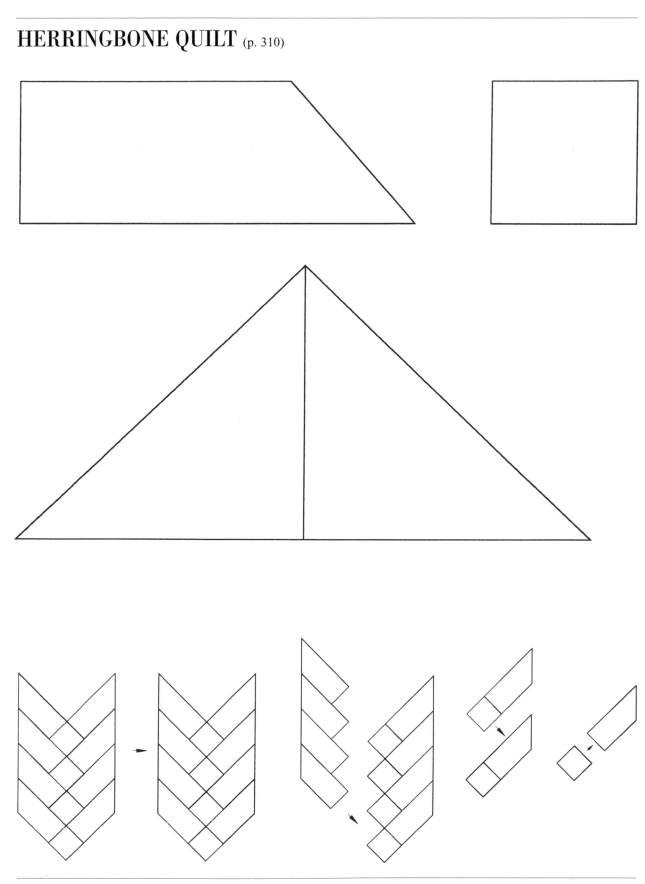

# LATTICE OF CATS QUILT (P. 312)

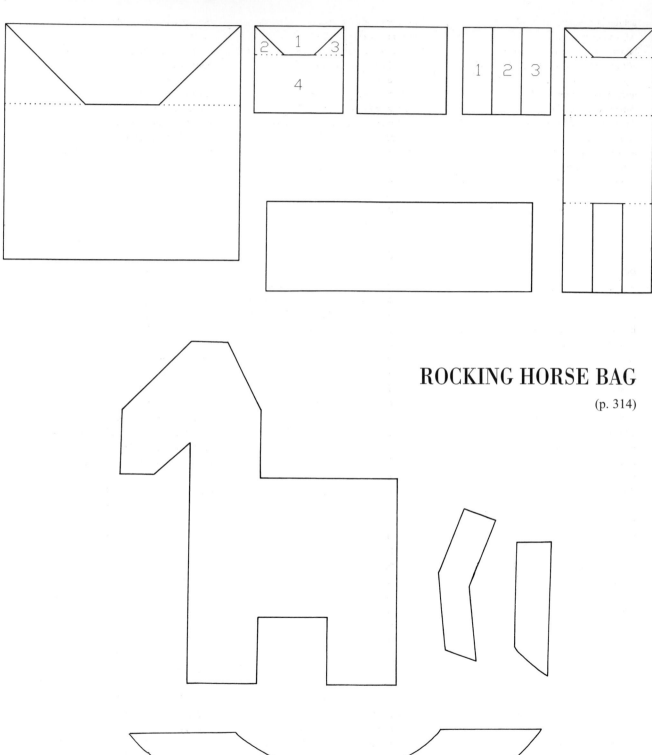

## ROCKING HORSE BAG

(p. 314)

# INDEX